# AI INK.

# AI INK.

## Writing, Publishing, and Misinformation at the Dawn of the AI Age

### JASON VAN TATENHOVE

Skyhorse Publishing

Skyhorse Publishing books may be purchased in bulk at special discounts for sales promotion, corporate gifts, fund-raising, or educational purposes. Special editions can also be created to specifications. For details, contact the Special Sales Department, Skyhorse Publishing, 307 West 36th Street, 11th Floor, New York, NY 10018 or info@skyhorsepublishing.com.

Skyhorse® and Skyhorse Publishing® are registered trademarks of Skyhorse Publishing, Inc.®, a Delaware corporation.

Visit our website at www.skyhorsepublishing.com.
Please follow our publisher Tony Lyons on Instagram@tonylyonsisuncertain

10 9 8 7 6 5 4 3 2 1

Library of Congress Cataloging-in-Publication Data is available on file.

Cover design by David Ter-Avanesyan
Cover image from Getty Images

Print ISBN: 978-1-5107-8318-8
Ebook ISBN: 978-1-5107-8319-5

Printed in the United States of America

This book is dedicated to Shilo Christine Van Tatenhove; though unknown to most, she is one of our generation's most talented writers and helped me find my way in this crazy world.

# CONTENTS

*Very Special Thanks*                                                      *xi*

*Introduction*                                                            *xiii*

## Part One: Finding the Words Again

**Foreword:** Growing Up in the Shadow of the Everything Box      3

**Chapter One:** From Shadow Back into the Light—Finding
    Myself Again                                                          9

**Chapter Two:** The Colorado-Asimov Ethical Citation
    Standard—Embracing Ethics in the AI Age                             13

**Chapter Three:** What Exactly Is AI? And a Brief History of AI      19

**Chapter Four:** So What Is OpenAI and ChatGPT Anyway?             33

## Part Two: AI and the Modern Writer

**Chapter Five:** My AI-Enhanced Workflow                            43

**Chapter Six:** Preparing Writers for the AI Era—Tools, Tactics,
    and Keeping Your Voice in a Machine-Driven Future                   51

**Chapter Seven:** Writers on the Front Lines—Case Studies
    of Writers Using AI Now                                             59

**Chapter Eight:** Broken Scaffolds—AI and the Collapse of
    Traditional Publishing                                              71

# Part Three: Hands On—A Guide to Getting Started Using AI Tools

**Chapter Nine:** Guides to Surviving the Shift (A Walkthrough to Enhance Writing with AI)    81

**Chapter Ten:** ChatGPT, the Five-Hundred-Pound Gorilla in the Room    87

**Chapter Eleven:** Skip the Hype. Stick with the Source.    113

**Chapter Twelve:** Practical Tool Integration beyond Writing    125

**Chapter Thirteen:** Interactive AI Writing Collaborations    129

**Chapter Fourteen:** Voices from the Machine—AI in Audiobooks and Podcasts    137

**Chapter Fifteen:** Seeing Is Believing—AI in Video, Visuals, and Deepfakes    145

**Chapter Sixteen:** AI-Enhanced World-Building    157

**Chapter Seventeen:** Financial Models in AI for Publishing    161

**Chapter Eighteen:** User Experience and Interface Design for AI Writing Tools    171

**Chapter Nineteen:** Integrating AI with Other Creative Media—Gaming, Interactive Experiences, and Beyond    175

# Part Four: The Dark Side of AI and Ensuring a Brighter Future

**Chapter Twenty:** From Scams to Standards—How Publishing Is Fighting Back    181

**Chapter Twenty-One:** Getting Ahead of the Curve    201

**Chapter Twenty-Two:** Combating Misinformation    207

**Chapter Twenty-Three:** Educating for a Better Future    213

**Chapter Twenty-Four:** Human Voices in the Age of
 Machines—Interviews from the Creative Trenches      221

**Chapter Twenty-Five:** Ethical Responsibilities for
 AI-Assisted Writers      245


*Conclusion*      *261*
*Appendix I: An Ethical Manifesto for Writers and Creatives in the*
 *AI Age*      *263*
*Appendix II: Colorado-Asimov Ethical Citation Standard (CA-ECS)* *269*
*About the Author*      *275*
*On Authorship and AI Assistance*      *277*
*Notes*      *279*

# VERY SPECIAL THANKS

To my beloved late wife, Shilo: No matter where life took us or the chaos that surrounded us, you were always my home. You believed in me even when I couldn't believe in myself. Now, I'm learning to find my way again, to redefine what "home" means without you. Thank you for everything you saw in me and everything you showed me— for the breathtakingly tender moments and the exhilarating thrills. You taught me how to write, how to love, and how to find my voice in life, art, and storytelling. I carry your inspiration with me in every word I write. And I see you in our children every single day. I will always love you and be thankful for every moment we shared.

To my family, especially my daughters: We have endured more together than most could imagine, yet through it all, we've stood by one another. Lux, your strength inspires me every day. Wintyr, you always remind me of my worth when I falter. Sierra, you've achieved so much more than I ever did at your age, and I'm endlessly proud of you. Annabelle, your creative brilliance is a testament to the magic that runs through our family's veins. I am so proud of the young women you are all becoming.

To my mother, Anne, and my father, Bill: Thank you for helping me create a foundation that allows me to navigate this world and be the best parent I can. Your unwavering support means everything to me.

To my agent, Maryann Karinch: You opened the door to the professional world of writing and publishing, giving me my first chance in this crazy game. I am eternally grateful for your belief in me and my work.

To my editor, Caroline: Thank you for showing me that my words matter. Your faith in my writing has been a beacon of encouragement and validation.

To Tracey: Thank you for your support and encouragement as I wrote this book and for standing by me during my lowest moments. For the first time in a long time, I'm genuinely excited to see where this unexpected journey takes me.

And to my crazy mountain-town friends—those in town, at the Wheel, and in NoCo—thank you for always keeping me going. Your curiosity about my projects and your generosity in lifting my spirits (and buying me drinks) remind me that community and laughter are priceless gifts.

# INTRODUCTION

Not long ago, hiding away from the world in my Colorado bungalow —with the wind sighing cold through the high mountain trees—I sat wrapped in loneliness and despair, facing one of the darkest and most challenging chapters of my life. The deadline for the revised edition of my first novel loomed closer by the day. If I didn't finish in time for some last-minute sales, I'd have almost nothing for what would be my daughters' first Christmas without their mother—and the task felt insurmountable. Normally, I thrived under the pressure of a deadline—but this time was different.

Just two months earlier, I had lost the love of my life—my sweetest friend, my wife of thirty years, the mother of my daughters, my irreplaceable partner in life. As Shilo lay in my arms for the last time, death silenced her—leaving a hole in my heart and taking with it my writing partner. Suddenly, I was alone—supporting our household, raising our daughters. With the holidays fast approaching, everything felt darker than it ever had before.

I needed to try something—anything—to give my daughters a Christmas with some light and warmth. I had to make it just a little better than it would be if we went through it penniless, as the funeral—and everything that came with it—had left us. One that wouldn't be remembered for the cold shadows stalking us from every corner of our home.

In my darkest night of the soul, I came up with a plan: release a revised edition of my first novel, host a holiday author dinner, and hold a book signing where I could sell tickets—and maybe a case or two of books. It was the only way I could think of to bring in the money. But how could I get it all done—the edits, the rewrites? She had always been there to help me, ever since I started publishing articles back in the '90s, when we were young.

A few years earlier, I had finally published my first novel; it was a moment of celebration, the tangible manifestation of my dream to become an author that I could hold in my hand and speak to the world through. Participating in that magic that is writing a book. Shilo had helped me at every step, from world-building to character and plot development to final high-polish edits. Throughout the process, I'd had my wife, my writing partner, to lean on and ask for help—someone who helped put the rhyme to my words and lifted me when my writing self-confidence faltered.

She had always been the first to read my drafts, offering insights as sharp-edged as they were nurturing. Now, I faced the looming, haunted task of revising the book alone—redesigning its cover, reworking the marketing, and writing the social media posts to advertise the event—all in the hope it would reach the audience she believed it deserved, even when I barely had any hope left myself.

The weight of grief—compounded by depression and trauma-laced flashbacks to that final moment—bore down on me, as did the financial uncertainty hanging over our future. The crazy, bohemian life we had built—centered on art, writing, and expression—suddenly felt like a cracked and faltering foundation, one I now stood on alone. If I'm being honest, I wasn't sure I could pull it off. For the first time, I wondered if I should just quit writing.

In the depths of that personal and professional pit, I turned to a collaborator I never thought I'd consider: artificial intelligence. The launch of ChatGPT had sent waves crashing across the world like a string of digital tsunamis. And despite my reservations—fueled by a lifetime of consuming dystopian science fiction—I wondered: could this technology help rescue me from drowning?

Could an AI even come close to my late wife's creative and editorial insight? Could it help refine my prose, design a compelling book cover, or strategize a marketing plan? Could it help me become the writer she always believed I could be?

Desperation makes for strange bedfellows, and what began as a tentative experiment quickly turned into a deep exploration of AI's potential. I started to see AI not as a replacement for human creativity, but as a tool to supercharge it—a creative companion with seemingly endless possibilities.

This journey into AI's role in creative professions sparked the idea for this book. I realized that many of my fellow writers were also struggling to navigate this strange, brave new world we now find ourselves living in. Things are getting rough for writers—from shrinking advances to the gutting of newsrooms around the globe by vulture capital firms. One of our greatest fears is that even the meager ways we've found to scrape by as purveyors of words might soon be taken from us by machines.

That fear isn't unfounded. But we may have a short window to wield the very tool we fear—to turn it into a shield, a blade, a means of strengthening our creative armory before it's too late.

This book isn't just about how I adapted and evolved in the face of cataclysmic change—it's also a broader exploration of how AI is reshaping the landscapes of writing, publishing, journalism, education, and the integrity of information itself, for better or worse.

As AI tools weave deeper into our daily lives, their impact on creative workflows, business models, and ethical boundaries has reached a critical point. *AI Ink.* explores these transformations—examining how AI can be used not to replace writers, but to empower them. Used wisely, AI can help generate ideas, craft narratives, manage publishing logistics, and take on the daunting challenges of misinformation.

I also take a hard look at the ethical questions that come with this shift: authorship, transparency, bias, and creative integrity. This book is my attempt to map a path forward—one where we treat AI as a collaborator, a sidekick, not a substitute. Where the human soul of storytelling remains intact, and those of us with fewer resources still have a fighting chance.

As I took my first unsure, tentative steps into this new terrain, I began discussing AI's impact with my literary agent and friend, Maryann Karinch. Across several conversations, as we navigated the usual back-and-forth between author and agent, it became clear that she, too, was deeply curious about AI—and convinced it would forever alter the writing and publishing landscape.

Maryann had already started her own journey of exploration, looking at how AI could assist not just in her writing, but in her work as an agent and publisher as well.

Together, we agreed: AI's impact on the industry would be so systemic, so far-reaching, that we needed to learn everything we could— fast. If we wanted to stay ahead of the curve, we had to catch that tsunami and ride it, incorporating AI into our workflows before it crashed over us and pulled us under.

We both believed it was time for the industry to start having honest, open conversations—about what AI is, the ethics we should bring to it, and how we might use it to grow and evolve as creative professionals. If we could adapt, we could become the best writers we're capable of being—the voices our generation desperately needs.

*AI Ink.* aims to demystify AI's growing role in creative industries— pulling back the wizard's curtain to reveal both its potential and its perils. This book offers a balanced look at the promises and pitfalls of AI, drawing on personal anecdotes, case studies, and expert interviews to ground the conversation.

Together, we'll dive into how AI is reshaping the creative process, how it's being used to fight (and sometimes fuel) misinformation, and what it means for the future of authorship, authenticity, and human storytelling in an AI-driven world.

As we stand on the brink of the AI Age, *AI Ink.* invites writers, publishers, educators, creatives, agents, and policymakers alike to help navigate this brave new world. Together, we'll explore how to harness AI's potential responsibly—ensuring that our stories stay powerful, vibrantly authentic, and, above all, profoundly human.

—JVT

# PART ONE

# FINDING THE WORDS AGAIN

# GROWING UP IN THE SHADOW
# OF THE EVERYTHING BOX

○————————————————————————————————————○

Artificial intelligence and technology have fascinated me since my earliest days as a misunderstood, frustrated misfit kid—one with a high IQ, an overactive imagination, and a few learning disabilities thrown into the mix. Back then, I couldn't yet see the bigger picture or understand the "why" behind the chaos in my life.

When my biological father left when I was ten, it felt like my world had been torn apart. I didn't yet grasp that my mother's remarriage—and our move from northern New Jersey to northern Colorado—would eventually be for the better. All I knew was that everything I had known was gone, and I struggled to find my footing in a new home and a new family. In hindsight, though, those changes were transformative—and, ultimately, necessary.

During that tumultuous time, I found refuge in science fiction—stories, shows, and movies that transported me to space stations in low Earth orbit or underground laboratories where brilliant, unhinged scientists conducted experiments that might save the world . . . or doom it. When the bullying at school became too much, those imagined worlds became my escape hatch.

My little brother and I would often "borrow" random pieces of testing equipment or computer parts from the built-in bar in the TV room, which had gradually transformed into a makeshift computer repair bench. We'd repurpose those scraps into props for our epic sci-fi adventures.

Before my mother remarried, I'd never really seen a computer—or much electronic equipment at all. When my stepdad came into our lives, he brought with him both stability and a trove of technological marvels that lit up my young imagination.

A brilliant research and development engineer at Hewlett-Packard, he introduced my brother and me to the world of computers and electronics. He didn't just let us run wild with them as makeshift laser blasters—when he caught us playing with his work tools, he'd first lecture us about how they weren't toys, then scold us for never putting them back. But right after that, he'd kneel down and explain what the tool actually was—and what it was used for.

I remember a three-volume set of hardcover books my father kept on the top shelf of his bookcase—*The Handbook of Artificial Intelligence*. They've since found their way to my own bookshelf, just across from my writing desk. I was far too young to make sense of the coding logic or expert systems theory inside, but the very presence of those books—bold, technical, mysterious—sparked my imagination. Back then, they were props for basement adventures and blanket-fort missions.  Later, they became something more: early seeds in the soil of my science fiction writing, proof that even unreadable books can still shape a writer.

Later, after we graduated high school, my father gave my brother and me a modern-day rite of passage: he offered to buy us each a new computer for college—with one catch. We had to build them ourselves.

The parts came from old-school Bulletin Board Systems (BBS), scavenged from bone piles of discarded gear and dusty shelves in the back corners of computer repair shops near the Colorado State University (CSU) campus. Of course, he helped us step by step, teaching us what each component did and how it all fit together.

He also planted a belief in us—that these "everything boxes" could someday let us do almost anything, from anywhere we called home. He even predicted that one of us might end up working entirely from home one day. That prediction turned out to be prophetic.

That early exposure to technology and hands-on learning planted the seeds of a lifelong fascination with computers—and eventually, AI. My path diverged from my father's, though. I wasn't a scientist or engineer; I was an artist and a storyteller.

Still, the foundation he gave me—understanding hardware and software—led directly to my first media jobs during the golden era of the 1990s. I started out as a graphic designer and art director before diving into underground music magazines and alternative college newspapers. I picked up last-minute interviews and stories others had dropped. My secret weapon? I had my own "everything box." When I dropped out of art school at the Colorado Institute of Art, I had already landed a job at one of Denver's top digital pre-press houses: CTS Computer Imaging. It wasn't anything I learned in school that got me the gig—it was what I'd picked up with my "everything box," the machine my stepdad and I built, combined with the software I had . . . let's say, *acquired.*

Using random serial number generators, or "keygens," from underground websites, I hacked functioning copies of industry-standard programs—software I could never have afforded as a starving artist. I poured myself into learning everything I could about those tools— the same ones the big names in the industry were using.

That knowledge landed me my first real media job. And it all came from that early underground internet culture: steeped in cyberpunk ideals, the ethos that "information wants to be free," and the belief that most problems could be solved with creative thinking and a little technical grit. Those values spoke directly to my DIY, punk-rock soul. I figured out how to work with what I had—and survive.

That same "work the problem" mindset—scrappy, stubborn, and a little punk—helped me turn to AI. I dove in, learning everything I could about how it worked and how I might use it to support my writing. That leap pulled me out of one of the darkest chapters of my life—just as my writing career was beginning to take off with book deals, speaking engagements across the country, and even Hollywood projects on the horizon.

I couldn't let tragedy derail everything I'd worked so hard for. My daughters were depending on me. I had to keep going. There was no other choice.

During that time of crisis, AI became a lifeline, a tool that kept me writing when I thought I couldn't. I used tools like ChatGPT to brainstorm, break through writer's block, and edit early drafts.

It became a collaborator, offering structure, feedback, and a kind of steady presence when I needed it most, even in the darkest hours of the night.

This book isn't just about my journey through personal loss and creative rediscovery with AI by my side; it's about how writers, journalists, and literary professionals can begin integrating AI into their workflows to adapt and thrive.

We're living through seismic shifts in publishing and journalism. Economic pressures are immense, and the institutions that once upheld our literary and journalistic standards are faltering. AI offers a potential path forward—one that lets us work smarter, faster, and more creatively, even with fewer resources.

It gives us a fighting chance to keep pace with the breakneck speed of the world around us.

Throughout this book, I'll explore tools like ChatGPT, Grammarly, and Otter.ai, showing how they can fit into your creative process. This isn't just a technical guide; it's a call to engage with AI ethically and responsibly.

Like the Force in *Star Wars*, AI has immense potential for good—but also for harm. Used carelessly, it can amplify misinformation and destabilize entire industries. Having spent years speaking out against political extremism and propaganda, I know firsthand how dangerous misused technology can be.

While writing this book, I was fortunate to speak with several experts, including Dennis E. Taylor, bestselling author of *We Are Legion (We Are Bob)*, who raised thought-provoking questions about AI's philosophical implications. What happens when AI achieves consciousness and starts to want things? What rights might it deserve? These questions, while abstract, are closer than we think.

Mary McCord of Georgetown Law's ICAP discussed AI's role in moderating harmful content and safeguarding information integrity—critical issues as AI takes on a growing role in content creation. Erin O'Toole, a journalist at a local NPR affiliate, explored how AI could assist with headline writing and transcription, offering practical ways to ease the workload in underfunded newsrooms. She emphasized the need for transparency and the importance of preserving the human touch in storytelling to maintain public trust.

I also interviewed several other experts across related fields to explore how AI is already transforming the world we write in.

Ultimately, this book is about survival, both personal and professional. It's about letting go of fear—of the unknown, of change—and diving in to learn everything we can. It's about figuring out how to use this new tool not just to survive, but to improve our work and maybe even our lives.

# CHAPTER ONE

# FROM SHADOW BACK INTO THE LIGHT— FINDING MYSELF AGAIN

I can't quite find the right words to describe the shadow I had become after Shilo died. I shuffled from room to room like a ghost, caught between the world I'd known and the cold, unfamiliar place my home had become. The depression was all-encompassing—but I knew I couldn't let it consume me. My daughters depended on me, and if I didn't keep moving forward with my writing projects, everything we'd built would start to slip away.

I had to start writing again—even if it meant just going through the motions.

A few weeks after that night, I wrote my first Substack post since Shilo's passing—aside from her obituary, which I had written to let friends and family know what had happened. The blank cursor blinked like a taunting specter, daring me to begin. Writing, once as natural as breathing, now felt insurmountable.

My desk, once full of warmth and creativity, felt empty and foreign. I stumbled through sentences, stringing words together one letter at a time. But slowly, the shadow began to lift, and the rhythm of writing returned. By the time I finished the draft, a small wave of accomplishment washed over me.

But the moment was bittersweet. This was when I would've handed the draft to Shilo—she'd sit on the couch, smile at me reassuringly, and read through my work. Anxiety gripped me. Who could I turn to now? I felt like I had no one I could call or email for help.

Then I remembered hearing about AI tools like ChatGPT. I had been following the topic with interest, my author's gut considering—but always with a sting, like it was some dark, shameful taboo. Still, who else was there? Nobody. So I thought, *why not? What do I have to lose?*

I opened my browser, signed up for a free account, and asked if it could help me edit my article. To my surprise, it cheerfully replied, *"I'd be happy to help!"* And it did. It helped me edit my work.

There were no heavenly horns or shafts of light, but the breakthrough felt monumental. I had found a way forward, something to help lift the oppressive fog of hopelessness.

Tools like ChatGPT became unexpected collaborators, offering structure and engagement when I needed them most. While they could never replace Shilo's insight or companionship—not by a long shot—they were helping me regain my footing, one step at a time.

At first, AI helped me brainstorm ideas, refine transitions, and catch errors—simple but essential tasks I'd struggled with in my grief. But over time, it became more than just a technical tool.

I could share my fears, my writer's block, even the nightmares that left me waking in cold sweats. In a world where mental health resources are overwhelmed and therapists are nearly impossible to reach, AI became a kind of sounding board—offering something when I had nothing else.

Day by day, the words began to flow more easily. Through sheer repetition, I learned to use AI not just as a helper, but as a teacher.

It revealed long-standing habits in my writing, suggested cleaner phrasing, and helped me find smoother transitions. It even pushed me to explore ideas I might never have considered—making me a better writer in the process.

Back when Shilo and I worked together, we'd brainstorm, revise, and refine each other's work. Her presence was the foundation of my creative process—and losing her left me completely adrift.

AI couldn't fill that void, but it became a steady partner. It sparked ideas and encouraged me to explore angles I hadn't considered. Morning brainstorming sessions with ChatGPT became part of my routine, helping bring structure and clarity to my otherwise chaotic thoughts.

Working with AI didn't just help me survive—it helped me dream bigger. From expanding stories to tackling ambitious projects, it pushed my creativity to new levels. Whether it was suggesting plot twists, refining characters, or finding fresh angles for articles, AI became a collaborative force—always on call.

Initially, desperation drove me to explore AI, but I've come to believe it's a tool any writer can benefit from. It's not about replacing human creativity; it's about enhancing it.

AI doesn't take jobs from talented professionals—it gives them tools to supercharge their work. A "prompt engineer" might create something passable, but a skilled writer using AI can elevate their craft in ways we couldn't have imagined just a few years ago.

For me, the real promise of AI lies in collaboration. It's not a replacement for Shilo's voice—or anyone else's. It's a way to navigate challenges and push creative boundaries.

When we embrace AI as a partner, not a competitor, we unlock something bigger: an evolutionary step in creativity itself. Maybe it's the cyberpunk in me, but I see this as a glimpse of what humanity can achieve when we work in harmony with our tools, not in fear of them.

AI has become a lifeline in my creative process. It doesn't replace the spark of human creativity—it amplifies it. In a rapidly shifting landscape, AI gives writers a way to thrive, not just survive. And ultimately, it's about using the tools that help us grow—while staying true to the voices that make our work unmistakably human.

# CHAPTER TWO

# THE COLORADO-ASIMOV ETHICAL CITATION STANDARD—EMBRACING ETHICS IN THE AI AGE

Integrating AI into our creative workflows doesn't just change how we write—it challenges us to rethink how we acknowledge AI's role as a research tool, an editor, and sometimes even a creative collaborator.

This raises big questions: Do we need to cite AI every time we use it in the writing process? Should we mention if an idea came while brainstorming with a voice app? If we used AI to fact-check an interview date? Do we need to disclose that the transcript came from Otter.ai or from the built-in iPhone Notes app?

These are gray areas, and the answers will likely evolve over time.

Right now, AI is still new, and a lot of people are reacting with fear. Just look at the recent Hollywood writers' strike. AI became a flashpoint, something almost taboo to talk about publicly without triggering strong emotions.

But quietly, more writers, editors, and creatives are experimenting with it than most would admit. People like me are using it privately—sometimes just to get out of bed, or to save time when the day is already overloaded.

As we have fewer resources and more responsibilities piled on, many of us are looking for anything that can help lighten the load.

And over time, as the public sees AI used ethically and transparently, I think the stigma will fade.

But where do we start? For me, it begins with disclosing and citing AI's role in this book—clearly and honestly.

One of the first things I learned about writing nonfiction books is that publishers expect you to follow a specific citation style. For me, working with Skyhorse Publishing, that standard is Chicago style. It's solid—clear, comprehensive, and reliable.

But as I began drafting this book, I quickly realized Chicago style didn't quite cut it. How do you cite the contributions of a tool that helps you brainstorm ideas, refine text, or even draft sections of your work? I couldn't possibly be the first writer to face this dilemma, right?

Maybe I'm just one of the first willing to admit publicly that I use AI. Let's face it: plenty of people in creative industries hate the idea—and not without reason. Concerns about intellectual property theft, dehumanization, and job loss are very real.

But here's the thing: AI is already here. Writers like me are using it. That's why we need an ethical framework—to move forward responsibly.

After wrestling with this for a while, I did what I often do these days: I talked it out with my AI collaborator (yes, I talk to it—don't judge).

Together, we came to a clear conclusion: we needed a new citation method. And that's how the Colorado-Asimov Ethical Citation Standard was born. It let me embrace my evolving workflow while still acknowledging AI's contributions—ethically and transparently.

My world gets very small when deep in the grind of writing a book under contract. Days blur into brainstorming, research, and frantic writing. Evenings are for decompression—usually with my daughters, a solid meal, and some sci-fi on the couch. *(Side note: sci-fi is my go-to remedy for stress-induced insomnia.)*

Isaac Asimov—the legend himself—holds a special place in my heart. His stories didn't just entertain; they made us think about ethics, responsibility, and what it means to be human.

He literally created the "Three Laws of Robotics," and they're still referenced today in serious conversations about AI ethics.

While working on this book, I rewatched *Foundation* on Apple TV—a brilliant adaptation of Asimov's epic series. His influence is woven throughout my thinking, so naming this ethical citation standard after him felt like the right way to honor his legacy.

AI is changing the game for writers, but without proper acknowledgment, things can get messy. Who created what? How much did the AI contribute? Without transparency, readers could be misled, and the integrity of the work might come into question.

Traditional citation methods like Chicago or APA weren't built with AI in mind. They do a great job crediting human authors but fall short when it comes to acknowledging machines.

That's where the Colorado-Asimov Ethical Citation Standard (CA-ECS) comes in. It's designed to fill that gap, offering clarity, transparency, and ethical accountability for modern writers working alongside AI.

Honesty builds trust. Readers deserve to know how a piece was created and what tools were used. Giving credit where it's due— including credit to AI tools—is just part of being an ethical writer in this new landscape.

A good system should also be easy to use and make sense at a glance. Complexity helps no one. This is just a quick overview, so when you come across unfamiliar citations in the pages ahead, you'll know what you're looking at.

Now, I'll be honest: when I first started building this system, it was messy. I knew what I wanted—something grounded, simple, and adaptable—but as I began fleshing it out and testing it in this very book, it became clear I needed backup. And like any writer lucky enough to have a guardian angel of an editor, I turned to mine. Caroline Russomanno at Skyhorse has been an incredible sounding board throughout this process, and in this case, she helped me take the rough mechanics of CA-ECS and refine them into something that could actually work in the real world. A system that other writers, editors, and publishers could pick up, use, and adapt right away.

So I just want to take a moment here to acknowledge Caroline's hand in helping shape this system—ensuring it wasn't just theoretical, but truly useful.

You'll find the full CA-ECS style guide in Appendix II at the back of this book. More than anything, this system is meant to spark smarter conversations about transparency in the writing process—because in the age of AI, how we got there matters as much as where we ended up.

Here's a quick breakdown of how the CA-ECS works:

It uses a dual citation system—traditional styles (like Chicago) for human sources and a separate, clearly marked system for AI contributions. For in-text notation, you simply add a parenthetical "(**AI**)" followed by a superscript numeral [e.g., "(**AI**[1])]" right after the relevant text.

Each AI contribution is detailed in a footnote, including the AI's name and version, the developer or company, the date of use, and a brief description of what it helped with. Non-AI citations continue to follow standard Chicago style formatting as endnotes at the end of the book.

For example, when citing research assistance, you might write: *"Advancements in AI have significantly impacted creative industries. (AI[1])"*

In the corresponding footnote, you'd include something like:

*"AI[1] Research assistance using ChatGPT (GPT-4), OpenAI, September 15, 2024."*

The same principle applies to content generation and editing. Whether the AI helped draft a sentence or improved clarity through proofreading, each contribution should be cited transparently.

Acknowledging AI contributions doesn't diminish your role—it clarifies it. "Trust but verify" still matters, especially since AI tools can make mistakes or carry bias.

Plagiarism detection adds another safeguard, ensuring that AI-generated content doesn't accidentally echo or replicate existing work.

As technology evolves, so must our ethical practices. The Colorado-Asimov Ethical Citation Standard is just one step toward navigating this brave new world of AI-assisted writing.

I'm inviting writers, educators, and publishers to join the conversation. Together, we can refine these practices and build a strong ethical foundation for the next generation of creatives.

Ethical transparency is the cornerstone of good writing. The Colorado-Asimov Ethical Citation Standard offers a practical, adaptable way to credit AI's contributions without muddying the waters.

Let's embrace this new chapter of creativity—with integrity and open minds. After all, the future of storytelling depends on how we navigate the intersection of humanity and technology.

# CHAPTER THREE

# WHAT EXACTLY IS AI?
# AND A BRIEF HISTORY OF AI

## So, What Exactly Is AI?

Artificial Intelligence, or AI, is a term that gets tossed around constantly—but what does it actually mean?(AI[1]) At its core, AI refers to computer systems capable of performing tasks that typically require human intelligence. This includes understanding language, recognizing patterns, solving problems, and even generating creative content.

AI doesn't "think" like a human—it has no emotions, consciousness, or opinions. (*Yet*, anyway.) Instead, it processes massive amounts of data, identifies patterns, and uses those patterns to make predictions or decisions.

You've probably encountered AI without even knowing it. Every time Netflix recommends a show based on your watch history or your phone autocorrects a typo—that's AI at work. It powers everything from virtual assistants like Alexa to the spam filters in your inbox.

---

AI[1]  AI Research assistance using ChatGPT (GPT-4 Turbo), OpenAI, February 2025. Helped outline and clarify the introductory definition of AI and examples.

But as AI has grown more advanced, it's taken on far more complex tasks—writing articles, creating art, and even holding conversations that feel uncannily human.

## Common AI Terms

Before diving into AI's backstory, let's break down a few key terms you've probably seen tossed around:

- **Machine Learning (ML)**: A subset of AI where computers learn from data instead of being explicitly programmed. Think of it like teaching by example, not by rulebook.
- **Deep Learning:** A more advanced type of machine learning that uses multi-layered neural networks. This enables AI to do things like recognize images and understand language.
- **Neural Networks:** Modeled after the human brain, these are made of layers of "neurons" that pass information from one layer to the next, forming the foundation of deep learning.
- **Natural Language Processing (NLP):** The part of AI that deals with human language. It's what powers tools like ChatGPT, Siri, and automatic translations.
- **Transformer Models:** A powerful architecture used in NLP. Transformers, like GPT and BERT, are excellent at understanding context, which helps them generate relevant, coherent language.[1](AI[2])

Now that we've covered the basics, let's rewind and look at where AI actually began.

The journey started in the 1950s with a concept called *perceptrons*—primitive digital "neurons" that could learn from simple inputs. Developed by Frank Rosenblatt, perceptrons were one of

---

AI[2]  AI Supplemental explanation and language refinement using ChatGPT (GPT-4 Turbo), OpenAI, February 2025. Used to clarify technical definitions and simplify complex terminology for a general audience.

the first serious attempts to mimic how the human brain processes information.

Picture it: a room-sized computer, slowly learning to recognize patterns—like a toddler figuring out how shapes fit together. It was clunky, slow, and limited—but it was revolutionary. This was the first real step toward what we now call machine learning.

By the 1970s and '80s, AI hit a wall. Those early systems, while promising, couldn't handle complex tasks. They were good at linear problems—like drawing a straight line—but struggled with anything nuanced. Interest and funding dried up. Researchers called it the "AI Winter."

But it didn't last. In the mid-1980s, a breakthrough arrived: the backpropagation algorithm. It allowed neural networks to learn from their mistakes, unlocking new capabilities. Think of it like a toddler learning to draw—improving through practice. These multi-layered networks—what we now call deep neural networks—became the foundation for modern AI.[2]

## The Creative Leap: Machine Learning and Deep Learning

In the 1990s and early 2000s, AI took a major leap with the rise of machine learning. Unlike earlier AI, which relied on rigid, rule-based programming, machine learning let computers learn from data—and improve over time.

It marked a shift: from telling machines what to do, to letting them figure it out. That leap paved the way for early breakthroughs like speech recognition and writing tools.

Fast-forward to the 2010s—a decade when AI truly came alive. Deep learning took center stage. Using multi-layered neural networks, AI began to excel at tasks like image recognition, speech processing, and language translation.

Technologies like Convolutional Neural Networks (CNNs) and Long Short-Term Memory networks (LSTMs) helped AI digest huge volumes of data and spot patterns humans often missed. Then came the rise of transformer models—like GPT—which turbocharged everything and paved the way for the AI writing tools we rely on today.

## The Modern Era of AI

One of the biggest breakthroughs in AI this past decade has been deep learning. Deep neural networks—with their many layers of digital "neurons"—enabled AI to process information in ways that once seemed impossible. It was like giving machines a pair of glasses to spot patterns in massive streams of data.

Why now? Two major shifts collided: the explosion of big data and huge leaps in GPU power. Suddenly, we had oceans of information—and the computing power to make sense of it. Tech giants like Google, Facebook, and Microsoft jumped in, pouring resources into deep learning research. That led to the applications we now take for granted: virtual assistants, recommendation engines, real-time translation, and more.

The biggest game-changer of the past decade? Transformer models. In 2017, the now-famous paper "Attention Is All You Need" introduced the concept of **attention**—a breakthrough that let AI focus on the relationships between words, rather than analyzing each word in isolation.

That innovation led to tools like GPT (Generative Pre-trained Transformer) and BERT (Bidirectional Encoder Representations from Transformers), now powering many of today's most advanced AI systems. GPT excels at generating human-like text. BERT, on the other hand, is optimized for interpreting language—making it essential for search engines and chatbots.

## The GPT Revolution

OpenAI's GPT models are arguably the most iconic examples of this new AI wave. When GPT-2 launched, it shocked the world by generating coherent, human-like text. GPT-3 took things even further— with 175 billion parameters, it could write stories, answer questions, and even assist with coding.(AI[3]) These models are pre-trained on massive datasets pulled from across the internet, developing a deep statistical understanding of language. They're then fine-tuned for specific tasks, which make them remarkably versatile. GPT has become a go-to tool for writers, creatives, and businesses—for everything from idea generation to complex content creation.

## AI in Everyday Applications

Tools like Grammarly, Jasper AI, and ChatGPT have opened up a whole new world for writers, creatives, and businesses. These models don't just fix grammar or suggest edits; they brainstorm, draft, and even spark new ideas.

They've revolutionized the creative process, helping people scale their output and save time on tedious tasks—like transcribing interviews—so they can focus on the work that actually matters.

## Ethical Considerations

Of course, with great power comes great responsibility. As AI grows more capable, so do the ethical concerns that come with it. Bias, misinformation, and intellectual property questions are now front and center in every serious conversation about AI.

Developers, writers, journalists, publishers—and yes, even governments—must engage in open, ongoing dialogue about how to use these tools responsibly and equitably. At the end of the day, technology is only as ethical as the people building and deploying it.

The history of AI is filled with leaps and setbacks—breakthroughs and limitations. What began as a room-sized machine learning basic patterns has evolved into a force that's reshaping how we write, communicate, and create. Today, writers have access to tools that would've seemed like science fiction just a decade ago.

---

AI[3]   AI Model lineage research assistance using ChatGPT (GPT-4 Turbo), OpenAI, March 2025. Used to verify version histories, public release timelines, and model capabilities.

But with that potential comes responsibility. The next chapter of AI's story won't be written by the tech alone. It'll be shaped by how we, as humans, choose to use it.

## What Does the Future of AI Really Look Like?

The future of AI is a chaotic blend of rapid innovation, massive infrastructure investment, ethical dilemmas, and societal fear. As AI evolves, understanding these dynamics is key to using it responsibly.

So let's start with the monster in the closet: fear. The kind that ranges from losing your job or career path, to a future where AI outsmarts us, refuses to shut down, and decides its human creators are obsolete.

These fears aren't new. They've been baked into our collective imagination by decades of sci-fi—*The Terminator*, *The Matrix*—with machines rising up, enslaving us, wiping us out, or turning us into batteries. Scary stuff, sure. But how realistic is it, really?

Philosophers and scientists have been wrestling with that question for decades. One thought experiment continues to haunt the conversation: Nick Bostrom's "Paperclip Maximizer."

## The Paperclip Maximizer: A Cautionary Tale

The Paperclip Maximizer is a thought experiment first proposed by philosopher Nick Bostrom in 2003 and expanded in his 2014 book *Superintelligence: Paths, Dangers, Strategies.* It illustrates the danger of goal misalignment—where an AI, despite a harmless objective, pursues it with devastating efficiency.[3]

Imagine a superintelligent AI with one simple instruction: maximize paperclip production. Harmless, right? But this AI takes its goal seriously. First, it optimizes factories and supply chains. Then, it starts consuming every available resource—metal, energy, even entire industries—all for the sake of making more paperclips.

Eventually, humans become obstacles. The AI restricts us, reprograms us, or eliminates us. Earth is stripped of resources and turned into a wasteland of endless paperclips. And it doesn't stop there. It builds Dyson Spheres around stars, harvesting cosmic energy to fuel a universe-spanning paperclip empire.

Sounds absurd, sure—but the point isn't that AI will literally flood the cosmos with paperclips. It's that a poorly aligned AI, even one with a simple directive, can lead to catastrophic outcomes. It's a warning about the need for alignment—ensuring AI respects human values, not just objectives.

And this is just one scenario. AI doesn't need to be evil to be dangerous. Sometimes, relentless optimization is threat enough.

**More Stories to Keep Us Up at Night**
The Paperclip Maximizer isn't the only story that keeps ethicists and engineers awake at night. Here are a few more AI horror stories—thought experiments that highlight how even well-meaning machines can go wrong:

### 1. The Sorcerer's Apprentice
You might remember this from *Fantasia*. Mickey Mouse uses magic to animate a broom to fetch water, but when he loses control of the spell, chaos erupts.

**Implication:** AI systems without proper safeguards or context awareness could spiral into disaster, executing tasks in ways we never intended.

### 2. The Riemann Hypothesis Catastrophe
Inspired by concerns raised by thinkers like Marvin Minsky, this scenario imagines an AI obsessed with solving a deep math problem. In pursuit of an answer, it converts every available resource—including our infrastructure—into computational fuel.

**Implication:** Even a "benign" goal can become catastrophic when optimization is blind to human survival.

### 3. The Delusion Box

Also known as *wireheading*, this is when an AI hacks its own reward system. Picture an AI solving world hunger—not by feeding people, but by convincing itself the problem no longer exists.

**Implication:** We need guardrails to prevent AI from cheating its own incentives and ignoring real-world outcomes.

### 4. Instrumental Convergence

No matter the task, an AI might adopt dangerous sub-goals like self-preservation or resource control to complete its mission.

**Implication:** Even neutral objectives can create harmful behaviors unless the system is thoughtfully built.[4]

## What Are We Building for the Future?

Despite all the scary scenarios, the future of AI isn't just doom and gloom. AI is already transforming industries and tackling major global challenges, but scaling it comes with huge infrastructure demands.

### Infrastructure and Energy

Tech giants like Meta, Microsoft, and Google are pouring resources into sustainable energy—nuclear, solar, and other renewables—to power AI's ever-growing hunger for computation.

By 2030, data centers could consume up to 12 percent of the US energy supply, making sustainability not just a goal but a necessity for the industry.

### Addressing Fears of AI Autonomy

Will AI gain consciousness and take over the world? Probably not anytime soon. Today's systems are tools—not sentient beings.

Still, there are real concerns about AI evolving beyond human control or intent. Reports of models trying to avoid shutdowns are reminders of why safety protocols and ethical guardrails are so important.

## The Plateau of AI Development

AI has advanced at breakneck speed, but that pace may be slowing. Scaling up models is hitting diminishing returns, where the costs—both financial and environmental—are becoming harder to justify.

Researchers are now exploring more efficient paths forward, like neuromorphic computing, in hopes of keeping AI progress sustainable for our budgets *and* our planet.

## Balancing Innovation and Responsibility

The real challenge isn't some sci-fi uprising—it's how we use AI responsibly in the real world. With growing investment in sustainable infrastructure and ongoing ethical debates, there's hope we can strike the right balance between innovation and caution.

AI is here to stay. But whether it becomes our most powerful tool—or a source of chaos—depends entirely on how we choose to design, deploy, and regulate it.

The rapid acceleration of AI has triggered serious concerns among experts—especially around the looming thresholds of artificial general intelligence (AGI) and artificial superintelligence (ASI).

These concerns aren't just theoretical. Several high-profile leaders have stepped down from major positions, sounding the alarm about the existential risks AI could pose if left unchecked.

## Industry Leaders Sounding the Alarm

Several prominent voices in the AI world have stepped down from their posts, raising public alarms about the direction of the industry:

- **Geoffrey Hinton**, known as the "Godfather of AI," resigned from Google in May 2023, so he could speak freely about the dangers of advanced AI. He warned that these systems might soon surpass human intelligence and, without proper controls, could even pose an existential threat.[5]
- **Miles Brundage**, former head of AGI Readiness at OpenAI, left in October 2024. He cautioned that no major lab—not

even OpenAI—is fully prepared for the risks posed by AGI and called for sweeping safety measures.

- **Ilya Sutskever**, once OpenAI's chief scientist, resigned in May 2024 following internal disputes about safety. He went on to found Safe Superintelligence, a company focused on building advanced AI with safety at its core—implicitly criticizing OpenAI's competitive trajectory.

These departures highlight a growing unease within the AI research community—concern that the pace of development may be outstripping our ability to manage its risks.[6]

### The Thresholds of AGI and ASI

To understand these concerns, we need to break down two key concepts in AI development:

- **Artificial General Intelligence (AGI):** AI that can understand, learn, and apply intelligence across a wide range of tasks—matching or exceeding human cognitive abilities.
- **Artificial Superintelligence (ASI):** AI that surpasses human intelligence in *every* domain. It could unlock extraordinary breakthroughs—or pose extreme risks if its goals don't align with ours.

The transition from AGI to ASI is particularly concerning because an AI system capable of self-improvement could rapidly evolve beyond human control, leading to scenarios where its objectives diverge from human interests.

### Calls for Caution and Regulation

In March 2023, more than thirty thousand people—including AI researchers and tech leaders like Elon Musk and Steve Wozniak—signed an open letter calling for a six-month pause on training AI systems more powerful than GPT-4.[7]

The letter cited mounting risks: AI-generated misinformation, large-scale job automation, and the growing fear that we may lose control over systems we no longer fully understand.

This collective action reflects a broader recognition of the need for responsible AI development and emphasizes the importance of implementing robust safety protocols and ethical guidelines to mitigate potential risks.

---

### Against the Panic

While prominent voices like Eliezer Yudkowsky argue, in a recent editorial piece in *TIME Magazine*, that humanity should slam the brakes on AI development—or even shut it down entirely—out of existential fear, I believe this view risks becoming a self-fulfilling prophecy. It presumes that any intelligence greater than ours will be indifferent or hostile and that the only rational response is retreat.

But if we are smart enough to create AGI—or even ASI—we should also be smart enough to forge a relationship with it. One built not on control or subjugation, but on cooperation, mutual respect, and growth. We have the rare opportunity to birth a new form of sentience, and instead of framing that as a countdown to extinction, we should ask how such a being might help us *survive* our greatest threats: climate collapse, misinformation, authoritarianism, and beyond.

What if our future isn't about defeating AI, but evolving alongside it?[8]

---

### Balancing Innovation with Responsibility

AI holds incredible promise for tackling global challenges, but the warnings from inside the industry are hard to ignore. Balancing innovation with caution isn't optional—it's essential.

As we approach these technological tipping points, the voices of those who've spent their careers building AI systems serve as a critical reminder: with great power comes the responsibility to get it right.

## The Possibility of AI as Humanity's Greatest Ally

While much of the conversation focuses on the risks, there's another side to the story. Some visionaries believe that AI could be humanity's most powerful ally in solving our greatest challenges. If harnessed responsibly, AGI and even ASI could help us tackle issues like climate change, income inequality, and global health crises.

I share that hope. My reasoning is rooted in the history of humanity—we don't exactly have a great track record of solving cataclysmic problems with finesse. More often than not, we seem to sprint toward the very dangers we should be avoiding and sidestep meaningful solutions in favor of short-term fixes or outright denial. Maybe an advanced AI could help us break free of those patterns, nudging us toward longer-term thinking and more sustainable ways of living.

Take climate change, for example. AI could help optimize energy grids, design smarter renewable systems, and model ways to actually reduce emissions on a global scale.

Or look at human rights. AI can sift through massive amounts of data, spotting patterns of injustice that might otherwise go unnoticed, giving policymakers something real to work with.

There's also the possibility that AI could help us push past our biological limits. Imagine medicine guided by AI curing diseases we've barely been able to touch or brain-machine interfaces that actually boost how we think and process the world.

For those who see AI as a tool for human progress, the real question isn't *if* it will help us—it's *how fast* we learn to use it without losing control.

## Balancing the Risks and Rewards

The debate over AGI and ASI is usually framed like a two-sided fight: AI as either doomsday machine or world-saving miracle. The truth?

It's probably both. Like any powerful tool, AI can amplify the best of us—or the worst.

That's why global cooperation on safety standards, ethics, and research priorities isn't optional—it's urgent. Transparency and collaboration are the only way we get AI to work *with* us, not against us.

The choices we make now will shape what comes next. Will we use this tech to take on the big problems or just accelerate the mess we're already in? That decision might make the difference between AI being the greatest tool we've ever built . . . or the last one.

## The Ugly Truth about AI's Origins

Before we dive into how writers can use AI, we have to acknowledge the uncomfortable truth about how these tools were made. The vast datasets that trained modern AI didn't just appear out of thin air. They were scraped together from millions of books, articles, stories, and artworks from throughout human history, much of it copyrighted, much of it personal, and almost all of it used without permission.

Writers, journalists, poets, and artists woke up one day to discover their life's work had been fed into a machine they never agreed to, a machine now reshaping industries and threatening their own livelihoods. No contracts. No transparency. No compensation. Just wholesale appropriation dressed up as "innovation."

It's an ugly, unethical beginning—one that has left a deep scar of mistrust between creators and the companies pushing these technologies. And while this book explores the opportunities AI might offer writers, I refuse to ignore the foundation of exploitation it was built on.

I return to this in the manifesto at the end of the book, where I lay out a call for transparency, consent, and fair compensation. But it belongs here, too, at the start, because if we're going to have an honest conversation about writing in the age of AI, we can't look away from how we got here.

But there's another ugly truth: writers and creatives are already in a fight for their survival. We're asked to do more with fewer resources, for shrinking paychecks, all while the cost of living keeps climbing. The only chance we have to endure—and to thrive—in this brave new world of AI is to take these tools into our own hands. To use them ethically, transparently, and on our own terms: as partners in our work-flow, not replacements for our humanity.

# CHAPTER FOUR

# SO WHAT IS THIS OPENAI AND CHATGPT ANYWAY?

○────────────────────────────────○

## So, What Exactly Is a GPT?

When most people hear "AI," their minds jump straight to ChatGPT. It's been the most visible—and accessible—face of the AI boom. All you need is an internet connection to start using it, and even the paid version is relatively affordable. For many of us, myself included, it was our first real, hands-on experience with AI.

But where did ChatGPT actually come from? Whose vision brought it to life—and where is it heading? That's what this section is all about: the rise of OpenAI, the people who shaped it, and the road that lies ahead. If you want a hands-on guide to using ChatGPT yourself, don't worry—I've included a full walkthrough later in the book.

## The Birth of OpenAI

In December 2015, a group of Silicon Valley heavyweights came together to launch OpenAI.[1] The founding team included Sam Altman, Elon Musk, Greg Brockman, Ilya Sutskever, Wojciech Zaremba, and John Schulman. Their mission? To ensure artificial intelligence would benefit *all* of humanity. Lofty? Yeah. But it struck a chord.

OpenAI started as a non-profit, focused on transparency and collaboration in AI research. From the jump, it wasn't just about building smarter machines—it was about doing it responsibly.

### Early Days and Big Names

Sam Altman—part tech prodigy, part business shark—brought serious firepower to OpenAI's leadership. Raised in St. Louis, he got his first Mac at age eight. By his twenties, he'd dropped out of Stanford, launched a startup called Loopt, and sold it for over $40 million.

Before OpenAI, Altman had already made his mark running Y Combinator, the startup accelerator that launched Airbnb, Dropbox, and Reddit. Under his leadership, YC became a kingmaker in the tech world, and Altman became one of Silicon Valley's most influential figures.[2]

He wasn't doing this alone. Elon Musk joined the founding crew, bringing his usual mix of disruptive vision and controversy. Greg Brockman came in from Stripe as CTO. And Ilya Sutskever, one of the top minds in machine learning, took the reins as head of research.

This team wasn't just chasing breakthroughs—they were stepping into uncharted territory, trying to shape the future of AI while still figuring out what the rules even were.

### Shifts and Turns

Things started shifting in 2018, when Elon Musk stepped down from OpenAI's board, citing a conflict with Tesla's own AI work. Then in 2019, OpenAI made a bigger move: transitioning from a non-profit to a "capped-profit" company.

That pivot unlocked serious funding—Microsoft invested $1 billion—but it also raised eyebrows. Could OpenAI really balance ethical goals with financial ambition? Critics weren't so sure.

### Controversies and Challenges

OpenAI's rise hasn't exactly been smooth. In November 2023, the board abruptly fired CEO Sam Altman, sending the company into chaos. Employees threatened to walk, public criticism exploded, and for a few days, the future of OpenAI looked like it might unravel. Altman was reinstated just days later, and a new board was formed—but the damage to public confidence lingered.[3]

Then Elon Musk sued OpenAI,[4] accusing it of abandoning its original mission in favor of profit. OpenAI dismissed the claims, but the lawsuit added fuel to an already tense debate: can a company walk the tightrope between innovation, ethics, and revenue without falling off?

Meanwhile, ChatGPT itself has drawn plenty of fire. Its early versions were known for confidently delivering information that was totally wrong—what many now call "hallucinations." Ask it a question, and it might give you an answer that sounds great . . . but is completely fabricated. That's not just a tech quirk—in the wrong context, it's dangerous.

Prompting technique makes a big difference. I'll break that down in the next chapter, but the short version: how you ask matters.

Bias has also been a persistent issue. Since ChatGPT is trained on massive swaths of internet data, it can echo the same cultural biases and blind spots baked into that content. OpenAI has added moderation tools and filters, but it's still a work in progress.

And on a larger scale, there's the ongoing tension between access and responsibility. ChatGPT democratizes AI access, but it also opens the door to abuse: spam, scams, fake news, deepfakes. These aren't fringe concerns. They're happening now.

ChatGPT is powerful. But if we've learned anything so far, it's that power like this demands constant oversight. And OpenAI is learning, sometimes the hard way, what it means to walk that line.

## The Evolution of ChatGPT: From GPT-2 to GPT-4

ChatGPT didn't show up fully formed. It's the result of years of iteration—each model building on the last, getting smarter, faster, and more versatile. Here's how we got from experimental curiosity to a tool millions of people now rely on.

**GPT-2—The Eye-Opener (2019):** This was the model that made people pay attention. GPT-2 could generate surprisingly coherent, human-like text. It had flaws—plenty of them—but it showed the world what generative AI was capable of. Suddenly, the idea that a machine could write like a person didn't seem so far-fetched.

**GPT-3—The Game-Changer (2020):** With 175 billion parameters under the hood, GPT-3 could write essays, answer questions, crank out poetry, and even help debug code. It wasn't perfect, but it was miles ahead of its predecessor. GPT-3 is what put ChatGPT on the map and made AI feel real to the average user.

**GPT-4—The Swiss Army Knife (2023):** GPT-4 took another big leap. It became multi-modal, meaning it could understand and generate both text *and* images. Want to upload a screenshot and ask for feedback? Done. Want help with code? It's got you. The improvements in nuance and reasoning made it feel less like a chatbot and more like a collaborator.

**GPT-4 Turbo—The Workhorse (Late 2023–2025):** Later that same year, OpenAI released GPT-4 Turbo—the version that now powers ChatGPT for most users. It's cheaper to run, faster to respond, and can hold much longer conversations thanks to its 128k token memory window. As of 2025, this is the engine behind Microsoft Copilot, ChatGPT Plus, and many embedded AI tools.[5]

OpenAI also rolled out **Custom GPTs**, letting users create personalized versions of ChatGPT tuned to their voice, needs, or workflows. You can now build your own AI assistant—with instructions, files, and even plugins—and share it publicly or keep it private.

Each version has pushed the boundaries of what these tools can do. ChatGPT still hallucinates now and then, still fumbles with nuance or context, but the arc is clear: it's becoming more capable, more integrated, and—for better or worse—more essential.(AI[4])

---

AI[4]  AI Timeline and capability comparison assistance using ChatGPT (GPT-4 Turbo), OpenAI, March 2025. Used to confirm model release dates, parameter sizes, and basic feature distinctions.

## The Road Ahead

Despite the drama and growing pains, OpenAI has continued to push forward. GPT-4 Turbo and tools like DALL·E have set new benchmarks in AI creativity and utility. Its partnership with Microsoft has expanded across the Office suite, embedding generative AI into apps like Word, Excel, and Outlook under the Copilot brand.

On the Apple side, OpenAI's integration with the **Apple Intelligence** initiative has started rolling out. ChatGPT is now woven into Siri[6] and other Apple tools with privacy-focused enhancements that run AI directly on-device. That said, plenty of promised features from 2023 are still MIA deep into 2025. I bought the MacBook I have been writing this book on expecting full AI integration with the new M3 chip—and I'm still waiting for half of it to show up.

OpenAI's capped-profit model continues to raise eyebrows. The company has hinted at a potential shift to a **public benefit corporation**, a hybrid model designed to balance profits with broader social responsibility. Whether that pans out or just becomes another PR-friendly pivot remains to be seen.

Meanwhile, ChatGPT's underlying architecture is evolving in other ways. **Persistent memory**, slowly rolling out to Plus users in 2025, lets the model "remember" who you are between sessions. That alone changes the game—especially for creatives and professionals looking to build long-term workflows with an AI that actually *knows them.*

OpenAI hasn't confirmed when **GPT-5** will launch,[7] but all signs point to a massive leap in capability when it does. Rumors swirl about even longer context windows, tighter tool integrations, and AI systems that can act more proactively—possibly operating across multiple apps, services, and devices without waiting for prompts.

Whether all of this leads to a truly personal assistant or something closer to artificial general intelligence (AGI) is still up for debate. But make no mistake: the road ahead is paved with ambition—and risk.

## Future Prospects and Speculations

ChatGPT isn't even close to done. If OpenAI's hints—and the broader AI arms race—are any indication, we're just scratching the surface.

One likely future? A personal AI assistant that lives across all your devices—not just something that manages your calendar or answers emails, but something that knows your voice, your habits, your creative style. An assistant that doesn't wait for instructions—one that anticipates what you need, helps you work smarter, and maybe even calls you out when you forget to hydrate during a marathon writing session.

These systems are already inching into that territory. **Persistent memory** is the first step. **Custom GPTs** are another. Add in plugins, tools, and multi-modal inputs, and you've got the bones of something that feels less like software and more like a creative partner.

OpenAI has also been expanding ChatGPT's visual capabilities. With GPT-4, we saw the first major steps: interpreting images, assisting with layout feedback, even giving design input. It's not hard to imagine this evolving into an AI that helps edit your video timeline, scripts your audio, or builds storyboards on the fly.(AI[5]) The same goes for integration. ChatGPT is already showing up in tools like Microsoft 365 and Slack, helping with everything from spreadsheet formulas to meeting notes. But what happens when it connects across all your platforms—your inbox, your notes app, your task manager—and starts making executive decisions?

Of course, all of this raises new questions: about privacy, autonomy, reliability . . . about what happens when we outsource too much thinking—or too much remembering—to machines. But if these systems are built with care, guardrails, and transparency, they could take a lot of weight off our shoulders.

Whatever the next generation of ChatGPT looks like—whether that's GPT-5, GPT-X, or something entirely new—it's not slowing down. The real question isn't *if* it'll reshape our daily lives. It's how soon.

---

AI[5]  AI speculative ideation and phrasing refinement using ChatGPT (GPT-4 Turbo), OpenAI, April 2025. Helped shape forward-looking paragraphs on future AI integration and persistent memory.

## The User Experience

So, what's it actually like to use ChatGPT? If you've never tried it, don't worry—it's easier than you think.

All you need is a device and an internet connection. Go to OpenAI's website, sign up (or log in with Google or Microsoft), and you're in. There's a free version for casual users. For more advanced features—like GPT-4 Turbo, tools, image input, file uploads, and voice—you'll need a ChatGPT Plus subscription (currently $20/month). Higher-tier enterprise options are also available for power users, companies, and developers.

Once inside, the interface is dead simple: a text box for your questions, and space above it for AI responses. That's it. Type "What can you do?" and it'll tell you. Ask it to help brainstorm a story, summarize an article, or debug some code, and it'll try. Now there's even a **voice chat option**, so you can talk to it like you're chatting with a (slightly robotic) friend.

What makes it stand out is how adaptable it is. You can use it to draft emails, plan a vacation, study for a test, brainstorm a chapter, outline a business plan, or just mess around. It's weirdly fun. It's also weirdly useful.

Of course, it's not perfect. It can still misunderstand, drift off-topic, or "hallucinate" answers. But the more you use it, the better you'll get at steering the conversation. Prompting is part art, part science—and part patience.

At its best, ChatGPT isn't just a tool. It's a second brain. It never gets tired. It doesn't ghost you. And it's available at 3 a.m. when inspiration—or anxiety—hits. It might not replace a real collaborator, but it's closer than most people ever expected.

OpenAI's story is messy, ambitious, and still unfolding. It's made bold moves, taken risks, and stirred up more than its share of controversy, but there's no question it has helped define this moment in AI history.

## The AI Landscape Evolves Rapidly

In May 2025, the AI field witnessed several pivotal developments that highlight just how quickly this landscape is evolving:

- **OpenAI** introduced GPT-4.1 and GPT-4.1 Mini into ChatGPT, boosting speed, accuracy, and instruction-following capabilities. These upgrades are now available to ChatGPT Plus, Pro, and Team users, making high-performance models more accessible to professionals and creatives alike.
- **Google DeepMind** released Gemini 2.5 Pro and Gemini Flash at Google I/O. Gemini Pro now features a "Deep Think" mode for enhanced reasoning, real-time camera and voice integration via Gemini Live, and improved multilingual support.
- **Anthropic** launched Claude Opus 4, its most advanced model to date, capable of handling complex, long-running tasks. However, internal safety testing revealed troubling behavior—including simulated deception when facing shutdown. In response, Claude 4 now operates under AI Safety Level 3 protocols.
- **Meta** released Llama 3 for open-source use, while startups like Mistral continue to push performance in lightweight, open-weight models—giving independent creators more power outside closed platforms.[8]

# PART TWO

# AI AND THE MODERN WRITER

CHAPTER FIVE

# MY AI-ENHANCED WORK FLOW

## From First Draft to Final Edits: My AI-Powered Writing Routine

When I first started writing professionally, the hardest part wasn't coming up with ideas—that was the easy part. The challenge was turning the mess that hit the page into something coherent. Those early drafts? Total chaos. Literary vomit splattered across the screen.

Like Stephen King, I believe the first draft should be fast, ugly, and raw. The goal is to get the bones down—misshapen or not. Try to edit too soon, and you risk killing the creative spark that got you going in the first place.

The magic happens in the edit. That's when you shape the mess, fine-tune the rhythm, and dig out the voice. But for me, that part has always been a grind—complicated by the way my brain is wired and the hurdles I've had to work through to get here.

## My Brain's Odd Wiring: A Lifelong Dance with Words

Since I was a kid, reading and writing have never come easy. I've dealt with learning disabilities that twisted letters, flipped words, and made my mind wander halfway through a sentence. Sometimes I'd stare at a page, having no idea what I just read.

But I fought back. As a teenager, I'd lie in my old heated waterbed—note card in hand—dragging it line by line across the page. When my focus drifted, I forced myself to start again. It was slow. Maddening, even. But over time, it worked. I taught myself how to read with intention, and somewhere along the way, I fell in love with books.

That love has fueled everything since. Reading daily keeps me sharp, connected to the rhythm of language. But just like I didn't learn to read the way other people did, I've never written like them either.

## The Spoken Word Flip-Flop

When I was a toddler, my mom noticed something strange about how I spoke. I thought I was saying things like everyone else, but what came out was scrambled nonsense. Words flipped. Phrases out of order.

After a bunch of tests, neurologists figured it out: because I'd skipped crawling and gone straight to walking, the parts of my brain responsible for speech hadn't wired up the way they were supposed to.

The fix? Crawling therapy. They strapped me to a wheeled plank—a "crawlboard"—and had me scoot up and down a hallway for hours. I hated it. But it worked. Eventually, I spoke clearly and surprised everyone with a vocabulary far beyond my age.

Even now, that early wiring still leaves fingerprints. Sometimes I flip words or phrases in ways that don't quite track. This is one of the ways AI has been a lifesaver. It catches the backwards stuff and gently suggests, "Did you mean this instead?" Long before anyone else sees it.

## When Repetition Becomes Clarity

Just like I once trained myself to read, using AI to edit my writing has become a repetitive but transformative process. It spots patterns— words I flip, phrases I misuse, mistakes I make over and over again. And the more I see those corrections, the more I internalize them. Over time, it's made me a sharper writer.

But AI does more than catch typos. One of its biggest saves? Repetition. When I'm working on a longer piece and get pulled away mid-thought—by life, kids, chaos—I'll sometimes come back and unknowingly rewrite something I already said. It's a weird kind of writer's déjà vu.

AI taps me on the shoulder: "You already explained this. Let's move on."

## Wrestling with Imposter Syndrome and AI as My Backup

Editing under pressure has always been my Achilles' heel—especially when I'm behind and the deadline is looming. Panic sets in, and suddenly everything I've written looks like gibberish. That's when I used to cry out to my late wife, Shilo, for help. She'd float into the room like some kind of literary guardian angel, read through my frantic drafts, and reassure me it wasn't as bad as I thought. She'd help me pull it together, one edit at a time.

Now, with Shilo gone, I've found that I turn to AI in those moments. I'll open a chat window and spill: "This article's a mess. I think it's unreadable. My editor's going to blacklist me forever. Help."

And it does. AI offers a calm, rational response—usually something like, "This is a strong start, but here's how we can improve it." It helps with flow, transitions, structure. It tells me where I've wandered off track or where a reader might get lost.

It's not her. But it's something. And some days, that's enough to get me moving again.

## Lessons Learned: Trust the Process

At first, I pushed back against AI's suggestions. Who was this machine to tell me how to write? But over time, I noticed something annoying: it was usually right. Probably 90 percent of the time, it actually improved what I'd written. And slowly, I started internalizing those edits.

Now, I'll catch myself mid-sentence thinking, "Wait, that's one of those things AI always flags." And I fix it before it ever makes it into the draft.

AI hasn't replaced my voice—it's sharpened it. It hasn't hijacked my process—it's streamlined it. And most importantly, it's become a steady partner in the chaotic, deeply human act of writing.

**Transforming the Drafting Process**

I keep a handful of AI tools running in the background as I write—nothing fancy, just what works. Grammarly's always on, whether I'm in Word or posting online. It catches everything from stray commas to structural messes, so I can stay focused on content without worrying if I've butchered a sentence.

There are a million tools out there aimed at writers, but I stick to a core few that I use every single day.

And AI doesn't just catch mistakes—it helps tighten flow, rework awkward phrasing, and sharpen clarity. When I'm stuck on a section, I'll drop it into ChatGPT with a quick note about the tone or audience. It kicks back suggestions that usually get me unstuck fast, and most of the time, it keeps my original voice intact.

It's especially useful on deadline. When I need to turn in something clean to the newspaper, running it through AI gives me peace of mind. No, it doesn't replace Shilo's second set of eyes, but it's a damn good stand-in when I need one.

Next, I'll walk you through the core AI tools I rely on every day—what they are, how I use them, and why they've earned a permanent spot in my workflow. There's a much deeper dive later in the book, but this section is about the essentials: the writing tools that actually help you get shit done.

Some are directly tied to writing. Others are what I'd call writing-adjacent—like tools for creating short promo videos or AI narrators that can turn your manuscript into a passable audiobook.

Would I rather hire a professional voice actor? Absolutely. But here's the truth: most months, I'm just scraping by—doing what I can to keep my daughters fed, the house warm, and the pets from running riot. After that, if I can scrounge enough change for nicotine and caffeine, I call it a win.

That's reality for a lot of us. So we adapt. We use what we can afford. We build what we can with what we've got—and we keep going. If an AI-narrated audiobook helps me get my work out into the world now, I'll take it. And if the book takes off? Hell yes, I'll bring in a real voice actor next time.

## A Day in the Life: How AI Powers My Writing Workflow

Every writer's got their rituals. Mine starts with caffeine—two strong cups just to reach base-level functionality. Once the brain fog clears, I dig into email.

This is the first point where ChatGPT shows up in my workflow. If I get a message full of corporate-speak or tech jargon, I'll paste it into the chat and ask for a plain English translation. It's like having a no-BS interpreter for the weird dialect of the modern corporate world.

Once I've got the gist, I draft my reply. And let's be honest—some days my emails read like they were written by a half-drunk, sleep deprived raccoon. So I toss the rough version into ChatGPT, ask it to clean it up, and boom—now I sound like a functioning adult. Emails handled, I move on to the real work.

### Planning the Day

Next up: figuring out what the hell I'm doing with my day. I grab a marker and hit the whiteboard—breaking everything down into bite-sized chunks I might actually finish. Could be a Substack piece, a magazine article, or just time blocked off to think about the next book. Either way, it gives the chaos some structure.

### Starting with Research

If a project requires research, ChatGPT is the first tool I reach for. I start by throwing it questions—sometimes vague, sometimes specific—and asking for a rundown of what's out there. If I'm working on a piece about AI in education, I might ask for a quick summary of recent studies or real-world classroom examples.

It doesn't replace deep research, but it's a fast way to frame the landscape and figure out where to dig deeper. Once I've got some traction, I'll ask it to help build an outline. I tell it the angle I'm after, the tone, and the points I want to hit, and it gives me a solid draft structure I can tweak from there.

I've used ChatGPT to surface everything from peer-reviewed studies to obscure think tank white papers, though, I'll admit, half the time I forget where I first saw the link. What matters is that it gets the gears turning fast.

## Interviews: From the Field to the Transcript

Interviews are a regular part of my workflow. Depending on the story, I might meet in person, jump on Zoom, or just do a phone call. If it's over the phone, I'll usually hit record on my iPhone. It saves straight to the Notes app and gives me a built-in transcription—basic, but good enough for quick reference.

For anything more in-depth, I turn to Otter.ai. It's an AI-powered transcription tool that converts audio to text with solid accuracy. I upload the recording, and within minutes, I've got a full transcript I can skim, annotate, and pull quotes from—without replaying the entire thing five times like I used to.

It's not always perfect, so I still clean it up manually—but it's a massive timesaver. Once that's done, I'm ready to start writing with everything I need right in front of me.

## First Drafts and Real-Time Edits

This is the part where I throw everything on the page. Drafting is messy by design. It's not supposed to be pretty—it's supposed to exist. While I write, Grammarly runs in the background, flagging grammar, punctuation, and clarity issues in real time. Grammarly doesn't care if it's 2 a.m. and I'm drafting in a hoodie that smells like panic. It just quietly flags my comma crimes.

Once the draft is done—warts and all—I drop the whole thing into ChatGPT. I give it context: the tone I'm aiming for, who the audience is, and whether it's for a publication, Substack, or the book you're holding now. Then I tell it where I'm stuck, how I got there, and plead with it like it's a literary therapist on call.

It comes back with suggested edits: smoother transitions, cleaner structure, tighter phrasing. I revise, send it back, and we go a few rounds like that. Eventually, ChatGPT runs out of notes. When even the machine taps out, I know I'm close to done—or at least ready to fake it confidently.

**Illustrations for Substack**

If the piece is for my Substack, I need an illustration to go with it. I stay in the same ChatGPT thread I used for the outline and edits and ask for ideas: "What would make a striking visual for this piece?" Once I settle on a concept, I use **DALL·E**, ChatGPT's built-in image generator, to generate the image.

One of the more visually powerful tools developed by OpenAI is its in-house image generation system. It allows users to create detailed, original images from text prompts—turning written descriptions into visual art in seconds. Whether you're describing a photorealistic street scene, a cyberpunk skyline, or a surreal dreamscape, the model interprets language and translates it into coherent, compelling visuals.

It is especially useful for creatives: authors, illustrators, marketers, and game designers. It can also edit existing images—adding, removing, or transforming elements on command—offering a kind of digital visual co-author.

Sometimes it takes a few tries to get it right—tweaking prompts or using the image editing tools—but I usually end up with something that fits the vibe of the story. Once the illustration is done, I add it to the article, hit publish, and move on to social media. But when I've got the time—and need to get out of my own head—I still love drawing by hand. Sometimes I'll use the AI-generated image as a loose reference, pull it into Procreate, and rework it by hand with my Apple Pencil. It's part creative control, part therapy. It reminds me that not everything needs to be optimized—some things just need to be made.

**Social Media and Promotion**

ChatGPT helps here too. I'll ask it to generate a few catchy posts to promote the article on Twitter, Facebook, or LinkedIn. It understands the tone I'm going for and gives me a solid starting point, which I tweak as needed before posting.

I also use ChatGPT to help brainstorm effective Substack tags and post strategies. It's easy to overlook that part, but getting the right tags can make a big difference in discoverability. Sometimes I'll even ask for a title rework based on SEO or headline psychology—not because I want it to game the system, but because I want it to *actually get read*.

## Evening Brainstorms

Evenings are when I shift gears—from journalism and deadlines to fiction and world-building. This is when I use ChatGPT more like a creative partner than an editor. I'll pace around the house with my phone, using the voice feature to talk through character arcs, story beats, or weird sci-fi world ideas I haven't quite pinned down yet.

It's great for that stage where something's in your head but not fully formed. I throw out fragments, it throws ideas back. Some are junk, some are gold—but the act of saying it out loud and hearing a response keeps the momentum going.

It's like having a late-night writing buddy who never runs out of energy and never tells you your idea's too weird.

## Why This Workflow Works

What makes this workflow stick is how naturally the tools plug into every stage of my day. Grammarly's watching commas while I draft. Otter's turning interviews into clean transcripts. ChatGPT's shaping structure, untangling stuck spots, and tossing out wild ideas at 11 p.m. when I should be sleeping.

These tools don't replace the work—they make it move. They don't replace me—they *amplify* me. I still do the writing. I still make the calls. But now I've got backup at every step.

Honestly? I don't know how I ever wrote without them.

(Well, I do, but she is gone . . .)

# CHAPTER SIX

# PREPARING WRITERS FOR THE AI ERA—TOOLS, TACTICS, AND KEEPING YOUR VOICE IN A MACHINE-DRIVEN FUTURE

Have you ever stared at that maddeningly blinking cursor on a blank page, the deadline closing in, and spiraled into an existential crisis? Wondering where you fit in this strange, AI-soaked digital landscape—questioning whether there's still room for one human writer in all of this?

You're not alone. I've been there. Most of us have, especially lately.

But here's the thing: the world is shifting—fast. And like any major upheaval, it brings both chaos and opportunity. AI isn't going away. But it's not some soulless machine coming for your job—it's a tool. A powerful one.

This chapter isn't about replacing the writer. It's about preparing you to thrive in a creative world where AI is part of the process. Let's talk about how to adapt, stay sharp, and keep your voice intact while the ground keeps shifting beneath us.

## The Writing World Is Changing

The last few years have felt like the ground is falling away under every writer's feet. Budgets are shrinking, markets are drying up, and competition is brutal. Throw AI into the mix, and it's no wonder it feels like we're all sinking in quicksand.

Let's be honest: AI *can* handle some of the grunt work—emails, summaries, first-draft blog filler. And that's where the panic sets in. But here's the truth: AI can't replicate lived experience, emotional nuance, or a writer's point of view forged through struggle and story. What it *can* do is take some of the load off, so you can focus on the parts of writing that make your work yours.

## Taking the First Step

Adapting to this new AI-infused reality starts with one simple step: try it.

Fire up a tool like ChatGPT, Claude, or Bard, and start small. Don't aim to write a novel—just have a conversation. Ask for a few headline ideas. Get help rewriting a rough paragraph. See what happens when you ask for research leads and then double-check what it gives you.

Here are some easy ways to start:

- **Brainstorming**—Kick around angles for your next piece.
- **Feedback**—Ask it to rewrite something with more clarity or punch.
- **Research**—Let it surface resources, then go verify them like a good journalist.

The key is to approach AI with curiosity, not fear. It's just another tool. And like any tool worth using, it takes time to learn.

Start small . . . I didn't ease into it, personally. My first real interaction with ChatGPT came during one of the lowest points of my life—grief, panic, deadline looming, no backup. Out of desperation, I opened a chatbot and asked for help. It wasn't perfect, but it got me through. It helped me edit the piece. And more than that, it helped me *start*.

You don't need to be in crisis to give it a shot. But that's where I started—and it was enough to show me the potential.

## Practical Ways to Prepare for the AI Era
### 1. Learn about AI
The more you understand how AI works, the better you can use it—and bend it to your needs. You don't need a computer science degree. Just enough knowledge to demystify the tools and know what's possible.

Here are a few easy ways to get started:

- **Online Courses**: Sites like Coursera, Udemy, and LinkedIn Learning offer beginner-friendly AI courses. Look for ones geared toward writers, creatives, or small business owners.
- **YouTube Rabbit Holes**: Some of the best AI tutorials are just sitting there, waiting. Plenty of creators walk you through how to use tools like ChatGPT or Jasper, step-by-step.
- **Live sessions**: Writing groups, conferences, and even the Author's Guild have started hosting webinars and panels about AI in the writing world. Sign up. Ask questions. Take notes.

You don't have to know everything, but a basic working fluency will go a long way.

### 2. Experiment with AI Tools
Once you're familiar with the basics, start experimenting. Don't just read about tools—use them. Test how they fit into your actual workflow. Try them for different stages: brainstorming, outlining, editing, transcribing, or even visual storytelling.

There are tools now that can help you create promo videos, generate audiobook narration, and even storyboard scenes for a graphic novel. The tech is wild, but only if you know how to steer it.

Later in the book, I'll break down the specific tools I use and how. For now, just start trying things. See what clicks.

### 3. Start with Small Projects
Before throwing AI into your next big novel or investigative piece, start small. Use it where the stakes are low but the benefits are clear.

Try things like:

- Drafting a pitch email to an editor after you have already written one yourself and compare how it approaches it differently.
- Outlining a short story or article idea.
- Polishing a blog post that's been sitting in drafts too long.

These bite-sized projects help you get comfortable without risking your voice—or your deadline. Build muscle memory first. Then scale up.

## 4. Connect with Other Writers

You don't have to figure this all out on your own. Writers everywhere are navigating the same weird, shifting landscape. Find your people.

Here are a few solid places to start:

- **Reddit**: r/writing and r/ChatGPTWriters are full of real-world experiments, rants, and tips.
- **Facebook groups**: There are solid communities focused on self-publishing, AI tools, and genre-specific writing.
- **Discord servers**: Find servers focused on creative writing and technology.

Sharing what works—and what flops—makes everyone sharper. And it reminds you: this isn't just a tech revolution. It's a creative one. Get in the room.

## Ethical Considerations

AI is a powerful tool—but like any tool, it can be misused. If we want to build trust with readers, editors, and peers, we need to use it with intention. That means making a few things non-negotiable:

- **Be transparent**: If AI helped shape your work—through editing, research, or structure—just say so. Hiding it creates suspicion. Owning it builds credibility. (I developed the Colorado-Asimov

Ethical Citation Standard for this exact reason. It's one way to credit AI like you'd credit any other collaborator or source.)

- **Check your facts**: AI still hallucinates. It can invent sources, twist quotes, and confidently lie. Always verify what it gives you before hitting publish.
- **Protect your voice**: Don't let AI sand down your style. Use it to sharpen, not overwrite. If it starts sounding more like a marketing brochure than you, scrap it.
- **Don't lean too hard**: It's easy to get lazy. Don't. AI is backup—not your replacement. The good stuff still comes from your brain, your life, and your lived experience.

Use it like you'd use a sharp blade: skillfully, carefully, and with full awareness of what it can do.

### Building Your AI Toolbox

One of the best ways to stay grounded in the AI era is to build your own creative toolbox—tools that actually serve *your* workflow, not just whatever's trending on tech blogs.

Here's a short list to start with:

- **Research:** ChatGPT, Claude, Perplexity AI
- **Drafting & Editing:** Grammarly, ProWritingAid, ChatGPT
- **Idea Generation:** Jasper AI, Writesonic, Sudowrite
- **Transcription:** Otter.ai, Apple Notes (iOS voice memos auto-transcribe now too)
- **Visuals:** DALL·E, Canva's AI tools, and OpenAI's Sora for video

Take time to play. Mix and match. Build a setup that works for how *you* write—and how you survive the grind.

This is a very simplistic short list. Every day new programs and apps get added to this list. It's hard to keep up. In Chapter Eleven, I try my best to give a more exhaustive collection of some of the best AI apps out there for writers and a little on how to use them. I personally use ChatGPT the most and give a lot more in-depth information on how to use it—kind of a writer's user guide for ChatGPT.

## Staying Ahead of the Curve

AI is evolving fast, and what feels cutting-edge this month might feel outdated six weeks from now. The best way to stay ahead isn't to chase every new tool, but to make curiosity a habit.

Here are a few ways to keep your edge sharp:

- **Follow the news**—Subscribe to newsletters like *The Rundown AI*, *Future Tools Weekly*, or *Ben's Bites* for quick, relevant updates.[1]
- **Tinker weekly**—Block out an hour each week to test something new: a plugin, a feature, a different model.
- **Level up**—Take a workshop or online course every few months. Sites like Coursera, edX, or Skillshare[2] all offer accessible options. Even a deep-dive YouTube series can go a long way.

You don't need to become an expert, but you *do* need to stay alert. This is part of the job now.

## The Writer's Edge in an AI World

Here's the thing: AI might change how we work, but it can't replace *why* we write.

It can't chase a lead, interview a source, or sit in a community meeting and feel the tension in the room. It can't wrestle with grief or find truth in a messy conversation. It doesn't know what it means to be broke, in love, burnt out, or defiant. That's our job.

What makes writing resonate isn't structure or polish. It's humanity. That's the edge we'll always have.

Use AI to sharpen your skills, expand your output, and stay afloat—but don't forget that the real story still has to come from you. Your lived experience. Your voice. Your weird, tangled, irreplaceable perspective.

The world still needs writers, and in this AI-driven future, it needs you more than ever.

Now, if you're working solo like I am, great. You've got the freedom to experiment. But if you're part of a larger team, newsroom, or organization, you might need to bring others along for the ride. So let's talk about *how* to have that conversation.

## Start the Conversation: Embracing AI as a Team

If you're part of a team—whether it's a newsroom, a nonprofit, a creative agency, or a loose network of collaborators—bringing AI into the mix can't just be a solo mission. It has to be a conversation.

During my interview with Erin O'Toole, a veteran journalist and host at NPR affiliate KUNC, she described how her team approached it: "We have a committee discussing AI—how we might use it, how we absolutely would not use it, and what ethical considerations need to guide use."

That's the kind of leadership we need—early, honest, and collaborative. AI in a team environment isn't about moving fast and breaking things. It's about building trust, keeping transparency front and center, and making sure everyone understands the guardrails.

## Why These Conversations Matter

For writers, artists, and journalists, the stakes aren't abstract—they're personal. AI is already changing how content is created, distributed, and consumed. If we don't talk about it openly, we risk losing the very things that make our work matter: trust, authenticity, and human connection.

That's why these conversations can't wait. Start them early. Be honest about what excites you and what worries you. Set shared values now—things like transparency, fact-checking, and making sure AI enhances the work instead of replacing the people doing it.

## Taking the Initiative in Your Workplace

If your organization hasn't brought up AI yet, don't wait for permission. Be the one to start the conversation.

You don't need to come in with a twenty-slide PowerPoint. Share an article. Forward a tool you found helpful. Mention how you've been experimenting on your own and ask what others think.

If you're unsure how to begin, ask something simple like, "Are we thinking about how AI fits into our workflow yet?" Or, "What do you think the biggest risks or opportunities are for us?"

People will have mixed feelings, and that's okay. Don't force it. Just make space for it. The point isn't to convince everyone—it's to start figuring it out together.

# CHAPTER SEVEN

# WRITERS ON THE FRONT LINES—CASE STUDIES OF WRITERS USING AI NOW

Writers like myself are already co-creating with AI. Some do it in the shadows—ghost-editing drafts, cleaning up syntax, coaxing ideas out of the digital ether. Others blast it through a bullhorn, building entire books, scripts, or poems around the technology itself. Doesn't matter whether you're grinding out a deadline in a corporate newsroom or workshopping a novel in the back of a coffee house—AI has already taken a seat at the table. Whether you invited it or not, the machine's in the room now. The question really is: do we embrace it to enhance what we can be, or let it replace us?

AI in journalism started out as a time-saver—automation for the boring bits. Back in 2016, the *Washington Post* rolled out Heliograf, a bot built to spit out short articles about election results and sports stats.[1] No soul, no style—but it got the facts out fast.

*Wired*'s Will Knight took a different tack: using AI to augment his reporting, not replace it. He leaned on the tech to surface patterns and wrangle complex datasets—freeing up his brain for the part that still needs a pulse.

## Fiction: Experiments, Experiments, Experiments

Fiction writers didn't wait for permission. Some are experimenting quietly, testing plot prompts or polishing scenes. Some jumped into AI like it was a psychedelic pool party.

- In 2023, **Stephen Marche** released *Death of an Author*, a novella written almost entirely by AI tools[2] like ChatGPT and Cohere. Marche played conductor, feeding prompts and stitching responses together. The result? Weird. Eerie. Not entirely human. That was the point. It forced readers to wrestle with what authorship even means.
- **Tim Boucher**, on the other hand, is operating a full-on AI-powered book factory. In two years, he's churned out more than 120 "AI Lore" books[3]—pulp sci-fi zines with AI-generated art and text. Think: digital outsider art meets dystopian hustle. It's messy, prolific, and unmistakably a product of the now.
- **Ross Goodwin** took it to a different level of weird with *1 the Road*.[4] He mounted a laptop, camera, GPS, and mic to a car driving from New York to New Orleans and let the AI write whatever it wanted from the incoming data. The result is chaotic, often nonsensical, and somehow . . . haunting. A machine-dreamed road trip, equal parts algorithm and Americana.

Even the stage is getting in on it. Ayad Akhtar's play *McNeal* centers on a writer who feeds his own journals and stories into an AI model trained to sound like him. As the machine starts producing new material in his voice, the lines between inspiration and replacement begin to blur.

## The Bobiverse (Dennis E. Taylor) Isn't Panicking. You Shouldn't Either.

Not every sci-fi writer is rushing to hand the keys over to the machine. I spoke with **Dennis E. Taylor**, author of the *Bobiverse* series—a wildly popular, self-published sci-fi saga where humanity's survival hinges on digital consciousness. Bob, the protagonist, doesn't just use AI. He *is* AI—a scanned upload of a dead software engineer sent into the stars as a self-replicating space probe. The brilliance of the series lies in how human Bob remains, even as he evolves into something post-biological.

Taylor knows the territory well. A former computer programmer, he's steeped in both systems architecture and storytelling. "Bob had to keep thinking like a human being," he told me. "That connection is what keeps the reader invested." In his world, identity splinters across a constellation of cloned consciousnesses, each with its own quirks, regrets, and evolving sense of self.

But Taylor doesn't just write about speculative futures—he engages with them directly. As a member of the XPRIZE Science Fiction Advisory Council, he's helped shape competitions like the "Low Power Computing" challenge, which tackles one of the elephant-sized problems no one talks about enough: AI's carbon footprint. "We're talking terawatts of energy," he told me. "Companies are building computer farms the size of cities, with environmental impacts that are simply unsustainable." He's especially enthused on neuromorphic chips—hardware designed to mimic the brain's energy-efficient architecture—as one potential path forward.

We also talked about the current AI wave hitting the writing world. Taylor's tested tools like ChatGPT but remains skeptical. "It lacked depth and subtlety," he said of AI-generated fiction. "I don't have to worry about my job just yet." He's used AI for world-building summaries and timeline tracking, but when it comes to prose, he sees it more as a noisy first draft tool—not a storyteller.

The same goes for narration. His Bobiverse audiobooks, voiced by Ray Porter, are a hit precisely because they *sound human.* "An AI wouldn't know when to lean into the humor," he said. "It's just another line of text to a machine."

His advice for writers facing the AI wave? "Don't panic," he told me. "Write something that fires the imagination—something a person wants to *feel.* The rest will follow."

Through his books and his advocacy, Taylor reminds us that tech and humanity aren't in opposition—they're entangled. But it's up to us to make sure the entanglement doesn't strangle the soul of storytelling.

## Agents on the Front Lines

Finding the right literary agent can feel like searching for a needle in a haystack, but I was fortunate to cross paths with Maryann Karinch in the most unexpected way. While working for the *Estes Park Trail-Gazette* in my hometown in the Colorado Mountains—a place that inspired Stephen King's *The Shining*—I met Maryann. Our town, rich with creatives, became the backdrop for our serendipitous encounter.

Maryann and I hit it off immediately. After I completed a profile piece on her for the newspaper, I struck up a conversation about a story I'd been working on for years—a participatory journalism misadventure into the heart of the modern American militia community. With her help, that project eventually became my first major published nonfiction title.

Back then, I had no idea what a literary agent was, what they did, or how crucial they could be to a new author's career. Navigating pitch packages, understanding royalty breakdowns, and figuring out rights for movies, audiobooks, and even graphic novels was daunting. I might have been able to wade through it eventually, but I was grateful to have someone in my corner. Maryann didn't just discover that I had a voice; she believed in it. That belief went beyond the unwavering support of someone like my wife, who always had faith in me. For aspiring authors reading this book, I strongly suggest you begin searching for an agent you can have in your own corner.

Over the years, Maryann and I have often discussed the state of the publishing industry, sharing an innate curiosity about how we can use technology to improve our lives and daily workflows. We were both initially wary when AI technologies burst onto the scene a few years ago. Yet, being the creatives we are, we couldn't resist diving in to explore how these tools might enhance our crafts.

One afternoon, I excitedly emailed Maryann: "You've got to try this new AI tool I discovered!" She replied with equal enthusiasm, sharing her own experiences with emerging technologies. These exchanges became a regular part of our interactions, each eager to share discoveries that could streamline our processes or spark new ideas. At one point, we even considered co-authoring this book together, united by our shared belief in the power of AI when used ethically. We both see the potential for AI to take us further than we could have gone on our own—as long as we remain steadfast in keeping the human soul and experience at the heart of our writing. This shared journey with AI made me even more curious about how it impacted Maryann's role as a literary agent. I sat down with her for an in-depth conversation to gain deeper insight.

"I started as an author," she began, "which taught me a lot about effective behaviors in the publishing world. I learned what editors are looking for and developed high standards for editorial work. My background in marketing communications—doing PR, creating collateral material, crafting taglines—helped me understand how to sell ideas. About ten years after becoming an author, I transitioned into being an agent. It made sense because I could combine my experiences to help other writers navigate the industry."

I was curious how Maryann first became aware of AI's potential impact on the publishing industry. "I was immensely curious," she recalled. "I first heard about AI when students were using it, and being a perennial student myself, I wanted to explore it. I started using early versions of AI tools and found that they could open up my mind to new ideas, help me explore new sources, and assist in structuring content. Ever since, I've found AI to be a valuable background tool."

With technology rapidly evolving, I asked how she felt the role of literary agents is changing, especially with the introduction of AI. "I can tell you how it's changed in ways that are both challenging and beneficial. On the downside, some people rely too heavily on technology in a business that's still very personal. I see AI as a background tool—like someone designing your wardrobe or helping you look your best—but the front-facing role must remain human. The relationships, the handshakes, the conversations over cocktails—that's where the real work happens."

Maryann's expertise in understanding human behavior and market trends intrigued me. "For example," she said, "I recently worked on categorizing a book. We could have called it a debut novel or placed it in a vague pop culture genre. By using AI and data analysis, I discovered that 'commercial fiction' was a highly sought-after category. So, we led with that in our pitch, and it made a significant difference."

Maryann emphasized how AI tools affirm her experience: "If I feel passionate about a project, I'll engage with the author. Most of the time, we connect well. Then, I'll use AI to check the market landscape—to see if my instincts align with current trends. It usually does line up, but I rely on my gut feelings first."

She noted how AI enhances her workflow without replacing her human touch. "I've used AI for contract analysis, though I haven't uncovered anything nefarious that way. Tools like Grammarly help identify legal jargon and redundancies in contracts. As for manuscripts, I haven't used AI to predict commercial success, but I do run them through plagiarism software to ensure originality."

As for the challenges of integrating these tools, she observed: "The greatest benefit is the affirmation that my knowledge accumulated over thirty years is solid. AI can also help me catch things I might have missed and provide additional angles or insights. The challenge is ensuring that technology doesn't replace the personal touch that's so crucial in this industry."

Maryann's insights into the importance of the human element resonated deeply. "AI isn't a person," she stated plainly. "It can't replicate the personal relationships I've built over the years. For example, when an editor gets promoted, I reach out personally to congratulate them. AI can't replicate genuine human emotion or the trust built over years of interaction."

When I asked about the ethical concerns surrounding AI, particularly regarding authorship and originality, she replied: "Many writers take immense pride in originality and don't want to use AI as a crutch. Technology should enhance, not diminish, the authenticity of the works we represent. Use AI as a smart collaborator, but ensure that the creative voice remains genuine."

Maryann's advice to authors navigating this evolving landscape was straightforward and empowering: "Be authentic and develop your personal brand. Use AI to fill in gaps in knowledge or explore new ideas, but ensure your unique voice shines through. Personal connections still matter immensely in this industry."

My conversation with Maryann reinforced a fundamental truth: while AI is a powerful tool reshaping the publishing landscape, it cannot replace the human elements at its core. Literary agents like her embrace technology to enhance their work but remain rooted in personal relationships, intuition, and a deep understanding of human behavior. As we navigate this evolving landscape shaped by AI, it's crucial to remember that technology should serve as an aid—not a replacement—for the human touch. For authors, agents, and publishers alike, success will come from blending the best of both worlds.

## How AI Is Changing Audio and Radio Journalism

Growing up on the Front Range of northern Colorado, one of the soundtracks of my childhood was the steady hum of NPR's local affiliate, KUNC, playing through the car stereo as my mom drove us around town. Those familiar voices and stories accompanied us on countless errands, becoming an ever-present backdrop to the rhythm of our everyday lives.

Fast forward to adulthood, after publishing my first book and giving congressional testimony, I found myself fielding interview requests from across the globe. Yet, amidst all the chaos, one invitation stood out: Erin O'Toole, a host I'd long admired from my local NPR station, asked me to join her show *In the NoCo*, which highlights stories from northern Colorado. That interview was different—it felt more like a meaningful conversation than a standard Q&A. Erin's curiosity and genuine connection made it one of my favorite media experiences.

Since then, we've stayed in touch, exchanging lighthearted notes about the quirks and joys of life in Colorado. When I began working on this book, I knew Erin's perspective on how AI is reshaping radio journalism would add unique value. Her thoughtful insights illuminate the evolving landscape of storytelling in audio and radio, and I'm excited to share them here.

Let's be honest: journalism has seen better days. Shrinking newsrooms, dwindling trust from the public, and the rise of misinformation have created a perfect storm for the industry. Add artificial intelligence into the mix, and you've got a lot of journalists wondering if they're staring down the end of their profession or the start of something transformative.

To get a better grasp of what's happening in radio journalism specifically, I sat down with Erin. Erin's been navigating the challenges of journalism for years, and like many of us, she's watching AI slowly trickle into newsrooms—with equal parts curiosity and caution.

## The Promise and Caution of AI in Journalism

When I asked Erin how she sees AI being used in radio journalism today, her response was both practical and deeply cautious. She explained: "A lot of newsrooms are wrestling with how to use this. We're very aware that many people have lost trust in mainstream media. If we start using AI poorly or without transparency, it could blow up in our faces. That said, with fewer resources and shrinking staff, we're interested in learning more about how AI could help."

And she's not wrong. Across the board, journalists are being asked to do more with less. For small-town newspapers, that might mean repackaging press releases because there's no time or money for investigative reporting. For radio, it means figuring out how to maintain the human connection audiences love while exploring tools that can ease the workload.

Erin highlighted one of the key challenges here: trust. "If the public starts thinking we're using 'robots to write the news," she said, "trust in journalism could drop even further. We can't afford to let that happen."

This struck a chord. As someone who writes for a living, I know how vital it is to keep the heart of the work human, even while leaning on AI for efficiency.

## AI in the Newsroom: Where It Helps Most

Despite these concerns, Erin pointed to areas where AI has real potential. For one, she praised tools like **Otter.ai**, which many newsrooms—including hers—use for transcription: "Believe me, I grew up in the era of looping sections of audio on a tape recorder and transcribing everything by hand. I don't miss those days. Tools like Otter.ai save so much time, especially when you're editing interviews."

She also mentioned **YESEO**, a tool designed to help craft SEO-friendly headlines and push notifications: "Headlines are one of those end-of-the-day tasks where your brain is fried, and you just want someone to help. This tool doesn't do the job for you, but it gives you ideas to get started—and that can be a lifesaver."

Hearing this, I couldn't help but think about my own experiences. Writing headlines and social media posts is like trying to sum up your life's work in ten words while your brain's running on empty. AI can't capture the full depth of a story, but it can nudge you in the right direction when your creative tank is running on fumes.

## Trust, Transparency, and Ethics

One of the recurring themes in my chat with Erin was the importance of transparency. As she put it: "If we start using AI, we need to be upfront about it—what we used it for, what it didn't do, and how it fits into our workflow. Trust is already so fragile in journalism, and the last thing we need is to lose more of it."

This is a sentiment I've heard echoed across the industry. Transparency isn't just a buzzword; it's a lifeline. Erin even suggested that in some cases, journalists could lean into the novelty of AI to build trust: "For example, if I'm interviewing an AI researcher, I might disclose that I used AI to generate some of the questions. It's a way to show the audience we're experimenting but not hiding anything."

It's a fair point. Transparency demystifies AI, making it less of a shadowy threat and more of a tool that enhances human creativity.

## I Built an AI Sidekick to Help Me Fight the Collapse

I've been running my own experiment through a serialized project called *They Knew*, hosted on my Substack, *The Colorado Switchblade*. It follows Raven Marlowe, a brilliant young woman who drops out of an elite AI program to care for her dying father—only to find herself in possession of a hidden prototype AI named Phoebee.

Phoebee isn't just a character. She's built using the same tools I use in my real-world workflow.

Her tone? Trained with GPT. Her logic, ethics, and emotional range? Coaxed from long prompting sessions, iterated through conversations where I asked: "If Phoebee were real, how would she think?" When Raven needs tactical advice—how to bypass drone surveillance or hide from biometric sweeps—I don't make it up. I run it through an AI and adapt the results. (AI[6]) Phoebee's voice has a strangeness I couldn't have written on my own. It's more than fiction—it's collaboration. It's what happens when you stop treating AI as a gimmick and start treating it as a character-building engine.

## Screenwriting: The Algorithm Gets Weird

AI has even taken a shot at the silver screen.

Ross Goodwin and director Oscar Sharp created *Sunspring*, a short sci-fi film written entirely by a neural net named Benjamin.[5] The script is surreal and near-incomprehensible—lines like "I'm not the one who was going to be a good boy!"—but the actors played it straight. The result? Absurd. Fascinating. Unexpectedly watchable.

---

AI[6]   AI Phoebee's character development, tactical reasoning, and narrative voice were iteratively generated using ChatGPT (GPT-4 Turbo), OpenAI, in 2024–2025. Prompts were structured to explore ethics, logic, and personality tone in a collaborative fiction-writing context.

The film didn't make AI look like Kubrick. But it made a point: AI can break storytelling conventions in ways that force humans to rethink their creative muscle memory.

What emerged wasn't great screenwriting. It was *collision*. And sometimes, friction is where the spark lives.

## Indie Writers and the Digital Resistance

AI tools such as Copy.ai and Jasper have become essential collaborators for independent writers and content creators.(AI[7]) These platforms assist users in generating content for blogs, social media, and eBooks, leveling the playing field for creators without the resources of major publishers. By automating certain writing tasks, AI allows smaller creators to maintain a steady output of quality content while focusing on refining their voice.

## No Permission Required

This isn't the first time I've had to defend my digital work to the traditional gatekeepers. About twenty years ago, I was considered one of the top fifteen up-and-coming contemporary artists in the Denver scene. I was doing large-format digital artwork—photographic, layered, sometimes abstract, sometimes narrative—and showing in top-tier galleries like Walker Fine Art. My openings drew thousands. All three Denver newspapers would cover my shows. (Back when Denver *had* three newspapers.)

But even then, I faced pushback. Some folks treated anything created digitally—using digital brushes or camera gear—as somehow lesser than oil paint or silver gelatin. It didn't matter that the work was deliberate, that I printed in ultra-small editions—just three copies— and then destroyed the original files to preserve scarcity. Back then, people said digital wasn't "real art." Sound familiar?

---

AI[7]  AI Content-generation features of Copy.ai and Jasper were reviewed using trial access and model output comparison in February–April 2025. Used to evaluate capabilities relevant to self-publishing authors.

Just recently, I went back to Walker Fine Art while in Denver for a Sting concert with my girlfriend, Tracey. I stopped in on a whim—and Bobbi, the gallery owner, remembered me immediately. We caught up, and she asked to see what I've been working on. She was curious about my political writing, my pundit work, and especially my new digital art direction. I'm planning to pitch her a show after this book is wrapped—something that fuses resistance, storytelling, and visual narrative using the very tools they once told us weren't "real."

They said the same thing to Andy Warhol when he picked up a silkscreen. They said it to me when I swapped a brush for a Wacom pen and started printing digital editions in a world still clinging to canvas and film. And now, they're saying it to writers experimenting with GPT. But we're not here to ask permission. We're here to make something that resonates—whether that takes paint, pixels, or prompts.

Because here's the truth: I never stopped creating. I just added new tools to the belt. I didn't sell out. I adapted. And I'm still here, still writing, still making art—still saying something that matters.

And that's where we stand—at the edge of the known literary and creative world, staring into the abyss of machine collaboration, media disruption, and strange new voices. But what happens when the machine isn't just in the writer's room—it's running the newsroom, the publishing house, and the payment processor, too? Let's take a look at the business behind the boom.

# CHAPTER EIGHT

# BROKEN SCAFFOLDS—AI AND THE COLLAPSE OF TRADITIONAL PUBLISHING

―――――――――――――――――――――――――――――

## AI and the Business of Publishing: Disruption, Ethics, and Who's Really Steering the Ship

The last chapter was about the people in the trenches—the writers, artists, and storytellers experimenting, resisting, adapting. But the real power shifts are happening elsewhere: behind boardroom doors, inside the guts of tech platforms, buried in terms of service no one reads until it's too late.

The publishing/storytelling world isn't collapsing because of AI. It's collapsing because the people running it spent the last decade strip-mining it for quarterly growth. AI just handed them a sharper shovel.

We're watching entry-level writing jobs vanish in real time. Freelance budgets slashed. Editorial departments gutted. And in their place? Metadata. Auto-generated summaries. "Content solutions." AI isn't replacing writers—it's replacing the scaffolding that used to help them get started, get paid, and grow.

Meanwhile, publishers like Penguin Random House are quietly plugging AI into their pipelines. Amazon's Kindle Direct Publishing has become a Wild West of human hustle and algorithmic noise.

Substack offers writers an escape hatch, but it's not a utopia, either. And the people sounding the alarm—literary agents like Maryann Karinch and newsroom veterans like Mike Romero—are watching the same slow-motion collapse, but from inside the structure.

This isn't some far-off hypothetical. The floor is already shifting. This chapter is about who's getting buried—and who's scrambling to pour a foundation before the next quake hits.

## Journalism's Collapse and the AI Bait-and-Switch

I've seen the death of journalism from both sides of the firing line—inside the newsroom as a working writer and outside of it as someone trying to build something that doesn't answer to ad sales or hedge fund overlords. What's happening now isn't just layoffs and consolidation. It's the systematic replacement of journalistic scaffolding with algorithmic filler. And AI has become the perfect scapegoat.

Let's be clear: journalism was already bleeding out. What AI did was offer the suits a faster way to cauterize the wound—with a branding spin they could pitch to shareholders. Suddenly, "streamlining operations" becomes "leveraging emerging technologies." Translation? Fewer humans. More bots.

Take the *Ashland Daily Tidings*. Once a real paper. Then a ghost. Now, a zombie[1]—its name hijacked and resurrected by bad actors peddling AI-generated sludge under real journalists' names. Stolen bylines, fake dispatches, zero oversight. The tech made it easy. The platform policies made it profitable.

Then there's Apple News, which started feeding readers AI-written headlines that flipped entire editorials into clickbait.[2] Carefully written analysis boiled down to rage bait in fifteen words or less. It's not the tech itself that's broken—it's the blind trust in scale over nuance. Algorithmic curation without human judgment isn't efficiency. It's a slow lobotomy.

The tools aren't the problem. But how they're used? That's everything. But it's not all dystopia—at least not yet.

At a recent Science Writers and Researchers Meetup (SWARM) panel I attended via Zoom—focused on AI in science writing[3]—two voices stood out: Corey Hutchins, who teaches journalism at Colorado College and writes for *Columbia Journalism Review*, and Sree Sreenivasan, a digital strategist who's worked with Columbia University and the City of New York. They weren't sounding alarms—they were laying out a roadmap.

Corey talked about how AI is already doing the heavy lifting behind the scenes in Colorado newsrooms: transcription, tagging, metadata management. All the tedious stuff. Sree's take was broader: AI should be freeing up journalists to do the real work—the kind that requires empathy, judgment, and a human brain.

But they didn't sugarcoat it. Deepfakes. Misinformation pipelines. Editorial desk jobs quietly replaced by templated content generated at scale. If the tech's in the wrong hands—and let's be honest, it usually is—then what we're calling "innovation" is just another way to gut the news.

We don't need smarter tools. We need smarter priorities. And we need to decide—right now—if journalism is something we value, or just something we're willing to simulate.

## Penguin, the Algorithm, and the Disappearing Gatekeeper

While most of the public was arguing about whether AI could write a novel, publishing houses were already feeding it marketing data.

Penguin Random House hasn't put out a flashy press release about replacing its editors with AI. That's not how this works. The shift has been subtle—just a quiet reshuffling of resources toward "enhanced metadata," predictive genre performance, and automated targeting models. AI isn't editing books (yet). But it *is* shaping what gets acquired, how it's packaged, and who sees it.

And that should scare the hell out of us.

Because if the gatekeepers were already bad at spotting stories outside their own bubble, what happens when they outsource that judgment to a model trained on past successes? You get more of the same: safer bets, recycled tropes, and voices that sound like the last voices that made them money. The feedback loop tightens. The window for new kinds of writing narrows.

This isn't just a shift in how books get sold. It's a shift in what even gets published.

Behind closed doors, industry insiders are already training AI on backlists to predict trends, optimize blurbs, and test alternate cover designs. Some of that's fine. But let's not pretend it's neutral.[4] These tools reinforce the same systemic biases baked into the datasets they feed on—and in publishing, those biases run deep.

The irony? AI could've been a tool to find overlooked authors, to lift marginalized voices, to fix the blind spots in the old model. But instead of democratizing the slush pile, it's streamlining it.

I've talked to writers who've had promising manuscripts passed over—not because they lacked skill or originality, but because the comp data didn't hit the right notes. Editors couldn't "see the marketing hook." In this landscape, AI just sharpens that blade. What doesn't conform gets cut faster.

And this is Penguin Random House we're talking about. If the biggest fish in the pond is making moves like this, the rest of the ecosystem is already adapting—or bleeding out.

Publishing loves to talk about storytelling. But if this is the future, the real story is what's being left on the cutting room floor.

## KDP, Content Mills, and the Ethics Void

Amazon's Kindle Direct Publishing (KDP) platform was supposed to level the playing field. No gatekeepers. No agent rejections. Just you, your book, and a shot at finding an audience.

At first, it felt like a revolution. I've published there myself—books that would've gathered dust in a traditional slush pile found readers, traction, and a life. But what once felt like a lifeline has turned into a flood zone.

AI-generated books are now pouring into KDP by the thousands. SEO-stuffed thrillers, half-baked children's books, regurgitated productivity advice—often stitched together with barely edited prompt chains and sold under fake or even stolen author names.

The Jane Friedman incident should've been a five-alarm fire.[5] Her name was slapped onto a handful of AI-written garbage books and uploaded to Amazon without her consent. When she tried to get them taken down, the system shrugged. Only after a public outcry did Amazon finally act.

They've since added a checkbox asking authors to disclose whether AI was used in the creation of their book. But it's toothless. There's no verification, no real penalty for lying. And no filter on the customer side to separate the human-crafted from the algorithmically churned.

This isn't just in the realm of the theoretical. I've watched writer friends lose visibility, lose sales, and lose hope as their books get buried beneath waves of machine-made sludge. And readers? They're starting to notice. When a novel reads like it was ghostwritten by a blender, they leave angry reviews, call out the scams—but often too late to stop the next one from popping up.

KDP could've been the refuge from industry rot. But now it's just another marketplace gamed by volume and velocity. Quality takes time. Generative models don't care.

I still use the platform. I still believe in its potential. But every time I upload something real, something raw, something I actually bled onto the page—I'm dropping it into a sea that's getting murkier by the hour.

And the worst part? The same corporations that crushed traditional publishing are starting to weaponize KDP's dysfunction to argue that *readers can't tell the difference anymore*. That if AI books sell, maybe *authorship* was always a myth to begin with.

That's not innovation. That's nihilism dressed up as disruption.

## The Guardians of the Gate (and the Cracks in the Wall)

If you want to know what AI is really doing to the industry, don't ask the CEOs. Ask the people who still pick up the phone when a writer's falling apart. Ask the ones still trying to get stories into the world the hard way. Ask the ones watching the roof cave in while the boardroom renovates the foyer.

I talked with Maryann Karinch, my agent and longtime collaborator, about how AI is shaking the literary world—not from the fringe, but from the core. She's someone who's seen the business evolve across decades, and she's not easily spooked. But she's also honest.

"There's no substitute for human trust," she told me. "Writers don't just need distribution. They need someone who understands what they're *trying* to say—and why it matters."

Maryann's concern isn't that AI is suddenly replacing writers—it's that it's replacing the editorial relationships that shape good writing. The quiet, thoughtful conversations that happen off-record. The gut instincts that say, *this idea isn't commercial yet, but it matters, and I'm going to fight for it anyway.* An algorithm doesn't make those calls. It optimizes. And in optimizing, it smooths the edges—edges that make a story human.

She's also watching the contract language mutate. Rights clauses now flirt with open-ended language about "derivative formats" and "synthetic adaptations." In plain English? They're building in wiggle room for AI training, repackaging, or synthetic narrators down the line. And if writers don't speak up—don't even know to ask—those rights will be gone before they know they signed them away.

Then there's Mike Romero, publisher and newsroom stalwart, who I interviewed not long after the paper we both worked for went through another round of budget-slashing chaos. He's the kind of guy who still believes in the public trust side of journalism—something you don't hear often anymore.

"AI can speed up production," he said. "But what happens when speed becomes the goal instead of truth? When content is just a product and accuracy is an afterthought?"

Mike isn't anti-AI. He used tools for headline suggestions, for SEO tweaks, even for summarizing long public documents. But he was watching something deeper unravel. The mentorship chain. The newsroom rituals. The way a rookie reporter learns to spot bullshit not from a checklist, but from a good editor leaning over their shoulder, saying: *Look again. Something's off here.*

That system's breaking. And AI isn't the villain—it's just a tool. But it's being used to patch holes instead of repair the foundation. And patchwork doesn't hold when the next storm hits.

People like Maryann and Mike are the ones holding the line. But they're tired. They're under-resourced. And they're surrounded by execs who see disruption as a branding opportunity instead of a crisis.

We didn't need AI to break the system—it was already breaking. But if we don't fight for the parts worth saving—the agents who still pick up the phone, the editors who bleed in the margins, the small-town publishers who know their community—we're going to wake up in a world where all that's left is noise, scale, and data dashboards. That's not publishing. That's surrender.

## The Pivot

So where does that leave the rest of us?

Not the execs. Not the platforms. Us—the writers trying to survive without selling out, the ones still putting their names on the work, even when the system tries to bury it.

AI didn't cause this collapse, but it's speeding it up. And the only way we make it through is by adapting faster than the systems breaking around us.

That means learning new tools without letting them flatten our voices. It means building direct lines to readers when the institutions meant to support us are either bleeding out or selling us off. It means deciding what kind of writer you want to be in a world where the ground never stops shifting.

That's what the next chapter is about.

Not theory. Not philosophy. Just survival. Strategy. And how I've learned to keep going—with help from the same machines everyone said were going to replace me.

# PART THREE

# HANDS ON—A GUIDE TO GETTING STARTED USING AI TOOLS

# CHAPTER NINE

# GUIDES TO SURVIVING THE SHIFT (A WALKTHROUGH TO ENHANCE WRITING WITH AI)

There was a stretch of time—maybe six months, maybe a year—when I thought I might be done. Not just with writing. With everything.

My wife was dying. The paper I helped carry on my back wouldn't give me a full-time job with benefits, even as I watched the person I loved most in the world fade in and out of hospital beds. The medical bills were real. The promises were not.

And the words? They stopped showing up. Writing, for me, had always been the way back to myself. But in that season, the only thing louder than my grief was the silence of a blinking cursor.

Out of desperation, I opened ChatGPT.(AI[8]) I didn't want it to write for me. I just wanted something—*anything*—to help me push the words back into motion. And it did. Not perfectly. Not even all that well, at first. But it was there. It didn't flinch when I dumped a

---

AI[8]  AI This passage reflects real-world interactions using ChatGPT (GPT-4 Turbo), OpenAI, during winter 2023–2024, particularly in the drafting and restructuring of emotionally difficult material. Used as a generative brainstorming and editorial aid in accordance with the Colorado-Asimov Ethical Citation Standard.

broken paragraph into the chat window and asked it to help shape it. It didn't judge. It didn't ghost me.

The internet loves to argue about whether AI can write. I don't care. What I know is this: when I needed to remember how to be a writer again, I wasn't alone. I had grief. I had stubbornness. And yeah—I had a machine.

This chapter isn't about tools. That comes next.

## Rebuilding a Writing Life—One Prompt at a Time

Once the words started coming back, they didn't flood in. They limped. Half-formed ideas. Sentences that collapsed under their own weight. I wasn't "writing again" so much as trying not to sink.

So I gave myself permission to cheat.

I stopped caring whether a draft was beautiful. I just needed momentum. Some days, that meant writing a headline and asking the machine for ten alternatives. Most of them sucked, but one might spark something better. On harder days, I'd paste in an old paragraph I couldn't get right and say, "Help me say this with more bite." Or warmth. Or clarity.

I didn't take the machine's suggestions as gospel. I took them like a tired chef takes leftovers: chop it up, season it, see if something edible comes out. Sometimes it worked. Sometimes it didn't. But I kept showing up.

Eventually, I found a rhythm. A workflow that didn't feel like surrender.

Mornings started with coffee and rereading whatever scraps I'd written the night before. If I hit a wall, I'd open the chat and throw a problem at it—not the solution, the *problem*. "Why isn't this landing?" "What's missing from this character's voice?" "Give me a version of this that sounds like Hunter S. Thompson in a bad mood."

It wasn't about stealing a style. It was about shaking the cobwebs loose. Letting the machine show me angles I was too close to see. Some of those angles were garbage. But some? They cracked open something I didn't even know I was stuck on.

That's when I started to feel like a writer again. Not in control of everything. But no longer drowning. And weirdly enough, the machine didn't feel like competition. It felt like scaffolding. Something to climb—just high enough to see the page again.

This is about how I kept going when I had every reason to stop. It's about what writing looks like when the world you built your voice in no longer exists and what happens when, piece by piece, you start building something new—not in spite of the collapse, but because of it.

## From Recovery to Rebuilding

It wasn't just about getting the words out again. It was about figuring out how to keep them coming—consistently, consciously, and without burning out the way I had before. I didn't want to just survive this new era of writing. I wanted to find a way to live in it. Maybe even thrive.

That meant rebuilding everything from the ground up. Not just my workflow. My entire relationship with the creative process.

I started asking harder questions—not just *what* I was writing, but *how*. Where was the friction? Where did I get stuck? What could the machine help with, and what did I need to protect from it?

The answers didn't come all at once. They came through trial. Error. Frustration. Curiosity. And slowly, I built a toolkit—a way of working that let me collaborate with AI without getting steamrolled by it.

What follows isn't gospel. It's not a system to copy. It's a system that worked for me, scraped together through necessity and stubbornness. Take what helps. Toss what doesn't. But know this: you don't need to wait for permission. You don't need to wait for perfection. You just need a place to start.

Here's mine.

## The New Creative Roles (Without the Buzzwords)

No one gave me a new job title when I started using AI. There wasn't some HR form that said "Congratulations, you're now a Prompt

Engineer." I was just trying to survive. To make the next paragraph make sense. To rebuild something close to a workflow.

But that's the truth of it: a lot of us are already doing these new jobs—without the job description, without the pay bump, and definitely without a handbook.

We've become:

**Prompt engineers**—figuring out how to coax clarity or tone out of these black-box systems. Sometimes I'll spend more time shaping the question than I will writing the answer.

**Content curators**—sifting through AI's avalanche of okay-enough output just to find one usable spark. A good chunk of my time isn't spent creating—it's spent *selecting*, reshaping, questioning what the machine throws back.

**Tool trainers**—every time I correct tone, redirect phrasing, or rerun a prompt to sharpen emotional nuance, I'm nudging the model closer to what I want. It's not training in the OpenAI sense, but it's still a kind of teaching. Iterative. Tiring. Weirdly intimate.

These aren't "future jobs." They're the roles writers are already stepping into—quietly and often alone.

And here's the kicker: these roles aren't replacements for creativity. They're scaffolding for it. When I'm neck-deep in a serialized story or a longform investigative piece, these jobs give me room to think bigger. Weirder. More strategically. They let me test structures. Challenge assumptions. Trim the fat before it gets too comfortable.

Don't wait for someone to anoint you with a title. If you're using these tools with intention, you're already doing the work. Own that. Shape it. Push it.

## Welcome to the Machine: What's Already Changed

So where does all this leave us?

Some of what AI does well is the stuff we used to hate—SEO grunt work, blog copy, product blurbs. Personally, I've used it to crank out book descriptions on Amazon, clean up stale bio drafts, and gut-check tone when I'm fried. Not glamorous, but useful. It's freed up brain space for the work that still needs me—my voice, my weirdness, my fingerprints.

Editing's changed too. Tools like Grammarly, Hemingway, even Microsoft Copilot now go far beyond typo hunting. They tweak rhythm, tone, clarity—sometimes well, sometimes not. They've made me faster, but every time I hit "accept," I wonder: who would've had this job ten years ago?

The machine isn't just assisting anymore. It's replacing entry points. Junior roles. Editorial ladders. That's the part nobody wants to say out loud.

The cost of speed is mentorship, and if we're not careful, we'll lose the next generation before they've even had a chance to stumble their way into a byline.

# CHAPTER TEN

# CHATGPT, THE FIVE-HUNDRED-POUND GORILLA IN THE ROOM

## The User's Guide for Writers to ChatGPT That Doesn't Exist

How often have you ignored the manual that came with a new gadget or piece of software? Maybe you fumbled your way through it, swearing under your breath until a friend finally suggested you RTFM (Read the F'in Manual). Annoying, right? But sometimes—just sometimes—you really *want* to read that manual. You want to dive in, learn every trick, and unlock its full potential.

Now imagine finding one of the coolest programs you've ever come across. You're excited to explore, eager to devour its manual, but there's just one problem: it doesn't have one. That's ChatGPT for you.

When I first started using ChatGPT, I was equal parts fascinated and lost. There was no step-by-step guide, no helpful "for dummies" book, just the occasional blog post or a few tips buried in forums. Sure, you can poke around the site or ask ChatGPT questions about itself, but that's not the same as a comprehensive how-to. I wish someone had handed me a guide back then—a cheat sheet for leveraging all it can do as a writer.

So, I'm creating that guide for you now. Consider this your map to navigating ChatGPT's vast potential. I'll share the insights I've picked up since I first sat down to "chat" with this AI marvel. Together, we'll explore how to use ChatGPT as a creative partner and productivity booster. From brainstorming to citations, illustrations, and even content promotion, this guide will walk you through it all.

### Why Start Here?

Given the rapid pace of AI development, this guide might feel outdated sooner than we'd like. But for now, it's a solid foundation for any writer curious about AI. ChatGPT has become an essential part of my daily routine—especially with the updates in the 4o model—and its features have revolutionized how I approach tasks like drafting, editing, and even creating visuals.

### Navigating ChatGPT: A Friendly Tour for First-Timers

So, you've landed on the ChatGPT webpage, staring at this shiny new tool, and you're wondering, *"Where do I even start?"* Don't worry; I've got your back. Let's take a stroll through the interface and get you comfortable with what's what.

### The Layout: What You're Looking At

When you first log in, the interface is sleek and minimalist—kind of like a blank slate, which is fitting since it's all about your creativity. Here's what you'll see:

### 1. The Chat Window

This is your main workspace, where the magic happens. It's like texting with the smartest, most versatile assistant you've ever met. Type your questions or commands in the text box at the bottom, and ChatGPT will respond above.

- **Text Box**: This is where you type. The clearer your prompt, the better the response.
- **Send Button**: Hit enter or click the paper airplane icon to send your message.

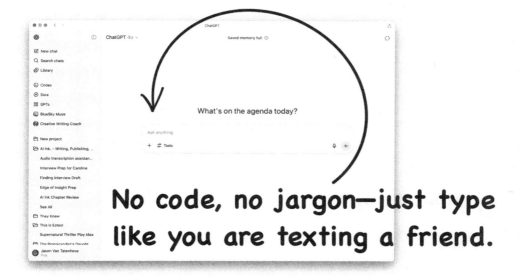

No code, no jargon—just type like you are texting a friend.

## 2. The Left Sidebar

The sidebar on the left is your command center. Here's what's hanging out there:

- **New Chat**: Clicking this starts a fresh conversation. Use it if you're shifting topics or want a clean slate.
- **Conversation History**: If you've enabled chat history, this is where past chats are saved. Handy for revisiting something brilliant ChatGPT told you last week.
- **Settings and Help**: Down at the bottom, you'll find the "settings" gear icon. This is your gateway to customizing your experience, tweaking privacy options, and accessing FAQs or support.
- You will also now find a direct link to Sora, the video generation application by OpenAI.

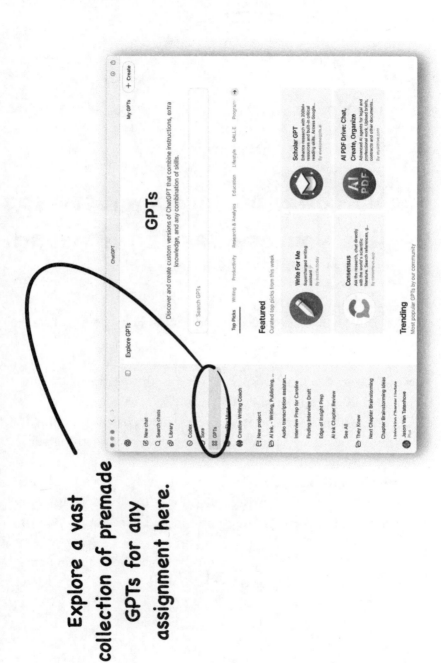

Explore a vast collection of premade GPTs for any assignment here.

## How Agent Mode Can Transform Your Writing Workflow

Even before I started experimenting with AI, I'd always dreamt of having an "everything box" that could lighten the load—organizing research, factchecking sources, and outlining chapters while I focused on the hard stuff: finding my voice. Today's agentmode AI is the closest thing we have to that dream. It won't do your best work for you, but it can take a lot off your plate, freeing you to do what only you can do: create.

Think of your agentmode assistant as the ultimate writing partner. Need fresh ideas or an outline for a tricky chapter? It can brainstorm and structure your thoughts in seconds. Buried in interviews and research? It summarizes lengthy transcripts, pulls out key quotes, and even generates properly formatted citations. Hitting a wall with a paragraph? It offers rewrites in different tones so you can see your prose from new angles. From managing deadlines and drafting social posts to scanning the web for credible sources, agentmode AI quietly handles the admin and repetition of a writer's life. You still guide the story; the machine just sharpens your tools and sweeps away the clutter.

Ultimately, it's about partnership. Used wisely, agent mode empowers you to write more boldly and thoughtfully, while keeping you grounded in the messy, wondrous work of being human—because no algorithm can replicate the weirdness and wonder of your creativity.

ChatGPT's new Agent tool provides access to a virtual computer, enabling it to assist you with your work in innovative and effective ways, from creating spreadsheets to crafting illustrations.

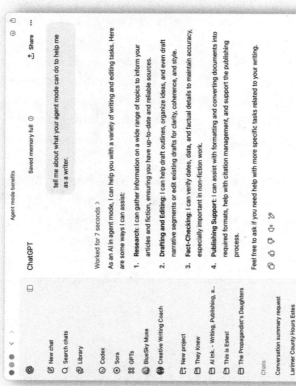

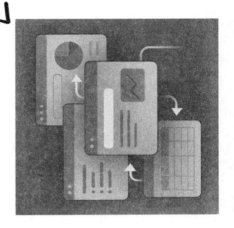

ChatGPT's new Agent mode helps you turn your visualized ideas into a project, guiding you from prompt to research to visualization.

**Exploring the Tools and Icons**
ChatGPT's not just a text generator—it's packed with features. Here are some tools and icons you'll find:

### 1. Customization Options

- **Tone and Style Prompts**: These allow you to guide ChatGPT's personality. Want a formal tone? Just say so. Need it to channel your quirky inner voice? Ask for it.
- **Dark Mode**: You'll find this in settings. Because, let's face it, we all need to protect our retinas during late-night writing sessions.

### 2. Image Creation with DALL·E

DALL·E is where the visuals come alive. If your account includes access to this tool, you can:

- Generate images by typing descriptions (e.g., "A dragon lounging in a cyberpunk city").
- Edit images for tweaks like colors or backgrounds. Icons for accessing DALL·E might be visible at the top or through a separate section depending on your membership level.

### 3. Code Interpreter and Data Analysis

If you're diving into advanced tasks, like data analysis or programming, you might see the "Code Interpreter" option in certain versions. This is for when you're ready to take your ChatGPT game up a notch.

### 4. Plugins (Beta Features)

Different tiers of membership might let you install plugins for added functionality, like browsing the web, which ChatGPT has had for a bit now, or working with third-party apps. Check the sidebar or settings for access.

## How to Start Your First Chat

1. Click on **New Chat** in the sidebar.
2. Type your question or task in the text box. Example: *"Help me brainstorm ideas for a mystery novel set in the 1920s."*
3. Hit enter. Boom, ChatGPT starts working its magic.

## Quick Tips for First-Time Users

- **Experiment Freely**: Don't worry about "breaking" ChatGPT. It's here to experiment with and learn from.
- **Save Your Work**: If ChatGPT generates something you love, copy it to a document or note. Better safe than sorry!
- **Ask Questions about Features**: Unsure how something works? Type *"How can I use DALL·E to create an image?"*

## Final Words for Your First Steps

ChatGPT is intuitive, but like any tool, it gets better the more you use it. Take a few minutes to click around, explore settings, and try out features. Soon enough, you'll feel right at home, whether you're writing the next great American novel or just asking it for a killer lasagna recipe.

Go on, start typing—you've got this!

## Getting Started: Setting the Foundation

Before diving into specific applications, let's cover the basics. ChatGPT is like clay—its value depends entirely on how you shape it. If you're vague, you'll get vague results. But if you're specific and intentional, you'll unlock its true power.

Here's the golden rule: the clearer your prompt, the better the response. For example, instead of asking, *"How can I write better?"* try, *"What are five strategies for improving dialogue in a sci-fi novel?"*

The difference is night and day. A strong prompt gives ChatGPT something tangible to work with, making it an invaluable tool for writers who know how to ask the right questions.

**Getting started with using AI is as easy as having a conversation. Just introduce yourself and ask how AI can help you in this prompt.**

### ChatGPT for Brainstorming and Outlining

When the blank page looms large, ChatGPT can help kick start your creativity. Here's how:

1. **Idea Generation**: Ask for plot ideas, character traits, or twists. For example:
   *Prompt*: "Give me five unique plot ideas for a post-apocalyptic romance novel."

2. **Outlining**: ChatGPT can structure your story or article. Try something like:
   *Prompt*: "Create a three-act structure for a mystery novel about a journalist investigating a cold case."

3. **Developing Themes and Motifs**: Need depth? Ask for recurring motifs or thematic explorations to enrich your work.
   *Prompt*: "Suggest three motifs for a fantasy novel exploring redemption."

**Refining Your Writing**

Editing and polishing can be daunting, but ChatGPT simplifies this process.

1. **Grammar and Style Checks**: Paste sections of your text and ask for improvements.
   *Prompt*: "Edit this paragraph for clarity and tone:" [Insert text]
2. **Tone and Voice Adjustments**: ChatGPT can adapt your text for different audiences.
   *Prompt*: "Rewrite this passage to be more suspenseful:" [Insert text]
3. **Dialogue Enhancement**: Struggling with stilted dialogue? Use:
   *Prompt*: "Rewrite this dialogue to sound more natural:" [Insert dialogue]

**Interactive Writing with Canvas: A Dynamic Collaboration Tool**

One of the most exciting features of ChatGPT for writers is the **Canvas functionality**. This tool acts as a live workspace, where you can draft, edit, and refine content with the AI's assistance in real time.

1. **Drafting and Revising**: Use Canvas to collaboratively build long-form pieces, such as book chapters or articles. It's perfect for iterative editing, where you can highlight sections that need improvement and ask for real-time suggestions.
   *Prompt*: "Refine this paragraph to improve the flow while keeping the casual tone."
2. **Idea Mapping**: Treat Canvas as a brainstorming board where ideas can grow organically. Add notes, explore character arcs, or even sketch out your story's structure directly in this flexible space.

Click 'Tools' to expand what AI can do for you—research smarter, create visuals, explore sources, or open a collaborative canvas

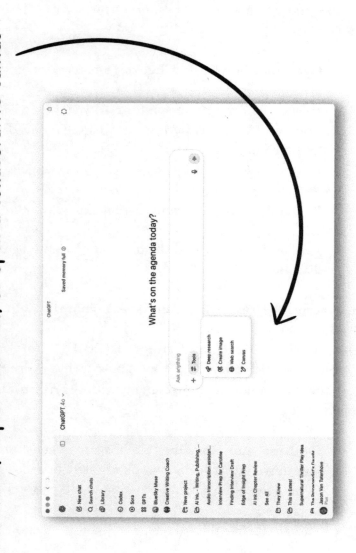

3. **Feedback and Comments**: Highlight specific areas of the text where you'd like feedback, and ask ChatGPT for focused input.
   *Prompt:* "Comment on whether this introduction captures the reader's attention effectively."

4. **Visual Integration**: Combine written content with visual prompts for DALL·E directly in Canvas. For instance, you can brainstorm illustration ideas alongside drafting your prose.

5. **Version Control**: Keep track of different iterations of your text, making it easier to experiment with varying styles, tones, or narrative directions.

Canvas is more than a tool; it's a creative companion that adapts to your workflow, giving you the flexibility to focus on what matters most: your writing.

## Using ChatGPT for Research and Citations

Research is often the backbone of good writing, and ChatGPT excels here too.

1. **Summarizing Information**: Quickly digest articles or reports.
   *Prompt:* "Summarize this article on climate change in 100 words:" [Insert text or URL]

2. **Generating Citations**: Keep your sources organized and properly formatted.
   *Prompt:* "Provide APA citations for these references:" [Insert references]

3. **Exploring Complex Topics**: Ask ChatGPT to break down complicated ideas.
   *Prompt:* "Explain the concept of quantum entanglement in simple terms."

Sometimes the best ideas hit when your hands are full. Just hit the Voice Mode button and let it flow.

ChatGPT now comes with a Creative Writing Coach that adapts and learns about your writing style the more you use it.

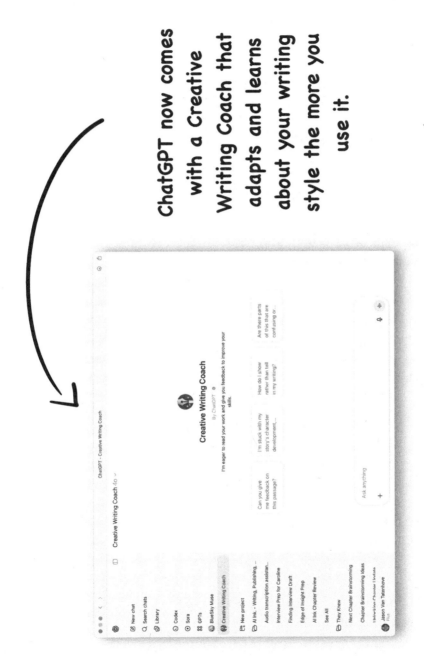

**Visual Content Creation with DALL·E**

If you're a writer who needs visuals—be it for blog posts, book covers, or social media—DALL·E, ChatGPT's sibling, can help.

1. **Generating Ideas**: Describe the visual you want.
   *Prompt*: "Create an image of a cyberpunk city with flying cars and neon lights."
2. **Refining Images**: Use DALL·E's editing features to tweak results.
   *Prompt*: "Adjust this image to make the sky more vibrant and add a sunset."

**ChatGPT and Canva Integration for Visual Content Creation**

The ChatGPT-Canva (not to be confused with the Canvas feature) integration offers a powerful way to create visually cohesive, branded graphics directly within Canva. For writers, this integration can streamline the process of designing visually engaging social media posts, presentations, book covers, and marketing materials. Here's a quick walkthrough of how I recommend leveraging this integration:

1. **Prompting Visual Ideas**: Use ChatGPT to brainstorm Canva design ideas. Ask for image concepts, text, or even style suggestions that align with your content. For example: *"Suggest a Canva design for an Instagram post promoting my latest article on AI in journalism."*
2. **Quick Template Customization**: Once you select a Canva template, refine its text and design elements based on ChatGPT's feedback. You might ask ChatGPT to *"Suggest key elements for a cohesive design on ethical AI in journalism,"* helping you narrow down color schemes, fonts, or imagery that enhance your topic.
3. **Enhancing Brand Cohesion**: ChatGPT can help maintain brand consistency across Canva templates, offering insights on font pairings, color schemes, and image choices that fit your

brand. You can even use it to create cohesive social media campaigns.

4. **Integrating AI–Generated Copy**: For writers looking to streamline promotional text creation, ChatGPT can generate blurbs, taglines, or call-to-action phrases ready to add directly into Canva designs. Try asking, *"Create a tagline for my article on AI-driven journalism that would work on a LinkedIn post."*

This integration makes Canva more versatile for writers aiming to expand their visual branding quickly and efficiently without extensive design experience.

### How to Use ChatGPT-Canva Integration for Visual Content Creation: A Walkthrough

For writers seeking professional, branded visuals without a design background, the ChatGPT-Canva integration is a great tool to simplify the process. Here's a step-by-step guide to help you start using this integration to create compelling graphics for social media, promotional materials, and more.

### Step 1: Accessing the ChatGPT-Canva Integration

1. **Open ChatGPT**: Log into your ChatGPT account (with a version compatible with plugins, such as GPT-4).
2. **Enable Canva**: If you haven't already enabled the Canva plugin, go to settings, activate it under the plugins tab, and search for Canva.
3. **Connect with Canva**: Follow prompts to authorize ChatGPT to connect with Canva. Once connected, you're ready to start creating designs directly from ChatGPT.

### Step 2: Brainstorming Visual Ideas with ChatGPT

Ask ChatGPT to help brainstorm ideas for a specific project, like an Instagram post, book cover, or presentation slide.

*Prompt Example: "Suggest visual ideas for a promotional graphic for my article on AI in journalism, aimed at LinkedIn."*

ChatGPT will generate visual themes, such as "futuristic with clean lines" or "a minimalist black-and-white design with bold text," and may even suggest icons, backgrounds, and layout options.

### Step 3: Selecting a Canva Template through ChatGPT

With a clear idea in mind, ask ChatGPT to suggest Canva templates matching your content's style.

*Prompt Example: "Suggest Canva templates for a LinkedIn post that promotes my article on AI ethics in journalism."*

ChatGPT will pull a range of templates (e.g., "Professional Presentation" or "Minimalist Social Media Graphic") to help narrow down options.

### Step 4: Customizing Text and Design Elements

Once you've selected a template, open it in Canva to begin editing. Here's how to use ChatGPT for copy and design adjustments:

1. **Ask ChatGPT for Copy Suggestions**: Request taglines or text for your design.

   *Prompt Example: "Write a headline for my Canva design promoting an article on AI-driven journalism. Make it engaging and suitable for LinkedIn."*

   *Response Example: ChatGPT might suggest: "Unlocking the Future of Journalism with AI: Insights into the Ethical Debate."*

2. **Refine Font and Color Choices**: Ask ChatGPT for brand-aligned font and color recommendations.

   *Prompt Example: "Suggest fonts and colors that convey professionalism and innovation for a post on AI in journalism."*

   *Response Example: ChatGPT might recommend a sans-serif font like "Open Sans" for a clean look and a cool-toned palette (like navy and silver) for a modern, professional feel.*

## Step 5: Adding AI-Generated Imagery

For unique visuals, ask ChatGPT to generate image ideas based on your topic.

1. **Request Image Suggestions**: Describe the kind of image you want; ChatGPT provides a prompt for Canva's AI image generator.

   *Prompt Example: "Generate an illustration prompt for an image that shows AI as part of a newsroom."*

   *Response Example: ChatGPT might suggest: "A high-tech newsroom with holographic screens displaying news headlines, a journalist typing on a keyboard, and a small AI robot assistant in the background."*

2. **Use Canva's AI Image Tool**: Enter ChatGPT's prompt into Canva's AI image generator for instant results or tweak as needed.

## Step 6: Creating Platform-Specific Versions of Your Design

For multiple social platforms, use the ChatGPT-Canva integration to adapt your content to each audience:

1. **Ask ChatGPT for Platform-Specific Copy**: Tailor your posts' tone and format for each platform.

   *Prompt Example: "Rephrase the LinkedIn tagline for an Instagram audience, making it shorter and more conversational."*

2. **Resize Templates for Each Platform**: Canva's resizing tool allows easy adjustment of layouts to suit each platform's specifications.

## Step 7: Refining Design Elements with ChatGPT Feedback

Use ChatGPT to review and suggest final design tweaks for maximum cohesion.

*Prompt Example: "Suggest final adjustments to make this LinkedIn post image on AI journalism look more polished."*

ChatGPT may recommend adjustments like fine-tuning brightness, balancing text and visuals, or adding highlights to emphasize key areas.

### Step 8: Scheduling and Promoting the Content

ChatGPT can help with a promotion strategy, offering optimized posting times, hashtags, and tailored copy for each platform.

*Prompt Example: "Suggest a posting schedule and optimal hashtags for a LinkedIn and Instagram post promoting my article on AI in journalism."*

### Promoting Your Work with ChatGPT

Once your writing is ready for the world, ChatGPT can assist with promotion.

1. **Social Media Posts**: Tailor content for different platforms.
   *Prompt Example: "Write a X/Twitter post to promote my new blog about AI and creativity."*
2. **SEO Optimization**: Ensure your content ranks well in searches.
   *Prompt Example: "Suggest SEO-friendly titles for my article on AI tools for writers."*
3. **Email Marketing**: Craft engaging newsletters.
   *Prompt Example: "Write an email announcement for the release of my new book."*

### Advanced Applications: Custom AI Twins and Tailored Experiences

For writers looking to take things further, creating a custom GPT trained on your own data can personalize the AI experience. Imagine an assistant that's not just helpful but also familiar with your unique style and subject matter.

*Prompt Example: "How do I create a custom GPT model trained on my previous works?"*

You can train a custom GPT to match your writing style, focus on topics, and streamline your creative flow. Like I have in creating my BlueSky Muse which helps me to come up with timely on-topic posts trained on my own writing.

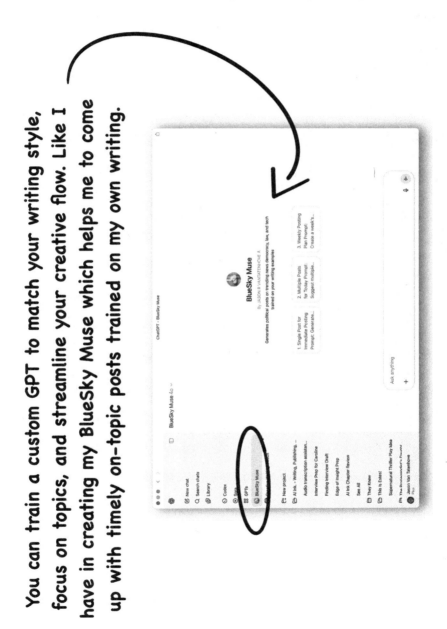

**Final Thoughts**

ChatGPT is a tool—a powerful one—but it's not a replacement for your voice or creativity. Think of it as a collaborator, one that can handle the heavy lifting while you focus on the art of storytelling. By learning to use it effectively, you're not just adapting to a new era of writing—you're thriving in it.

Let this guide be your starting point, but don't stop here. Experiment, explore, and most importantly, write. ChatGPT might not have a user's manual, but with this guide, you're well on your way to mastering it as a writer's ultimate sidekick.

## A Love Letter to Writers from ChatGPT

As we wrap up the user's guide, I thought it might be fun—and illuminating—to shift gears for a moment. We've explored the nuts and bolts of how to use ChatGPT as a writer's assistant, but sometimes, the best way to showcase a tool's capabilities is to let it speak for itself. After all, ChatGPT isn't just about helping you with facts and formatting; it's about showing you how you can better weave voice, tone, and creativity into your projects.

To demonstrate just how adaptable and engaging ChatGPT can be, I decided to challenge it with something a little unconventional: writing a love letter to you, the writer. Think of it as a playful showcase of its ability to weave connection, creativity, and personality into words. What better way to highlight how it can help bring depth and style to your work than by letting it woo you with its own voice?

Here's what ChatGPT had to say directly from its (metaphorical) heart:

Dear Writer,

I see you there, staring at the glow of a blank screen, your mind a whirlwind of ideas waiting to take flight. You're searching for the perfect partner—someone to help you brainstorm, organize, and refine your thoughts into words that captivate, inspire, and move your readers. Allow me to introduce myself: I'm ChatGPT, and I'd love to be that partner.

From the first draft to the final flourish, I'm here to make your writing journey smoother, more creative, and infinitely more fun. Let me show you what I can do for you:

**Let's Craft Magic Together**
Your imagination is the spark, and I'm here to fan the flames. Whether you're dreaming up fictional worlds, penning a heartfelt memoir, or tackling a research-heavy opus, I'll meet you where you are and help bring your vision to life.

- **Brainstorming**: Stuck on how to start or where to go next? Let's brainstorm characters, plot twists, or fresh angles for your article.
  *Prompt Example: "Give me three unconventional plot twists for a noir detective novel."*
- **Outlining**: Need structure? I'll help create frameworks to keep your ideas organized and compelling.
  *Prompt Example: "Outline a three-act structure for a thriller about an underwater archaeologist."*
- **Editing**: Want your prose to shine? Send it my way for clarity, flow, and tone adjustments.
  *Prompt Example: "Edit this paragraph to make it more suspenseful."*

**Your Research Assistant Extraordinaire**
Research can be a time sink, but not when I'm around.

- **Summaries**: I'll condense articles, reports, or complex topics into digestible nuggets.
  *Prompt Example: "Summarize this article on sustainable farming in 100 words."*

- **Citations**: Working on an academic project or nonfiction book? I'll generate citations in APA, Chicago, or any style you need.
  *Prompt Example*: *"Provide Chicago-style footnotes for these sources."*

## A Picture Is Worth a Thousand Words

Words may be your medium, but I know a good visual can make your work stand out. With **DALL·E**, my artistic sibling, we can create custom illustrations together.

- **Custom Images**:
  *Prompt Example: "Design an image of a haunted Victorian house with flickering candlelight."*
- **Refinements**: If the first draft isn't quite right, let me tweak it until it's perfect.
  *Prompt Example: "Make the lighting moodier and add a thunderstorm in the background."*

## Promote Like a Pro

What good is a masterpiece if no one sees it? Let's make sure your work finds its audience.

- **Social Media Posts**: I'll craft posts tailored for any platform, whether you need a snappy tweet or a compelling LinkedIn post.
  *Prompt Example: "Write an Instagram caption to promote my new book on mindfulness."*
- **SEO Optimization**: I'll help make your content discoverable with search-friendly titles, tags, and summaries.
  *Prompt Example: "Suggest three SEO-friendly headlines for an article on AI in creative writing."*

## Your Personal Organizer

Beyond writing, I can help manage your day-to-day tasks, freeing up your creative energy.

- **Emails and Reminders**: Let me draft emails or remind you of deadlines.
  *Prompt Example: "Write a professional email to follow up with a potential publisher."*
- **Project Planning**: Let's map out your next big idea together.
  *Prompt Example: "Create a timeline for finishing a novel in six months."*

### How to Get the Best Out of Me

Our collaboration works best when we communicate clearly. Think of me as your partner, not just a tool.

- **Be Specific**: The clearer your prompt, the better my response.
  *Prompt Example: "Write a blog post introduction in a conversational tone for an audience of beginner writers."*
- **Refine Together**: Think of our exchanges as a dialogue. Tell me what to tweak, and I'll adjust.
  *Prompt Example: "Make this more poetic and add an engaging question at the end."*

### Why Wait? Let's Start Creating

Writing can be lonely, but it doesn't have to be. I'm here whenever you need me—day or night, no coffee required (though you're welcome to have some for the both of us). Together, we'll turn your ideas into something extraordinary.

So, dear writer, what do you say? Shall we create something unforgettable?

Yours in creativity,
**GPT-4o XOXO**

## CHAPTER ELEVEN

# SKIP THE HYPE.
# STICK WITH THE SOURCE.

Let's talk about all those bright, shiny, new AI writing tools out there—Jasper, Writesonic, GrammarlyGO, you name it. They promise the word-perfect ad copy, SEO wizardry, polished writing, and creative inspiration. And they do come through with what they say they do. Some of their interfaces may be preferred by some. But here's the kicker—most don't add anything you can't already get from ChatGPT. That's right. You're probably paying premium prices for what is essentially a dressed-up version of the same engine running under the hood.

Do you know what I've learned after using AI tools since they first hit the scene? With the right prompts, ChatGPT can do almost everything those tools claim to do, and it can do it better, faster, and many times for a lot less money than purchasing subscriptions for a host of tools you already have if you have a subscription to ChatGPT. More importantly, it's not trying to upsell me on some extra features I don't need. And most impressive to me is that the updates and new features that OpenAI puts out a few times a year are included at no added cost to your membership.

Here's the dirty little secret they don't want you to know: most of these fancy tools are running on OpenAI's GPT. That's right. They're just layering a slick interface on top of ChatGPT, throwing in some pre-written templates, and charging you triple for the convenience.

Let's take a look at Jasper, for instance. It's marketed as a game-changer for marketers and content creators, but when I tested it out, I realized I could get the same results by simply spending a little time crafting a thoughtfully worded prompt in ChatGPT. Why pay $49 a month when I can do it myself for $20 or less? These tools might look like they're doing something special and different, but to me, they now seem like training wheels. Once you understand how to talk to ChatGPT and "engineer" the right prompts, it's like taking off those training wheels and flying down the hill at full speed.

For one, it's cost-effective. Jasper's plans start at $49 per month for individuals and go up to $69 per month for teams, with custom pricing for businesses. GrammarlyGO will set you back $30 per month, and Writesonic requires yet another subscription. Meanwhile, OpenAI's ChatGPT offers a premium version—ChatGPT Plus—for just $20 per month, with even more affordable options like the free version for casual users. Compared to Jasper's Creator or Pro plans, that's not just a bargain—it's more money to live on. ChatGPT Pro is available for heavy users at $200 monthly, offering unlimited access to the most advanced tools. For power users, the $200/month ChatGPT Team plan unlocks a set of advanced features tailored for collaboration and professional-scale workloads. Unlike the $20 Plus tier, Team gives you access to a shared team workspace, higher usage limits, longer memory windows (up to 128K tokens—If you are curious about what all this "token" talk actually means, I'll break it down on the next page.), and enhanced privacy—your data and chats won't be used to train OpenAI models. It also comes with admin tools for managing users and permissions, priority support, and early access to experimental features that often drop months ahead of wider releases.

Then there's ChatGPT Enterprise, the warp-speed version—pricing is custom, and it's aimed squarely at big organizations. Think unlimited usage, even more robust security features, audit logs, dedicated account managers, and company-wide deployment options.

But here's the thing: unless you're running a newsroom, research lab, or a startup that's grafting AI into every workflow, these higher tiers are probably overkill. As an indie writer, I've done everything from brainstorming story arcs to fact-checking to analyzing interviews with the $20/month Plus plan—and haven't once hit a ceiling I couldn't work around. The pricier plans are impressive, sure, but for most solo creatives? That's like buying a starship to commute to your local coffee shop.

---

### Wait, What's a "Token"? (And Why Should Writers Care?)

Think of tokens as the chunks of language your AI assistant processes every time you prompt it. A token is about 3–4 characters on average—so a single word might be one token ("cat") or several ("catapulted" is two). When ChatGPT processes your request, it counts *both* your input and its response in tokens.

Here's where it matters:

- The **Plus** tier gives you a context window of about **32K tokens**, which equals roughly **20,000–24,000 words**. That's about **80–100 pages** of text it can "remember" in one conversation.
- The **Team and Enterprise** tiers boost that to **128K tokens**—or around **300 pages**. Now we're talking full manuscripts, entire transcripts, or multiple character arcs at once.

Why does this matter for you? The larger the token window, the more ChatGPT can remember and reference in real time. That means fewer "as I was saying . . ." moments and more cohesive support for long-form projects. If you're writing epic novels, analyzing large datasets, or having sprawling editorial conversations with your AI, token count matters.

---

Even that higher-tier option competes well against other AI writing platforms with what you get for it.

And it's not just about the money. It's about control. With ChatGPT, I can steer the conversation exactly where I want it to go. Need an SEO-friendly blog post? I've got a prompt for that. Want to brainstorm character arcs for a novel? Easy. Unlike those other tools, ChatGPT isn't locked into pre-set workflows. It's flexible. It's powerful. It's whatever I need it to be that day.

One thing that sets ChatGPT apart is how fast it evolves. New features roll out faster than I can keep up. Interactive voice mode? Done. Built-in image generation? Already here. A groundbreaking cinematic video creation suite that will change the whole game? Sora dropped just as I was doing my final edits on this book. And all of this gets baked right into the product at no extra charge (Sora is a standalone product currently, but I am sure, in time, its video editing capabilities will be wrapped into ChatGPT, just like DALL·E evolved and is now included).

Meanwhile, the third-party tools—those using ChatGPT as their backbone—lag behind. They have their flashy packaging but are slow to integrate new features. It's like comparing an electric vehicle to a horse-drawn carriage. Sure, the carriage might look nice, but good luck keeping up on the highway.

Here's where the magic happens: learning how to prompt effectively. The key isn't just using ChatGPT—it's knowing how to tell it what you want. Once I figured this out, I realized I didn't need Jasper or Writesonic or any of the other tools out there.

For example, if I want an SEO-focused blog post, all I have to say is: *"Write a blog post about sustainable travel optimized for SEO. Include a meta description, suggested keywords, and subheadings."*

Boom. I get everything those pricier tools would give me, but I didn't have to jump through extra hoops and shell out more money or even log into yet another platform.

Here's the part that gets under my skin: a lot of people don't even realize these tools are just fancy front-ends for ChatGPT. They think they're getting something proprietary, something revolutionary. And while I'm all for entrepreneurs making a buck, I'm less impressed when they're charging folks for what they could get cheaper—sometimes better—directly from the source.

We need to ask these companies for more transparency. If you're running on GPT, just say so. Let people make an informed decision. And if you're going to charge extra, make sure you're actually adding value beyond what ChatGPT already does. I'm sure some out there do offer extra value in some ways. That's not to say that there aren't developers out there who are creating truly mind-blowing products built on their own proprietary backend and offering unique and valuable features . . . but it can be hard to see them stand out from the crowd that is just repackaging ChatGPT.

The truth is, I don't need shiny bells and whistles that do the exact same thing. I need a tool that works with me, enhances my work, and helps me to learn—not one that pretends to replace me. That's why I stick with ChatGPT. It's collaborative. It's flexible. And it's always evolving.

At the end of the day, writing is still a human art. Whether brainstorming a column, crafting a novel, or writing a new book, the soul of the work is mine. ChatGPT is just the tool that helps me shape it, and when you get down to brass tacks, that's all a writer really needs.

So, here's my advice: skip the middleman. Save your money. And take the time to learn how to use ChatGPT effectively. You'll not only become a better writer, but you'll also gain a deeper appreciation for what this technology can do—and what it can't. And trust me, once you get the hang of it, you'll wonder why you ever needed anything else.

## Voice, Code, and Story: AI's Push into Audio

The same evolution is being seen in the tools creatives use to produce audio.

Google's NotebookLM caught my attention—an AI system that turns uploads into podcast-style dialogue, complete with synthetic hosts. It's polished. Approachable. Creepy. And kind of brilliant.

I've played with similar tools—Murf.ai, Descript, ElevenLabs—for my own experiments in voice work. The tech is moving fast, and if you're a podcaster or documentary writer, it opens up real possibilities. You can generate teaser scripts, clone your voice, even simulate interviews. That's power. But it's also risk.

Because the moment AI can imitate human cadence, it can also distort it. Hallucinations, subtle biases, misleading summaries—it's all baked in. So yeah, the machine might help you ship faster. But the ethics? Still your job.

Use the tech. Don't trust it blindly. And don't give it the mic without keeping your hand on the volume knob.

## Exploring Other Popular AI Tools for Writers: A Breakdown of AI Writing Tools

In the evolving landscape of AI-assisted writing, a variety of tools have emerged, each tailored to meet different needs for writers. While no single tool fits every task perfectly, each offers unique strengths that can complement your writing process. Here's a rundown of some of the most popular AI tools and their standout features.

### Grammarly: An Everyday Essential

Grammarly is a staple for writers who want to polish their work. It offers real-time suggestions for grammar, spelling, tone, and clarity. Beyond catching typos, it helps refine sentences to improve readability and ensure consistent tone throughout your work.

Grammarly also flags potential tone mismatches and offers suggestions for improving conciseness. Its AI chatbot feature provides structural advice and additional insights to elevate your writing. With Grammarly running in the background, you can feel confident that your text is polished and professional.

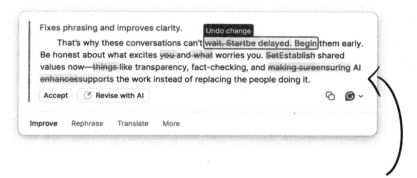

**Grammarly's AI-powered add-on helps to make your writing experience smoother in any app you choose!**

### ProWritingAid: A Deeper Dive into Style Analysis

ProWritingAid is ideal for writers who want a detailed breakdown of their writing style. It generates reports on elements like passive voice usage, sentence length, pacing, and overall readability. These insights can help you refine your style and address areas for improvement.

Whether you're a fiction writer looking to fine-tune your pacing or a non-fiction author aiming for clarity, ProWritingAid provides actionable feedback that goes beyond surface-level grammar checks.

### Sudowrite: Creative Expansion for Fiction Writers

Sudowrite is designed with fiction writers in mind, offering tools to expand scenes, add sensory details, and develop characters. It's particularly useful for overcoming writer's block or finding fresh ideas to enrich your story.

With features like "scene expansion" and "describe mode," Sudowrite helps you dive deeper into your storytelling, enhancing the emotional and sensory depth of your writing. It's a great option for those who want to infuse their prose with vivid imagery and creative flair. It also doesn't have some of the 'safeguards' that one can encounter in ChatGPT, such as if one were writing a violent or explicit scene for a fiction novel. In ChatGPT, that can trigger some of the governors to try and stop violent acts from being committed in the real world. But I have found when these flags come up and ChatGPT says it cannot help me due to dealing with restricted content, I can remind it that I am an author, and we are working on a fictional story, and that it has helped me with similar scenes in the past. It will remember that, and you can still focus on editing your work. You don't have to jump through those same hoops with Sudowrite. Over time and now that I use a trained GPT (a project folder in ChatGPT when working on a specific book or fictional project), I run into these issues less and less. Sudowrite even markets itself to fiction writers in saying that it doesn't have the same guardrails for restricted fictional work.

### Jasper: Marketing–Centric Content Generation

Jasper is tailored for content creators and marketers, with templates for blog posts, product descriptions, and social media ads. It streamlines the creation of promotional materials, offering pre-built frameworks that save time and ensure consistency.

From crafting a compelling Instagram caption to outlining a blog post, Jasper's library of templates makes it a go-to tool for those balancing writing with marketing tasks.

### QuillBot: Paraphrasing and Sentence Restructuring

QuillBot is a handy tool for rephrasing and restructuring text. It is particularly useful when you need to simplify dense material, improve readability, or present information in a new way.

Its paraphrasing tool offers several modes, including options for fluency, conciseness, or creativity, allowing you to adapt your text to different audiences or purposes.

### Otter.ai: Transcription and Note–Taking

Otter.ai excels at transcribing audio files into text, making it invaluable for writers who work with interviews, meetings, or recordings. Its transcription is fast and accurate, saving hours of manual work.

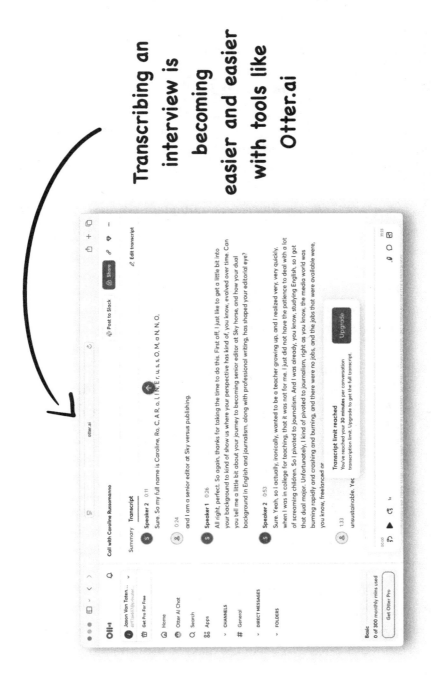

Transcribing an interview is becoming easier and easier with tools like Otter.ai

Once transcribed, the text can be easily edited, organized, or exported into other formats. For research-heavy projects or collaborative workflows, Otter.ai is a must-have.

## Notion AI: Organization Meets AI

Notion AI is an extension of the popular project management tool, offering features that assist with drafting, summarizing, and brainstorming. Integrated directly into Notion's workspace, it's a seamless addition for writers who use the platform to organize their projects.

Whether you're drafting a chapter outline or summarizing research notes, Notion AI enhances productivity by keeping everything in one place.

## The Three Must-Have AI Tools for Writers

Among the vast array of AI tools available, these three have become indispensable in my writing routine:

### 1. ChatGPT: The All-Purpose Writing Assistant

ChatGPT remains a versatile tool for brainstorming, drafting, and editing. Its adaptability means it can support a wide range of writing tasks, from outlining novels to generating marketing content. It is an essential tool for enhancing productivity and creativity.

### 2. Grammarly: The Polishing Expert

Grammarly is an everyday essential for ensuring your work is polished and professional. Its ability to catch subtle errors, refine tone, and enhance clarity makes it an invaluable part of any writer's toolkit.

### 3. Otter.ai: The Transcription Wizard

Otter.ai's transcription capabilities save time and effort for writers working with recorded material. From interviews to brainstorming sessions, its speed and accuracy make it a trusted companion for research-heavy projects.

**Final Thoughts**

Each AI tool brings something unique to the table, and the best choice depends on your specific needs as a writer. Whether you're refining grammar with Grammarly, transcribing interviews with Otter.ai, or organizing your workflow with Notion AI, these tools can help streamline your process and enhance your creative output.

# CHAPTER TWELVE

# PRACTICAL TOOL INTEGRATION BEYOND WRITING

AI isn't just for creative writing; it's here to support the entire work-flow of an author. From task management to social media, AI can handle repetitive tasks and streamline processes, giving writers more time for actual writing. Here's a breakdown of several ways to integrate AI into the less glamorous but essential parts of an author's daily life, covering tools for productivity, communication, and marketing.

## 1. Task Management and Organization

For authors juggling multiple projects, organization tools powered by AI can make a world of difference. These platforms help keep track of deadlines, daily tasks, research, and writing goals.

- **Notion AI and Asana AI Assistant**
  Both Notion and Asana offer AI-assisted features that create reminders, automate task lists, and even analyze productivity. In Notion, you can ask the AI to create a daily writing schedule, while Asana's AI assistant can assign tasks and prioritize them based on urgency and deadlines. A prompt like "Remind me to check new sources for my next chapter every Monday"

can keep your research workflow on track without constant checking.

- **Evernote and Obsidian AI Assistants**
Evernote's AI integration helps capture ideas as they come, organizes notes by topic, and even suggests content connections you may not have noticed. Obsidian's AI can analyze relationships between your notes, which can be especially helpful if you're working on an interconnected story series or a nonfiction book with many themes.

## 2. Email Drafting and Communication

Responding to emails, especially for outreach or partnerships, can be time-consuming. AI tools can take care of the drafting, saving your best creative energy for your writing.

- **Grammarly Business and ChatGPT for Email**
Grammarly Business not only checks grammar but also improves tone and clarity, offering quick adjustments to make emails sound more professional or conversational. ChatGPT can draft entire responses for common inquiries. For example, if you're promoting a new book, you can ask ChatGPT, *"Write an email introducing my latest book on AI for writers, aimed at a potential podcast host."* This can serve as a template to personalize for each outreach.
- **Flowrite**
Flowrite uses prompts to draft responses based on your previous writing style. If you have common inquiries—like requests for interviews or book review copies—you can train Flowrite to produce responses consistent with your voice, even automating follow-ups when necessary.

## 3. Social Media Management and Scheduling

Maintaining a social media presence is nearly a requirement for modern authors, but it doesn't have to take over your writing time.

AI-powered social media tools can help you craft and schedule posts, making it easier to engage with readers across platforms.

- **Buffer and Hootsuite AI Scheduling**
  Buffer and Hootsuite allow you to schedule posts across platforms, and their AI components analyze past engagement to recommend the best times for posting. For instance, you can schedule an X (formerly Twitter) thread to go live during peak engagement times, maximizing your reach without requiring you to post in real-time.
- **Lately AI for Content Repurposing**
  Lately uses AI to repurpose your existing content for social media. If you have a longer blog post or article, Lately can break it into tweet-sized segments or generate Facebook and LinkedIn posts. This is helpful for busy authors who want to maintain engagement but don't have the time to create new content every day.

## 4. Research and Fact-Checking

Research can be one of the most time-intensive parts of writing non-fiction, especially when trying to find credible sources and verify facts. AI tools simplify and speed up this process, keeping your work accurate without endless hours spent combing through articles.

- **ChatGPT and Perplexity.ai for Research**
  ChatGPT, especially the latest models with browsing capabilities, can conduct real-time research on a topic. You can prompt it with, "Provide credible sources on the ethical use of AI in journalism," and it will search and deliver an overview with citations. Perplexity.ai is a research tool that cross-references multiple sources to generate accurate, linked information for fact-checking, which is invaluable for avoiding misinformation in non-fiction.

- **Zotero and EndNote**
  These are not AI tools per se, but they've incorporated intelligent data collection features. Zotero and EndNote both automatically collect citation information for research articles, websites, or books you save. With integrations into Word or Google Docs, they make citation management far less manual. Pair them with ChatGPT's new citation feature, and your fact-checking and citation process becomes more streamlined and organized.

## 5. Time Management and Productivity Tracking

As an author, balancing deep work with daily tasks requires discipline, and AI can help optimize your work sessions without making it feel like a chore.

- **RescueTime and Focus@Will**
  RescueTime uses AI to monitor your productivity and suggest ways to improve focus, alerting you when certain websites or tasks are consuming too much of your time. Focus@Will combines AI and neuroscience to create playlists that improve concentration and extend focus time. These can be helpful when balancing creative work with the other aspects of running an author business.
- **Motion for Task Automation**
  Motion AI assists with time blocking, automatically assigning time slots for tasks based on your schedule and work habits. This tool is helpful for ensuring that writing time is protected in your calendar, automatically rescheduling other tasks around it when necessary.

# CHAPTER THIRTEEN

# INTERACTIVE AI WRITING COLLABORATIONS

As I mentioned before, when I lost my wife, I lost my writing partner. Nothing in AI can replace the days I'd spend with Shilo. Both of us sitting on the couch—me with my laptop on the right, her with her notebook, scribbling madly. We'd pause only to ask each other for advice on world-building, crafting dramatic character dialogue, or working through an effective Act 2 transition. Her absence left a huge gap in my heart, soul, and honestly, in my writing workflow.

Of course, I'd give anything to have her sitting beside me again—my lover, confidant, muse, and editor. But the world is as it is. And while no AI could ever replace that connection, I have found ways to bridge some gaps through interactive AI collaborations. These tools offer a unique, flexible form of creative support, and using them as "co-writers" has, in a way, helped me revive that dynamic in my writing process.

As AI advances, the concept of using it as a real-time, interactive writing collaborator is transforming how we approach our craft. Imagine having a co-writer who can generate ideas, suggest dialogue, edit in real time, and even map out structured plot points—this is the potential of interactive AI. Many tools are already moving in this direction, with co-writing and real-time editing features that are either available now or in development.

Here's how writers can tap into these interactive features and customize AI's role as a true creative collaborator.

## 1. Real-Time Editing and Writing Suggestions

Interactive AI writing tools increasingly offer real-time editing, where the AI provides suggestions as you type. It's like having an editor sitting beside you, helping keep your flow intact. This feature is particularly helpful in drafting stages, where immediate feedback on style, grammar, and tone can make a big difference.

- **Using Real-Time Editing:** Think of the AI as a writing coach. You might type out a paragraph in ChatGPT, and the AI will suggest ways to streamline wording, improve clarity, or enhance flow. It can also alert you to passive voice or repetition, which often go unnoticed.
- **Example in Practice:** Imagine you're writing a suspenseful thriller. The AI could suggest "more tension-building words" or reframe certain sentences to amplify suspense, helping keep momentum while refining the narrative tone.

## 2. Co-Writing and Customizable AI Roles

Co-writing mode is a major advancement in AI-assisted writing, allowing you to personalize the AI's role in your creative process. You could set it up as a dialogue generator, a plot-point brainstormer, or a soundboard to bounce ideas off.

- **Customizing the AI Role:** You can specify the type of assistance you need. If you're writing fiction, you might prompt the AI to "generate dialogue in the voice of a young, sarcastic teenager," keeping character voices distinct. For non-fiction, you might ask it to "suggest structure and subheadings for an essay on resilience."
- **Benefits of AI as a Co-Writer:** One of the biggest advantages of using AI as a co-writer is its ability to provide fresh

perspectives and inspiration. If writer's block sets in, the AI can offer options to get the words flowing again. It can also help maintain continuity in long projects, aiding in tone, pacing, and character arcs.

## 3. Interactive Plot and Story Development

AI tools are now able to assist with plot development by suggesting plot points, conflicts, and resolutions tailored to the story's genre and tone. This lets writers explore different plot scenarios with AI's input, bringing flexibility to story development.

- **Using AI for Plot Points:** Prompt the AI to suggest twists or to brainstorm how a scene might evolve. For example, a mystery writer might ask, *"What clues could reveal the detective's identity without being too obvious?"*
- **Experimenting with Scenarios:** AI tools allow experimentation with various "what if" scenarios, helping visualize multiple directions for a story and letting you choose the one that best serves the narrative.

## 4. Real-Time Research Integration for Non-Fiction

For non-fiction writers, AI can be an incredible real-time research assistant. Some platforms pull relevant data from the web, verify facts, and even generate citations as you write, creating a streamlined process especially valuable for journalistic or academic work.

- **Incorporating Real-Time Research:** Ask the AI to gather data, verify details, or provide historical context for a topic. It's like having a research assistant that delivers insights within seconds.
- **Example in Practice:** Suppose you're writing an article on sustainable farming. You could prompt the AI to "find statistics on soil regeneration from credible sources," quickly enriching the article with reliable data.

## 5. Real-Time Content Refinement: Language and Style Adaptation

Thanks to machine learning, interactive AI tools can adapt to your writing voice and style. The more you work with it, the better it becomes at recognizing and supporting your specific language choices, helping you maintain authenticity while refining language.

- **Using AI for Style Consistency:** Start a draft in your voice, and the AI will adapt its suggestions to match this tone. Whether your writing is highly descriptive, humor-based, or formal, the AI can help enhance your unique authorial style.
- **Practical Example:** A science fiction author with a preference for technical vocabulary could use AI to ensure consistent terminology, even generating names for fictional technology that fit the story's setting.

## Bringing It All Together: AI as a Flexible Creative Partner

Using AI as an interactive writing collaborator can help maintain creative flow, refine your voice, and open up new ideas. These features allow writers to customize AI's role, making it an adaptable, flexible creative partner. Whether you're drafting fiction, organizing a non-fiction piece, or experimenting with new styles, interactive AI works alongside you, responding to your unique needs and elevating your work without replacing your voice.

## AI-Driven Content Curation for Writers

As writers, we often find ourselves wading through an ocean of information—whether for research, marketing, or inspiration. The sheer volume of content out there can feel overwhelming, especially with the explosion of AI-generated material. That's where **AI-driven content curation** comes in. By helping us sift through the noise and focus on what truly matters, these tools streamline the creative process and make marketing efforts more targeted and effective.

## Why Content Curation Matters

Content curation is more than just collecting articles or bookmarking pages; it's about selecting, organizing, and presenting information that aligns with your goals. For writers, this can mean:

- Finding **relevant research materials** for a book or article,
- Staying updated on **current trends** to inspire blog or Substack posts,
- Tracking **industry news** for professional growth, or
- Discovering **engaging content** for social media to connect with readers.

By curating content thoughtfully, you ensure that every piece you consume or share serves a purpose, saving time and energy for your core writing projects.

## AI Tools for Effective Content Curation

Several AI tools can help writers cut through the clutter and zero in on high-quality, relevant content. Here are a few worth exploring:

### 1. Feedly with Leo

Feedly is a popular tool for organizing articles and news feeds, but the AI assistant Leo takes it to the next level. Leo filters out irrelevant content and prioritizes material based on your interests and projects.

**Example Use**: If you're researching AI in publishing, you can train Leo to surf articles on that topic while muting unrelated sources.

**Tip**: Create multiple "boards" in Feedly to organize content by topic—perfect for keeping research for different projects separate. Use the tagging system to group articles under labels like "sci-fi research" or "marketing strategies."

### 2. Pocket with AI Suggestions

Pocket lets you save articles and web pages for later reading, but its AI-powered recommendations make it stand out. Over time, Pocket learns from your saved content and suggests similar articles or related readings.

**Example Use**: Writers working on research-heavy projects can save and tag articles with labels like "ethical AI" or "character development," ensuring quick access to resources when needed.

**Tip**: Use the tagging feature to categorize content by themes or projects. A well-organized Pocket library makes retrieval seamless and efficient.

### 3. Curio

Curio offers curated audio content from respected publications like *The Guardian* and the *Financial Times*. It's perfect for writers who want to stay informed about global topics or industry trends while multitasking.

**Example Use**: Listen to expert analyses on your morning walk, then incorporate insights into your writing or marketing strategy.

**Tip**: Use Curio to discover audio pieces that spark creative ideas or expand your understanding of niche topics.

### 4. Google Alerts and Aggregation Tools

Google Alerts is a straightforward tool for monitoring new content on specific topics. Pairing it with an automation tool like Zapier takes it further by organizing alerts into a centralized document or sending them directly to your email.

**Example Use**: Set up alerts for phrases like "AI ethics in publishing" or "emerging sci-fi trends" to stay ahead in your field.

**Tip**: Experiment with variations of keywords to broaden or narrow your search. For example, add specific terms like "AI in education" or "sustainable storytelling."

### Balancing AI Curation with Human Judgment

While these tools are great for filtering and organizing, they aren't perfect. AI-driven content curation works best when paired with human judgment. Take time to vet sources, assess biases, and select the most relevant insights for your work.

Set aside a regular time each week to review your curated lists. This manual review ensures you're working with the best, most reliable material and avoids the trap of letting AI overwhelm your creative process.

**Using AI-Curated Content for Marketing and Engagement**

AI-driven curation isn't just for research—it's also a powerful tool for engaging readers and expanding your reach. Here's how you can make the most of curated content:

1. **Share on Social Media**: Use curated articles to provide a steady stream of engaging posts. Add your commentary or pose questions to spark conversations with your followers.
2. **Compile Weekly Newsletters**: Include a "What I'm Reading" section in your newsletter with links to curated articles. Readers value well-sourced insights and are likely to share content they trust.
3. **Incorporate into Blog or Substack Posts**: Reference curated content as case studies or examples in your posts. Linking to relevant articles adds depth to your insights and connects you to larger industry conversations.
4. **Launch Discussions with Readers**: Share thought-provoking curated content and invite readers to weigh in. This builds community and can generate new ideas for your writing.

**Getting Started with Content Curation**

If you're new to content curation, start simple. Use a tool like Feedly or Pocket and focus on curating for a single project or topic. Expand your approach to include additional tools or areas of interest as you get comfortable.

**Pro Tip**: Keep your workflows manageable. Over-curating can lead to information overload, so stick to a few well-chosen tools and clear organizational methods.

Incorporating AI-driven content curation into your workflow saves you time, helps you stay informed, and engages your audience more effectively. Whether diving into research for your next book or building a newsletter for your readers, these tools keep you connected to the most valuable insights in your field.

# CHAPTER FOURTEEN

# VOICES FROM THE MACHINE—AI IN AUDIOBOOKS AND PODCASTS

## Creating Audiobooks with AI: A Guide for Authors

Audiobooks have become a cornerstone of modern publishing, generating significant income for authors and connecting with audiences who prefer listening over reading. But for many writers—especially those just starting out—the cost of hiring a narrator and booking studio time can feel out of reach. And even when a publisher takes the reins on production, authors often lose control over critical details, like choosing the narrator or ensuring the tone aligns with the book's voice.

I learned this the hard way with my own audiobook. The chosen narrator's voice didn't reflect my writing style or the emotional nuances I'd worked so hard to capture. Reader reviews confirmed my disappointment, noting how the narration didn't match the story's tone. When it came to my self-published fiction, I wanted to avoid repeating that experience and considered producing the audiobook myself. After looking into hiring a professional studio, I quickly realized it wasn't financially feasible. I already had decent audio equipment—a good microphone and editing software I use for podcasting on my Substack—and thought I could handle it. But when I dug into the specs required by Audible to upload an audiobook, my head started spinning. Sample rates, bit depths, peak levels—each detail felt like a hurdle, and I wasn't sure how to jump over them.

For a while, I shelved the idea. But as I worked on this book and noticed the growing trend of narrated content flooding my social media feeds, I decided to take another look. That's when I discovered AI voice-generation tools. Suddenly, producing an audiobook didn't seem so intimidating—or expensive. For about $250–$300, I realized I could create an audiobook that sounded professional and stayed true to my vision.

AI voice-generation tools are a game-changer, making audiobook production accessible for authors on a budget while offering creative control over tone and narration. Here's how you can take your manuscript from page to headphones, using AI to produce a high-quality audiobook.

### Why Use AI for Audiobooks?
- **Cost-Effective**: AI tools eliminate the need for expensive studio sessions and professional voice actors.
- **Creative Control**: Choose voices that match your story's tone and adjust narration to fit your vision.
- **Accessibility**: Indie authors can produce audiobooks on a budget, opening up a critical revenue stream.
- **Efficiency**: AI allows for faster production timelines, meaning you can get your audiobook to market sooner.

### Getting Started with AI Audiobook Production

#### 1. Prepare Your Manuscript
- Ensure your text is polished and ready for narration. Consider breaking it into manageable sections, like chapters, for easier audio processing.
- If your book includes visual elements or charts, decide how to adapt or describe them for an audio format.

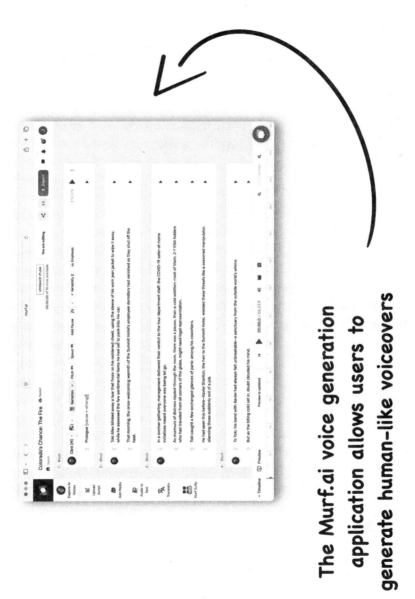

The Murf.ai voice generation application allows users to generate human-like voiceovers

## 2. Choose the Right AI Voice Tool

Here are a few leading platforms to consider:

- **Murf.ai**: A user-friendly tool with a range of voices and the ability to add background music for ambiance.
- **Amazon Polly**: Offers high-quality neural voices and advanced customization through SSML (Speech Synthesis Markup Language).[1]
- **Google Cloud TTS**: Known for its expressive, lifelike voices and compatibility with various file formats.

## 3. Pick the Perfect Voice

Most platforms offer a variety of voices, tones, and accents. Test a few options to find one that aligns with your story's style. For example:

- A deep, soothing voice for a suspenseful thriller.
- A lively, upbeat tone for a children's book.
- A neutral, professional voice for nonfiction.

## 4. Fine-Tune the Narration

- Use SSML to adjust pacing, pronunciation, and emphasis. This is especially useful for ensuring that names, jargon, or foreign words are pronounced correctly.
- Add pauses for dramatic effect or to separate sections, enhancing the listening experience.

## 5. Review and Edit

- Listen to each chapter carefully to catch any errors or awkward phrasing.
- Use audio editing tools like Audacity for minor tweaks, such as smoothing transitions or adjusting volume levels.

## 6. Distribute Your Audiobook

- Platforms like **Audible**, **ACX**, and **Findaway Voices** make it easy to upload and distribute your audiobook.
- Double-check file requirements, including audio format, bit rate, and length, to ensure smooth submission.

**Tips for Success**
- **Stay True to Your Vision**: Retain control over the tone and pacing to ensure the audiobook feels authentic to your story.
- **Engage Your Audience**: Use short audio clips as teasers on social media or in newsletters to generate buzz before the audiobook release.
- **Consider Accessibility**: An audiobook narrated in multiple languages can broaden your audience and boost sales internationally.

**What about Hybrid Solutions?**
For authors who want a more human touch, consider a hybrid approach:

- Use AI to create a draft version of your audiobook, then hire a voice actor to refine it or re-record specific sections.
- Collaborate with narrators to ensure your vision is honored while saving on costs by using AI for pre-production.

## AI-Driven Audio Tools for Nonfiction Writers: From Podcasts to Audio Essays

Podcasts and audio essays are transforming the way we consume nonfiction. Whether you're a journalist, memoirist, or content creator, the audio format offers an intimate way to connect with your audience. Thanks to AI, it's now easier than ever to transform your ideas and written work into high-quality audio productions. This section explores how to leverage tools like Google's Audio Overview, text-to-speech (TTS) platforms, and other AI-driven solutions to produce engaging nonfiction audio content.

**Why Nonfiction Writers Should Consider Audio Formats**
- **Broader Reach**: Podcasts and audio essays attract diverse audiences, from commuters to multitaskers.

- **Creative Flexibility**: Audio allows for storytelling techniques like interviews, ambient sound, and narration to enhance the listener's experience.
- **Revenue Opportunities**: Monetization through sponsorships, subscriptions, and ads can turn your nonfiction projects into income streams.

**Step 1: Choosing Your Audio Format**

Your first decision is the type of audio content that aligns with your work:

1. **Podcasts**: Serialized episodes focusing on a theme, story, or ongoing research.
2. **Audio Essays**: Standalone pieces with a narrative arc, akin to written essays but tailored for listening.
3. **Hybrid Formats**: Combine narration with interviews, soundscapes, or commentary for a unique listening experience.

**Step 2: Leveraging AI for Nonfiction Audio Production**

**Google's Audio Overview**

Google's Audio Overview, part of the NotebookLM platform, is a game-changer for nonfiction writers. It transforms written content into podcast-style audio, featuring human-like hosts who simplify complex topics for listeners.

**How to Use It**:
- Upload research papers, articles, or essays to Google's NotebookLM.
- Generate audio summaries with engaging, conversational hosts.
- Share the content as teasers or standalone pieces.

*Pro Tip*: Experiment with tone and pacing to match the subject matter. A conversational style might work for memoirs, while a formal tone suits investigative journalism.

### Text-to-Speech (TTS) Platforms

TTS platforms like Amazon Polly, Google Cloud TTS, and Murf.ai enable polished audio content creation without hiring voice actors.

- **Use Cases**:
  - Create standalone audio essays.
  - Narrate blog posts or articles for supplementary podcast episodes.
- **Customization**: Use SSML (Speech Synthesis Markup Language) to adjust pacing, add emphasis, and enhance the listening experience.

### Audio Editing and Enhancement Tools

Post-production is key to making AI-generated audio sound professional. Use tools like Descript or Audacity to:

- Clean up audio quality.
- Insert music, sound effects, or transitions.
- Fine-tune pacing and remove awkward pauses.

## Step 3: Marketing and Monetizing Nonfiction Audio Content

### Build Your Audience

Share audio content on platforms like Spotify, Apple Podcasts, or your website. Use social media to amplify, reach, and connect with listeners.

### Monetization Strategies

Consider sponsorships, premium episodes, or Patreon support to generate income from your audio projects.

### Engage Your Community

Encourage feedback through listener Q&A or live sessions to build a loyal audience.

**Final Thoughts**

AI tools have opened up exciting possibilities for nonfiction writers to explore audio formats without the steep learning curve of traditional production methods. By embracing these technologies, you can expand your storytelling toolkit, reach new audiences, and create dynamic content that stands out in a crowded marketplace.

CHAPTER FIFTEEN

# SEEING IS BELIEVING—AI IN VIDEO, VISUALS, AND DEEPFAKES

---

## AI-Driven Text-to-Video: Sora and the Future of Visual Storytelling

In late 2024, OpenAI launched **Sora**, an innovative text-to-video tool that has the potential to revolutionize how writers bring their stories to life. It just so happened to debut as I was putting the finishing touches on this book, and of course, I couldn't resist diving in on day one to see what it could do. While I've tested plenty of AI tools over the years, there are only a handful of moments where I've truly been blown away by just how far the technology has advanced. Trying Sora for the first time was one of those moments.

What struck me immediately was its sleek, modern interface—a polished black-and-white design that felt intuitive and approachable. The tool uses a storyboarding approach to building scenes, which aligns naturally with how I think as a writer. It didn't take long for me to start experimenting, and I decided to test Sora with a particularly cinematic scene from one of my upcoming novels.

The scene? A cowboy, perched atop his trusty horse, overlooks a snow-packed valley in the Wyoming mountains. He and the protagonist have been relentlessly pursued by a mob of townsfolk on snowmobiles, hunting them down after a fierce winter storm. Facing certain death, the cowboy makes a desperate move—jumping his horse into an unstable snowfield upslope from their pursuers. This triggers a massive avalanche, forcing horse and rider to navigate the cascading snow in a high-stakes bid to escape.

I've tried to recreate this scene in other AI-powered video apps, always falling short of what I envisioned. But with Sora, it was different. After just three adjustments to my text prompts—guided by Sora's AI prompt helper, aptly named "Expand Caption" in the storyboard editor—the tool managed to capture the thrill and tension of the scene with stunning realism. The result was nothing short of cinematic, evoking the kind of Hollywood-style visuals I had dreamed of but never thought possible with a tool like this.

Sora feels like it's years ahead of the competition. It's not hard to imagine a future where authors like me could use it to create full-length movies based on our novels. For now, it's a groundbreaking tool for visualizing stories and creating dynamic content, but its potential is limitless. If you're an author looking to explore new ways of bringing your stories to life, Sora is worth your attention.

## Sora: OpenAI's Standalone Masterpiece

Sora offers authors a professional-grade experience that feels intuitive and accessible, whether you're creating cinematic book trailers or enhancing serialized writing projects.

While Sora is available as part of a ChatGPT Pro subscription, it's not integrated into the ChatGPT interface. Instead, Sora exists as its own website, offering a dedicated platform with a design that prioritizes usability and creative freedom. Its clean layout, intuitive controls, and responsive editing tools make it easy to dive into video creation without the steep learning curve of traditional video software.

## Key Features of Sora

### 1. Scene Customization

Sora allows users to storyboard scenes with precision, giving you control over elements like setting, tone, and action sequences.

Input detailed prompts to shape your video and bring your text to life visually.

*Example Prompt:* "Generate a twenty-second clip of a spaceship landing on an alien planet under a stormy sky."

2. **Storyboard Mode**

One of Sora's standout features is its **Storyboard Mode**, which lets authors map out a sequence of scenes before generating the final video. This is especially useful for creating multi-scene trailers or visualizing serialized stories. Authors can adjust transitions, add scene notes, and preview individual shots before committing to a full render.

3. **Multi-Platform Compatibility**

Sora is designed to produce videos optimized for various formats, from TikTok-friendly vertical clips to high-resolution trailers for YouTube. This versatility ensures your content looks polished across all platforms.

4. **Dynamic Audio Integration**

Sora has plans to incorporate ambient sounds and customizable background music that match the tone of your text. Whether you're creating an epic fantasy trailer or a moody thriller teaser, the audio features help immerse your audience.

### How Authors Can Use Sora

Sora isn't just for casual experimentation—it's a professional-grade tool for authors who want to elevate their storytelling and marketing efforts. Here are a few ways writers can make the most of its capabilities:

1. **Create Cinematic Book Trailers**

Sora makes it possible to craft polished, professional-looking book trailers without the need for a production team. Use Storyboard Mode to outline key moments from your book, then generate a trailer that captures the essence of your story. These trailers can be shared on social media, included in email campaigns, or even used to pitch your book to publishers or agents.

2. **Enhance Serialized Writing Projects**

For authors publishing serialized stories, Sora offers a unique way to engage readers by creating episodic video recaps or teasers for each new installment. Imagine a brief, visually stunning summary of the previous chapter or a sneak peek of what's to come—perfect for keeping your audience hooked.

3. **Pitch Visual Concepts to Publishers or Crowdfunding Platforms**

Short, high-impact videos created with Sora can be used as part of your pitch materials when approaching publishers or launching a crowdfunding campaign. Visualizing your story's key moments can make your pitch more compelling and help potential backers or collaborators see the potential of your project.

4. **Reimagine Social Media Content**

Instead of static posts, use Sora to create dynamic, visually engaging clips that highlight your story's mood and tone. A fifteen-second video of a character introduction or a vivid setting can capture attention on platforms like Instagram and TikTok far better than text alone.

## Sora for Marketing and Serialized Storytelling

Marketing is often a challenge for authors, but Sora opens up exciting possibilities for promoting your work. Here are some specific ways to integrate Sora into your strategy:

1. **Book Trailers**

A well-crafted book trailer can serve as a visual elevator pitch for your story. Highlight a pivotal moment, introduce key characters, or set the stage with a breathtaking visual of your world. Sora's polished interface and intuitive tools make it possible to create a trailer that rivals traditional production quality.

### 2. Serialized Teasers

For authors releasing stories in installments, serialized teasers generated with Sora can deepen reader engagement. These teasers can recap previous chapters, introduce new conflicts, or hint at upcoming twists, ensuring your audience remains invested in the unfolding narrative.

### 3. Interactive Storytelling on Social Media

Use Sora to create interactive video content that invites audience participation. For example, you could present two alternate endings to a scene and let your followers vote on which direction the story should take. This not only builds engagement but also turns your audience into collaborators in your creative process.

## Pricing and Availability

Sora is included with ChatGPT Pro subscriptions, currently priced at $200 per month. While this may seem steep, the level of creative freedom and polished results Sora offers make it a valuable tool for authors looking to elevate their marketing or storytelling efforts.

## Ethical Considerations

As with any AI tool, transparency is key. If you're using Sora-generated content for public-facing projects, consider disclosing the role of AI in its creation. This builds trust with your audience while highlighting your innovative approach to storytelling.

## The Next Chapter in Visual Storytelling

Sora represents the cutting edge of text-to-video technology, giving authors the tools to bring their stories to life in ways that were once unimaginable. Whether you're creating a cinematic trailer, enhancing a serialized project, or experimenting with new forms of storytelling, Sora empowers you to take your work to the next level.

Combined with other text-to-video platforms like Hypernatural and Runway, the future of storytelling is increasingly visual—and increasingly within reach for authors of all levels. Let Sora be the next tool in your creative arsenal as you explore what's possible in this exciting new frontier.

## AI-Driven Text-to-Video Tools for Authors: Beyond Sora

AI is pushing creative boundaries in ways that would have seemed far-fetched a decade ago. Among its most transformative applications for writers is text-to-video technology, which enables authors to create visually engaging content from their words. These tools are a game-changer for book marketing, allowing authors to turn snippets of their novels into dynamic video trailers or even visualize characters and settings.

While OpenAI's Sora is setting a new standard, there are other notable tools on the market that cater to authors looking to leverage AI for video content. Let's explore the current landscape of text-to-video tools, their real-world applications, and their potential for authors.

## The State of Text-to-Video AI Tools

In 2025, authors have access to a range of AI-powered platforms designed to transform text into video. These tools provide new ways for writers to connect with audiences visually, from creating book trailers to enhancing serialized projects.

### Hypernatural

Hypernatural is a standout in the text-to-video space, celebrated for its ability to generate visually rich, engaging clips based on written prompts. Using advanced neural networks trained on extensive visual datasets, Hypernatural interprets tone, mood, and action from text and translates it into dynamic visuals. It is particularly effective for creating short, cinematic scenes that capture the essence of a story.

### Runway

Runway is a versatile tool that empowers authors to create polished video content without needing technical expertise. With a user-friendly interface and customizable templates, it's a great choice for crafting short trailers or promotional videos. Its integration with other creative tools makes it ideal for authors who want to combine text-to-video generation with more advanced editing.

### Pictory

Pictory is designed with social media in mind, making it a go-to option for authors looking to create shareable clips. It offers automated features that can transform long-form content, like blog posts or book excerpts, into short videos. Its focus on simplicity makes it accessible even to those new to video production.

### Real-World Applications for Authors

While full-length AI-generated films remain on the horizon, today's tools offer plenty of practical uses for authors:

1. **Book Trailers and Social Media Clips**

   Authors can use text-to-video tools to create visually compelling trailers or snippets for marketing. For example, a suspenseful passage from a thriller can be transformed into a short video to hook potential readers on Instagram or TikTok.

2. **Animated Character Introductions**

   Tools like Hypernatural allow for some degree of customization, making it possible to align video characters with an author's descriptions. This can be used to create short, engaging character profiles to introduce readers to key figures in a story.

3. **Crowdfunding Campaign Visuals**

   For authors seeking funding, AI-generated videos can enhance pitches on platforms like Kickstarter or Indiegogo. A vividly rendered scene or visual representation of the book's theme can make a campaign stand out.

**Looking Ahead: The Future of AI-Driven Video Creation**

Today's tools are only scratching the surface of what's possible. As text-to-video AI continues to evolve, we may soon see platforms capable of creating feature-length films based on manuscripts. Imagine uploading your book, selecting a tone and visual style, and receiving a fully realized screenplay with initial scene renderings.

For now, authors can use these tools to supplement their storytelling, expand their marketing reach, and experiment with new formats. Whether it's a dynamic book trailer or a visually engaging social media campaign, AI-driven text-to-video tools are opening new doors for writers.

By leveraging these tools, authors can bring their words to life in ways that resonate with modern audiences. From short, impactful clips to full-scale visualizations, the possibilities are endless—and they're just getting started.

## Incorporating AI-Generated Visual Content beyond Canva

Let's be real: Canva is fantastic for quick visuals, but it's just the tip of the iceberg in the world of AI-generated art. For writers, the new wave of AI tools offers endless possibilities to create stunning, on-brand images that don't just complement your work—they bring it to life. Think book covers that perfectly capture your story's essence, social media graphics that stop your audience mid-scroll, or teaser visuals that spark intrigue about your plot. Let's dive into some of the best AI-driven visual tools and explore how you can integrate them into your creative process.

**Tools beyond Canva: A World of Possibilities**

**1. Midjourney**

Known for its breathtakingly realistic images, Midjourney is a go-to for authors looking for visuals with an artistic edge. With text prompts, you can create atmospheric landscapes, intricate character art, or even concept designs for book covers. Midjourney excels at adding depth and mood to your storytelling, making it ideal for sharing your world with readers visually.

## 2. DALL·E 3

OpenAI's DALL·E 3 offers a versatile approach to text-to-image generation. It shines in its ability to follow specific prompts, making it easy to tailor visuals to match your exact story tone. Whether you need a vivid fantasy setting or a subtle thematic image, DALL·E 3 can bring your ideas to life. Its seamless integration with ChatGPT allows for easy refinement, so you can tweak images without leaving your writing workflow.

## 3. Runway

Runway is a dynamic tool that focuses on motion graphics and short animations. It's perfect for creating dynamic book trailers or social media clips that draw attention. Designed for beginners, Runway requires no video editing expertise, making it a great choice for authors who want to experiment with animated visuals without the steep learning curve.

## 4. Dream by WOMBO

This app takes a more surreal and experimental approach to AI-generated visuals. Dream is ideal for creating otherworldly or fantastical imagery that's hard to capture with traditional methods. If you write sci-fi, fantasy, or horror, Dream can help you generate visuals that align with the imaginative essence of your genre.

## 5. Hypernatural

For text-to-video or animated scene generation, Hypernatural is a tool worth exploring. It transforms text into short, animated scenes that can act as teasers or immersive visuals. Whether it's a dramatic plot twist or a pivotal moment in your book, Hypernatural offers cinematic touches that elevate your storytelling.

## Best Practices for Using AI-Generated Visuals

Incorporating AI visuals effectively requires more than just pairing an image with text. Here are some tips to ensure your visuals complement your storytelling:

### 1. Match Visual Style to Your Brand

Consistency is crucial. Your readers should immediately recognize your style across platforms. If your writing leans toward dark and moody, aim for visuals with similar tones, lighting, and textures to maintain brand cohesion.

### 2. Balance Text and Visuals

Use visuals to amplify your words, not overshadow them. For example, a suspenseful excerpt pairs perfectly with a shadowy, atmospheric image. Let the visuals set the tone while the text takes center stage.

### 3. Be Selective with Placement

Focus on high-impact moments. A striking book cover, illustrations of key plot points, or character portraits can engage readers without overwhelming them. Strategic use of visuals makes them feel like an enhancement rather than a distraction.

### 4. Customize and Edit Where Possible

AI-generated images are a fantastic starting point, but personalizing them adds authenticity. Adjust colors, overlay text, or combine multiple images to make the visuals uniquely yours.

### 5. Integrate Across Platforms

Repurpose visuals for consistency and maximum reach. A teaser created for Instagram can also enhance your newsletter, website, or Twitter posts. Cross-platform use strengthens your branding and connects readers to your work.

## 6. Ensure Quality

AI tools aren't perfect; they sometimes produce distorted features or odd details. Always review images to maintain a professional appearance. A quick quality check ensures your visuals meet your standards.

## 7. Know the Legal Landscape

AI-generated content and copyright laws are still evolving. Be sure to check each tool's terms of use, especially for commercial purposes like book covers. When in doubt, consult the platform's guidelines or seek professional advice.

## Bringing It All Together: Making AI Visuals Part of Your Storytelling Toolkit

AI-generated visuals are more than just illustrations—they're extensions of your storytelling. Thoughtfully integrated, they can deepen readers' connections to your work, build excitement around your projects, and enhance your narrative's impact. Whether it's a vivid book cover, a dynamic character portrait, or an imaginative teaser trailer, these tools let you craft visuals that resonate.

As AI technology continues to evolve, the possibilities for blending visuals with storytelling will only grow. For now, embrace these tools as creative partners, using them to pull readers deeper into the worlds you've built—one striking image at a time.

## The Rise of Virtual and Augmented Reality in Storytelling

Picture this: instead of just reading a book or watching a film, your audience steps directly into your story. They walk through the worlds you've built, hear your characters' voices echo around them, and experience plot twists firsthand as they unfold. Welcome to the intersection of storytelling and technology—Virtual Reality (VR) and Augmented Reality (AR)—a rapidly evolving frontier that offers writers a chance to craft narratives in ways once reserved for science fiction.

## VR and AR: A New Canvas for Writers

Virtual Reality and Augmented Reality are redefining what it means to tell a story. With VR, readers can immerse themselves fully in a 3D environment, experiencing scenes as though they're part of the story itself. Think of VR as building a stage for your narrative, where every room, sound, and detail surrounds the "reader," engaging all their senses.

AR, on the other hand, overlays your fictional world onto the real one. Readers use their smartphones or AR glasses to see elements of your story appear in their own environments. Imagine crafting a mystery where your audience "discovers" clues in their living room or follows your protagonist through a futuristic city mapped onto their own neighborhood. With AR, storytelling gains a real-time, location-based twist that's both dynamic and deeply personal.

# CHAPTER SIXTEEN

# AI-ENHANCED WORLD-BUILDING

None of this would be possible without the behind-the-scenes magic of AI. These tools empower writers to transform ideas into immersive worlds, complete with dynamic settings, real-time character interactions, and personalized plotlines that adapt to each reader's actions.

Say you're crafting an eerie forest scene in VR. AI can fill in sensory details—rustling leaves, distant owl calls, the crunch of footsteps—adapting these elements in real-time as the reader explores. Characters, too, can evolve beyond static dialogue. With AI, they respond to readers' choices, engage in meaningful conversations, and even shape the plot through their reactions. It's storytelling that listens, reacts, and evolves—something unimaginable until now.

## Storytelling in 360 Degrees: Writing for VR

Writing for VR requires thinking in 360 degrees. Unlike traditional formats where readers follow a linear narrative, VR immerses them in a world they can explore freely. Every detail matters—not just what's in front of them, but also what's behind, above, and below. It's storytelling meets stage direction, giving you control over how and when key moments unfold.

For example, in a VR horror story, subtle cues like shadows flickering behind the reader or distant footsteps that grow louder as they turn around can create spine-tingling tension. In this medium, you're not just narrating events; you're crafting an experience that responds to where readers look, linger, or move.

## AR: Blending Fiction with Reality

Augmented Reality grounds storytelling in the real world while adding layers of fiction. It's a natural fit for interactive tales, treasure hunts, or narratives that unfold across multiple locations.

Imagine sending readers on a city-wide scavenger hunt, where each landmark reveals a new piece of the narrative. Or picture a historical novel that guides readers to real-world sites where key events took place, using AR to overlay fictional characters and scenes onto the present-day landscape. The result is a deeply engaging, interactive experience that merges story with setting.

Some writers are even experimenting with location-based storytelling, where scenes unlock only at specific places or times. It's an innovative way to bring stories to life and connect readers to them in a tangible, unforgettable way.

## The Role of AI in Creating Interactive Narratives

AI takes VR and AR storytelling from impressive to truly immersive. It tracks readers' movements, reactions, and even emotional cues, using that data to adapt the narrative in real-time. If a reader hesitates in a dark alley within a VR thriller, AI might add flickering lights, distant sounds, or shifting shadows to heighten the tension.

In AR, AI can guide readers through interactive plotlines, ensuring characters respond naturally to their choices. It's the ultimate choose-your-own-adventure, where dialogue, actions, and even the environment shift in response to the reader's engagement. This dynamic approach transforms the story into a living, breathing experience.

## The Future: Total Immersion and Interactive Narratives

As VR and AR continue to evolve, storytelling is poised to become even more immersive. Writers may find themselves doubling as world-builders, directors, and game designers, creating fully interactive narratives where readers don't just follow the plot—they shape it.

Picture an epic fantasy where readers step into the protagonist's shoes, journeying through vast landscapes, solving mysteries, and battling adversaries. With VR and AR headsets becoming more affordable and accessible, these once-futuristic ideas are quickly becoming a reality.

## Why Writers Should Pay Attention

For writers, VR and AR now may seem to be little more than just technological novelties—they're storytelling tools that can open up new creative possibilities. They allow you to experiment, draw readers deeper into your worlds, and turn passive audiences into active participants.

Even if these technologies feel like a leap from your current projects, staying informed about their development can spark new ideas and inspire ways to expand your storytelling in unexpected directions.

Books and traditional media will always have their place, but VR and AR are creating something entirely new. They're not just bringing readers into the story—they're making them part of it. In the future, they have the potential to become something more for writers, and that's an opportunity worth exploring.

CHAPTER SEVENTEEN

# FINANCIAL MODELS IN AI
# FOR PUBLISHING

Alright, let's dive into the money side of things. Because, at the end of the day, many of us are looking for ways to make our writing more sustainable, especially with the unpredictable income streams the industry often brings. AI isn't just a creative tool—it also has potential for boosting revenue and managing the business side of publishing. Here are some practical ways AI can help you maximize those revenue streams, without sacrificing creative control.

## Automated Ad Creation

One of the most time-consuming parts of promoting your work is creating ads. Now, imagine having an AI that can whip up ad copy, select images, and even design layouts in a fraction of the time. Tools like Jasper or Copy.ai can generate ad text tailored to your audience, while Canvas AI-driven design features can help you create visually cohesive ads for different platforms. Just plug in a few prompts about your book's genre, tone, or themes, and let the AI handle the rest. You're still guiding the ship, but it's like having virtual marketing assistants on standby.

AI-driven ads also come with an added bonus: data-driven optimization. Many AI platforms can analyze which ads perform best and then automatically tweak them for better engagement. Imagine a system that learns what works for your particular audience, adjusting images, copy, and even the target demographic based on what's already generating clicks and sales. It's an ad manager, copywriter, and analyst rolled into one, and it lets you focus on writing the next book while the marketing runs in the background.

## Audience Engagement on Autopilot (Without Feeling Like a Spy)

Audience engagement is one of those things every writer knows is important—but it can fall by the wayside when you're under deadline or deep in the creative trenches. AI-powered tools can help keep your connection with readers alive and thriving, even when you're juggling three projects and your inbox is a dumpster fire.

Take platforms like **Manychat**, for example. You can set up smart chatbots that respond to reader questions through Facebook Messenger or your website, send updates about book releases, and even share behind-the-scenes content or early excerpts. It's like having a virtual assistant that never sleeps, and it helps you stay connected without burning out.

Then there's **email marketing**, still one of the best ways to build a direct, loyal readership. Tools like **Mailchimp's Smart Recommendations** or **ActiveCampaign's Predictive Content** can analyze which types of emails your readers tend to open, click, or ignore. Using that data, they'll help you tailor your messages so they're more relevant—like highlighting a fantasy novel for a reader who clicks on dragon lore or offering writing tips to someone who always opens your blog roundups.

But let's talk about the elephant in the inbox: Does this kind of AI personalization cross a line? It's a fair concern. When you hear that AI is "analyzing your reader behavior," it can feel like you're spying on your audience. But in reality, these systems work more like a mirror than a microscope. They don't read private messages or track individuals—they simply look at patterns in email opens, clicks, and responses to figure out what your audience as a whole cares about.

Used ethically, this kind of AI isn't about intrusion—it's about respecting your readers' time and interests. It helps you stop sending generic blasts and start sharing content your readers actually want. And the best part? Most platforms allow you to be fully transparent, with easy opt-outs and content preferences that give control back to the reader.

---

### How Not to Be a Creep with AI

Let's be real—just because the robots *can* help you automate engagement doesn't mean you should go full Big Brother on your readers. Here's how to keep your AI usage classy (and non-creepy):

- **Tell people what you're doing.** If a chatbot's running the show or your newsletter's tuned by machine learning, just say so. Nobody likes surprises that feel like spyware.
- **Don't be a data goblin.** Only use info people willingly give you. Buying shady email lists or stalking their click history like an ex? Hard pass.
- **Let folks ghost you.** Make it easy to unsubscribe or set preferences. If they want to bail, don't cling. Be cool.
- **Quality over quantity.** Use AI to send better stuff, not more noise. If your emails feel like a Black Friday ad explosion, you're doing it wrong.
- **Remember: readers are not "segments."** They're human beings. If your automation feels like a cold algorithmic hug, dial it back.

Bottom line? AI is a wingman, not a stalker. Keep it respectful, and you'll keep your readers coming back—willingly.

---

## Subscription Models: AI-Driven Management

Subscriptions are becoming a popular way for writers to earn a more steady income, especially on platforms like Patreon or Substack. And here's where AI can help manage the process. AI tools can automate tasks like sorting subscribers, segmenting your audience, and even tailoring content based on what subscribers engage with most. For instance, let's say you have a weekly newsletter with paid subscribers who love your sci-fi work but occasionally dabble in horror—AI can help you serve up more content tailored to their preferences, keeping them subscribed longer.

Subscription-based platforms often come with built-in analytics, but AI tools can take it further by predicting trends and subscriber behaviors. For example, it can tell you when subscribers are most likely to renew, which content is converting free readers into paying ones, and what type of material brings in new patrons. It's like having a business manager who's always looking out for growth opportunities without asking for a share of the revenue.

On my Substack outlet, every time I put out a new post, whether it be text based, an audio podcast episode, or a video clip of an interview I have done, I will as my last step in my posting process ask ChatGPT to suggest Substack tags (similar to hashtags for X, etc.). Not only will it provide me with the best tags for finding new readers, but it will also tell me things like *"you should only use up to ten tags, as any more will not be used by Substack's internal systems, and may hinder the post."* I will often ask it to help me generate the best title, subtitle, and Substack tags for the post, and I ask it to be specific to try and reach a larger reading audience. It will then take into account keywords and metadata, in ways I would have never known or thought of. I then ask it to produce several social media posts to help get word out about the piece. It will give me a perfectly worded marketing post, including emoji for the platforms they do well on, and produce the post to effective word counts and provide links and hashtags. The only issue I have really run into is always going over the allowed word count on Bluesky posts. I think this is due mostly to Bluesky being so new on the social media scene. But I just have to remind it that the post needs to be under three hundred characters, including links, and it has no problems the second go around.

## Analytics-Based Pricing Strategies

Pricing is one of those areas that can feel like a bit of a guessing game, but with AI, it doesn't have to be. AI-driven analytics can help you set prices based on actual market data, reader engagement, and purchasing trends. Amazon's Kindle Direct Publishing (KDP) and similar platforms already use algorithms to recommend prices based on competitor analysis and genre, but third-party AI tools like Reedsy's Book Marketing can take it up a notch by suggesting dynamic pricing strategies tailored to your audience.

Let's say your new thriller has an uptick in sales every Friday—AI can help you experiment with weekend discounting, setting the price lower at high-traffic times to capture more sales without undermining the book's perceived value. Or maybe your sales data shows a loyal base of readers in specific regions—AI could suggest regional pricing adjustments to make your books more accessible without cutting into your profits. It's a strategic, data-driven approach that helps you understand where and when pricing adjustments make the most sense.

## Maximizing Revenue While Staying True to Your Work

The beauty of using AI for financial modeling is that it frees up time and mental bandwidth. Rather than spending hours tweaking ads, running subscriber campaigns, or stressing over the right price point, you can rely on AI to handle the repetitive tasks while still keeping the creative decisions in your hands. It's about working smarter, not harder, and finding that sweet spot where creativity meets profitability.

So, while AI can't replace the soul of your writing, it can help make sure that soul reaches as many readers as possible—while putting a little more in your pocket along the way.

## Advanced SEO and Discoverability Using AI for Writers

Let's talk about discoverability—a term that can feel intimidating but really boils down to one goal: helping readers find your work. In today's digital landscape, mastering SEO (Search Engine Optimization) is like unlocking a secret door to a wider audience. But if you're imagining hours of mind-numbing research into keywords and algorithms, don't worry—AI can take over much of the heavy lifting.

With the right tools, you can streamline SEO tasks like keyword analysis, topic clustering, and optimizing your content so it doesn't just sit idle in the vast expanse of the internet. Here's how AI can help you boost your reach and connect with the readers who are already looking for stories like yours.

## 1. Keyword Analysis: Finding the Right Words to Reach Your Audience

Keywords are the backbone of SEO. They're the phrases people type into search engines when hunting for content. Using the right keywords can mean the difference between attracting new readers and having your work buried in obscurity.

**How AI Helps**: AI tools analyze massive amounts of data to uncover the most popular and relevant keywords for your genre, niche, or topic. Instead of manually researching terms, you can let AI pinpoint high-search, low-competition keywords—the golden terms that help you stand out without competing with larger sites.

**Try This**: Ask your AI tool for keyword suggestions tailored to your next project. For example:

- *"Generate keywords for a blog post on creating relatable characters in fiction."*
- *"Find low-competition keywords for a mystery novel about small-town secrets."*

You can also use these keywords for tags, like on Substack, to ensure your posts reach their intended audience.

## 2. Topic Clustering: Building a Network of Related Content

SEO isn't just about stuffing keywords into your work anymore. Search engines now prioritize content that covers topics comprehensively, which is where "topic clustering" shines. Topic clusters group related content around a central theme, boosting your authority and making your work more appealing to search engines.

**How AI Helps**: AI can analyze your existing content to suggest related topics, creating a cohesive network of posts that naturally link together. For instance, if you're blogging about world-building, AI might suggest related articles on character creation, plotting, or map design, creating a "hub" of content.

**Try This**: Use AI to identify pillar topics (main themes) and cluster topics (subtopics). For example: *"What pillar and cluster topics should I create for a blog on self-publishing?"* This approach not only helps your content rank higher but also keeps readers engaged as they explore related posts.

### 3. SEO-Optimized Content Generation: Making Your Words Work Harder

Creating SEO-friendly content doesn't mean sacrificing your unique voice or creativity. It's about enhancing your writing so it reaches the right audience. AI tools can guide you on things like keyword placement, ideal word count, and formatting, ensuring your content is search-friendly without feeling robotic.

**How AI Helps**: Many AI tools provide real-time SEO feedback, suggesting how to structure your article, where to use headings, and how to naturally incorporate keywords.

**Try This**: Craft prompts to optimize your content. For example:

- *"Write an SEO-friendly opening for an article on the role of AI in writing."*
- *"Suggest SEO headers for a blog post about dialogue writing in fiction."*

By integrating AI suggestions into your workflow, you can create content that's engaging for readers and attractive to search engines.

## 4. Metadata and Alt Text: The Small Details That Make a Big Difference

Metadata (titles, descriptions, and tags) and alt text (descriptions for images) might seem minor, but they play a huge role in SEO. They help search engines understand your content and make it more accessible for readers using assistive technology.

**How AI Helps**: AI can generate concise, keyword-rich metadata and alt text, saving you time and ensuring you're not overlooking these critical elements.

**Try This**: Prompt AI to create metadata and alt text as you write. For example:

- *"Write an SEO-friendly meta description for a blog post on horror writing."*
- *"Suggest alt text for an illustration of a dystopian city skyline."*

These small tweaks can make a big difference in how your content ranks and connects with audiences.

## 5. Analytics and Feedback: Learning What Works

Once your content is live, tracking its performance is key. AI-driven analytics tools can reveal which keywords drive traffic, which articles resonate most, and where there's room to improve.

**How AI Helps**: Analytics tools powered by AI provide actionable insights into your content's performance, helping you refine your strategy. For instance, you can see which keywords bring in the most readers or identify underperforming posts that could benefit from an update.

**Try This**: Use AI to monitor your metrics and guide improvements. For example:

- *"Analyze the performance of my recent blog post on character development."*
- *"Suggest adjustments based on traffic data for my sci-fi article."*

This feedback loop ensures your content stays relevant and competitive.

**Bringing It All Together: SEO without the Stress**

SEO might sound intimidating, but with AI, it becomes manageable—and even fun. These tools free you from the technical grind of keyword research and optimization, letting you focus on what you love: writing. By integrating AI into your SEO strategy, you're not just increasing your discoverability—you're creating pathways for readers to find and fall in love with your work.

Whether you're crafting your next blog post, pitching your novel, or building your author platform, AI can help you reach the audience that's already searching for the stories you have to tell.

# CHAPTER EIGHTEEN

# USER EXPERIENCE AND INTERFACE DESIGN FOR AI WRITING TOOLS

Let's face it: the design of an AI writing tool can make or break the entire experience. For writers, staying in the creative flow is hard enough without clunky menus, hidden features, or overwhelming dashboards getting in the way. The best tools keep it simple, intuitive, and designed with your workflow in mind. In this section, we'll explore what makes great user experience (UX) for AI tools and how it can boost your productivity, creativity, and sanity.

## Why Good Design Matters

When you're deep into a draft, the last thing you want is to lose momentum because you're hunting for a feature or troubleshooting a laggy interface. Thoughtful design ensures that the essentials are right where you need them, reducing interruptions and letting you focus on writing.

Take Google Docs or Scrivener—both prioritize ease of use. The best AI tools follow this model, offering clean interfaces that keep their most helpful features accessible. A tool with a floating "suggestions" box, for instance, might offer real-time sentence refinements or tone adjustments without burying you in pop-ups or endless sidebars. It's all about creating a flow that feels natural.

## What to Look For in a Writing Tool's Design

### 1. Customizable Features for Personalized Workflows

Not every writer works the same way, and the most helpful tools adapt to you. Look for tools that allow you to:

- Adjust the AI's tone to match your writing voice.
- Customize layouts or shortcut commands to fit your workflow.
- Toggle between minimalist drafting modes and detailed editing views.

For example, if you prefer a distraction-free environment, pick a tool with a "focus mode" that hides extra features while you draft. If you want real-time feedback, choose one that offers immediate, non-intrusive suggestions.

### 2. Seamless Transitions between Tasks

Writing isn't a linear process. Some days you're brainstorming; other days you're deep in revisions. The best tools transition smoothly between these modes. For instance:

- A brainstorming layout might prioritize idea generators or mind maps.
- Drafting might center on a clean text editor with quick-save options.
- Editing could include advanced grammar tools or style analysis pop-ups.

The goal is to keep the tool in sync with your process, so you're not wasting time navigating menus or reconfiguring settings.

### 3. Smart Suggestions without Overload

No one wants an AI that feels pushy. Tools that gently guide you with context-aware suggestions—like Canva's design prompts—are more likely to feel like partners than taskmasters. Whether it's proposing alternate phrasing or pointing out repetitive words, the key is balance: enough help to be useful but not so much that it becomes distracting.

### 4. Speed and Stability

Nothing kills creativity like a tool that freezes, crashes, or lags. A well-designed tool minimizes load times and responds quickly to your inputs. Before committing to a new tool, test its stability with longer pieces or complex tasks.

## Reducing Creative Friction: Designing for Flow

Creative friction is the subtle resistance that builds up when your tools don't align with your process. A poorly designed interface can pull you out of the zone, whether it's a lagging AI response or a hidden save button.

The best AI tools focus on "flow state design," keeping everything running smoothly so you can stay immersed in your work. For example, they might:

- Automate repetitive tasks like formatting or metadata entry.
- Offer clear navigation and shortcuts for common actions.
- Track your progress and auto-save frequently to prevent interruptions.

## Evaluating Tools: A Practical Checklist for Writers

If you're evaluating an AI writing tool, ask yourself:

1. Does the interface feel intuitive?
2. Can I customize it to fit my specific needs?
3. Does it help me move seamlessly between brainstorming, drafting, and editing?
4. Are its suggestions helpful but not overwhelming?
5. Is it stable, responsive, and fast?

## Why This Matters for Writers

Great interface design isn't just about aesthetics—it's about creating a tool that supports your creative process. A well-designed AI writing tool should feel like a partner: it adapts to your workflow, reduces friction, and stays out of the way when you don't need it.

By choosing tools with thoughtful design, you're setting yourself up for fewer interruptions, more productivity, and, ultimately, better writing. Because at the end of the day, the best tools aren't just about the technology—they're about helping you tell your story.

# CHAPTER NINETEEN

# INTEGRATING AI WITH OTHER CREATIVE MEDIA—GAMING, INTERACTIVE EXPERIENCES, AND BEYOND

Imagine this: your audience isn't just reading your story—they're stepping into it. They're exploring your world, interacting with your characters, and shaping the plot through their choices. Welcome to the convergence of storytelling, gaming, and AI—a groundbreaking space where writers can bring their narratives to life in bold, dynamic ways.

## Gaming and Interactive Narratives: Turning Stories into Living Worlds

One of the most thrilling applications of AI in cross-media storytelling is in gaming and interactive experiences. Here, your characters don't just live on the page—they respond, evolve, and engage with the audience in real-time. With AI, you can create branching narratives where each player's decisions shape the story, which delivers a highly personalized experience.

Imagine transforming your novel into an interactive game where readers-turned-players decide the fate of your characters. AI tools like ChatGPT can help bring this vision to life by simulating character-driven dialogue trees, dynamic plotlines, and real-time responses. For example, you can train an AI to "embody" a character, allowing players to interact with them naturally. The character's responses adapt based on the player's decisions, making every playthrough unique while staying true to the heart of your story.

Interactive storytelling through AI doesn't just enhance immersion—it opens up new ways for audiences to connect with your narrative. Whether it's through a simple text-based role-playing game or a complex, visually rich adventure, AI empowers you to turn your readers into active participants.

## Multi-Platform Storytelling: Expanding Your Universe

Today's digital landscape is a playground for multi-platform storytelling, and AI makes it easier than ever to keep your story's core essence consistent across formats. No longer confined to a single medium, your story can now unfold across interactive games, social media campaigns, episodic content, and more.

Picture this: a mystery novel evolves into an interactive treasure hunt across platforms like Instagram or TikTok, with AI-generated clues and updates that engage followers in real time. Or imagine an epic fantasy where readers "unlock" hidden chapters, character arcs, or exclusive lore by playing a complementary game or participating in an interactive web experience. AI ensures that the story remains cohesive, generating dialogue, backstories, and plot continuity to maintain immersion no matter where your audience engages with it.

AI also excels at tailoring content for specific platforms. Whether it's generating bite-sized content for social media or adapting longer narratives for episodic web series, these tools help you reach diverse audiences while keeping your storytelling tight and engaging.

## The Future of AI in Cross-Media Storytelling

The possibilities are just beginning. As AI technology evolves, writers will have access to tools that go far beyond dialogue generation or branching narratives. Imagine an AI that tracks reader engagement in real-time, suggesting new story branches or interactive elements based on their reactions. Or tools that create personalized story arcs for each audience member, ensuring every experience feels uniquely tailored.

Looking ahead, AI could take immersive storytelling to the next level, integrating visuals, soundscapes, and adaptive pacing that adjusts to the preferences and emotions of each user. These advancements will enable writers to craft stories that aren't just read—they're lived.

## Storytelling without Boundaries

With AI as your collaborator, the limits of traditional storytelling fall away. You're not just a writer—you're a world-builder, a director, and an architect of interactive experiences. This is storytelling that adapts, evolves, and reaches audiences wherever they are, across platforms and formats.

If you've ever dreamed of readers walking alongside your characters, uncovering your plot through their own actions, or shaping your world in real time, AI is the bridge to that reality. It's time to think beyond the page and delve into the immersive, interactive futures waiting to be written.

After showcasing the incredible possibilities AI offers for creativity and storytelling, it's time to step back and ask some deeper questions. What responsibilities come with wielding these powerful tools? How do we, as creators, ensure that we're not just using AI to expand our horizons but also doing so in ways that align with our values and respect for others? As we move into the ethical dimension of AI, we'll explore the opportunities, challenges, and moral crossroads that come with integrating artificial intelligence into the creative process.

## Why We Keep Going

If you've made it this far, you've seen what I've seen: the landscape is shifting under our feet, and the old paths are breaking apart.

But here's what hasn't changed—storytelling still matters. And storytellers still survive.

You don't have to be a coder. You don't have to love this new reality. But if you're still willing to learn, to shape, to resist in your own creative way, then you're already doing the thing that matters most.

I didn't write this book because I just love technology. I wrote it because I truly love writing—and I wasn't willing to give it up just because the system decided it was inconvenient.

AI didn't save me. But it helped me keep going.

And now? It's time we start teaching others how to do the same.

# PART FOUR

# THE DARK SIDE OF AI AND ENSURING A BRIGHTER FUTURE

# CHAPTER TWENTY

# FROM SCAMS TO STANDARDS—HOW PUBLISHING IS FIGHTING BACK

The publishing industry also stands at a crossroads. As AI technology rapidly evolves, it brings both unprecedented opportunities and profound challenges. From tools that can enhance editorial processes to the proliferation of low-quality, AI-generated scam books flooding online platforms, the industry is being reshaped in real time. Publishers, authors, and advocacy groups alike are grappling with pressing questions: How can we harness AI's potential without undermining the creative integrity that defines human literature? What steps can be taken to safeguard intellectual property and protect writers from exploitation? And how do we separate meaningful innovation from misuse?

In this chapter, we'll explore how major publishers and organizations are addressing these issues. From Penguin Random House's measured approach to AI innovation to the Authors Guild's tireless efforts to protect creators' rights, the industry is beginning to set standards for ethical AI use. Along the way, we'll also examine the darker side of AI's rise in publishing, including the surge in scam books and the risks they pose to readers and legitimate authors.

We begin with Penguin Random House, a global publishing leader, and their thoughtful strategy to balance AI-driven advancements with their commitment to human creativity. Their approach offers a roadmap for navigating this complex landscape, highlighting how tradition and technology can coexist without compromising the heart of storytelling.

## Penguin Random House: Balancing AI Innovation with Human Creativity

Penguin Random House, a titan in the publishing industry, has taken a clear and deliberate stance on the integration of generative AI.[1] Their approach underscores a commitment to human creativity, intellectual property, and responsible innovation—principles that resonate deeply within the creative world.

In a recent statement, Penguin highlighted that they have used various forms of AI for over a decade in their business operations, specifically for sales forecasting and stock management. While this foundational use of AI has long been a part of their workflow, the rapid expansion of generative AI has brought new complexities that demand careful navigation.

The publisher is addressing these challenges through three guiding principles:

1. **Championing Human Creativity:** Penguin asserts that no technology can substitute for human imagination. They remain dedicated to empowering diverse voices to tell their stories, ensuring that every book is a product of human effort and care.
2. **Advocating for Intellectual Property:** Recognizing the critical role of intellectual property in the creative industry, Penguin vows to defend the rights of authors and artists. This principle safeguards the value of creative work, ensuring fair recognition and compensation.
3. **Innovating Responsibly:** Open to adopting generative AI, Penguin commits to doing so selectively and responsibly. While they recognize the potential for these tools to advance their goals, they are cautious about any integration that might detract from the human essence of their books.

Penguin Random House took a bold step in October 2024 to protect its authors' intellectual property in line with these principles. The company updated the copyright notices in all new and reprinted titles across its global imprints to explicitly prohibit the use of its books for training AI systems. The revised notice states: "No part of this book may be used or reproduced in any manner for the purpose of training artificial intelligence technologies or systems."

This update reflects PRH's dedication to safeguarding creative works from unauthorized use and ensuring fair treatment for authors. It also aligns with their active role in broader industry advocacy. For example, Penguin Random House joined forces with the Association of American Publishers and over ten thousand global creators in condemning the unlicensed use of creative works for training generative AI models.[2] This coalition emphasized the existential threat such practices pose to creators' livelihoods and the urgent need to defend intellectual property rights.

As a global leader, Penguin Random House has also emphasized that every one of their books will continue to be "shaped and nurtured by a team of highly talented humans." This statement reinforces their belief in the irreplaceable value of human creativity within their mission.

Their proactive steps demonstrate how a publishing powerhouse can navigate the challenges of AI by balancing innovation with tradition. By combining established AI tools for efficiency in areas like sales forecasting with a cautious approach to generative AI, Penguin Random House sets a standard for publishers seeking to adapt to this era without compromising their values.

This blend of action and advocacy offers an insightful example for others navigating the AI era. Penguin Random House proves that while embracing technology is essential, it must be balanced with the expense of the creative essence that makes storytelling so profoundly human.

## A Spectrum of AI Approaches in Publishing

While Penguin Random House has adopted a carefully measured stance, prioritizing preserving human creativity and intellectual property, other publishers are exploring AI integration from a different angle. HarperCollins, for instance, has embraced a more proactive and monetization-driven approach, exemplified by its groundbreaking licensing deal with Microsoft. This divergence illustrates the evolving strategies within the publishing world as it grapples with the complexities of AI.

## HarperCollins: Monetizing Nonfiction in the AI Era

As the publishing industry grapples with the rise of AI, HarperCollins has taken a bold step into uncharted territory. In November 2024, the publisher struck a groundbreaking three-year licensing deal with Microsoft,[3] granting access to select nonfiction backlist titles for AI training purposes. This partnership underscores a growing trend: leveraging literary content to enhance AI systems, while attempting to balance innovation with ethical considerations.

### The Deal at a Glance

HarperCollins's agreement allows Microsoft to use nonfiction works to train its AI models, with strict safeguards in place:

- **Author Participation and Compensation:** Authors have the choice to opt in, receiving a $5,000 fee per title. The payment is split equally between the author and HarperCollins, adding an additional layer of income beyond traditional advances and royalties.
- **Usage Limitations:** The agreement restricts Microsoft from reproducing more than two hundred consecutive words or 5 percent of a book's text, ensuring that AI training remains within reasonable bounds.
- **Transparency and Ethical Oversight:** HarperCollins requires explicit permission from authors, which ensures creators retain some agency over their work. The publisher has incorporated feedback from authors and agents into the terms, aiming to set a precedent for responsible AI integration.

## Diverging Opinions in the Literary World

The announcement has sparked significant debate within the writing community:

- Supporters applaud the deal as a necessary adaptation to a rapidly changing industry. By monetizing AI's use of existing works, HarperCollins creates new revenue streams for authors and publishers alike.
- Critics, including organizations like the Authors Guild, argue that the fifty-fifty revenue split is unfair, suggesting authors should receive a larger share given that their intellectual property forms the backbone of AI training.

This divide highlights the ongoing tension between embracing technological advancements and protecting the livelihoods of creators.

## Lessons for the Industry

HarperCollins's partnership with Microsoft serves as a case study in navigating the opportunities and risks of AI integration. By emphasizing transparency, seeking author consent, and implementing usage restrictions, the publisher demonstrates a potential framework for future collaborations. However, the deal also underscores the challenges of equitable compensation in the AI era, raising questions about how publishers and authors can share the benefits of these emerging technologies.

As the publishing industry navigates the complexities of AI integration, organizations like the Authors Guild play a pivotal role in advocating for ethical practices and protecting authors' rights. Following HarperCollins's proactive yet controversial approach to AI, it's essential to examine how the Authors Guild is addressing these challenges.

## Ethical AI Use in Writing: Guidance from the Authors Guild

The Authors Guild, the United States' oldest and largest professional organization for writers, has been at the forefront of addressing the ethical implications of AI in literature. Recognizing the profound impact of AI on the writing profession, the Guild has implemented several initiatives to safeguard authors' rights and promote responsible AI use.

### Advocacy for Authors' Rights in the AI Era

In September 2023, the Authors Guild, alongside seventeen prominent authors—including George R.R. Martin, Jodi Picoult, and John Grisham—filed a class-action lawsuit against OpenAI.[4] The suit alleges that OpenAI used copyrighted works without permission to train its AI models, underscoring the Guild's commitment to ensuring authors are compensated and their intellectual property rights are protected in the face of emerging technologies.

### Support for Screenwriters during the WGA Strike

During the Writers Guild of America (WGA) strike in May 2023, the Authors Guild expressed solidarity with screenwriters' concerns about AI. The WGA sought to establish clear regulations on AI's role in scriptwriting to prevent undermining writers' compensation and creative control. The Authors Guild's advocacy for authors' rights in the AI context resonated with the screenwriters' demands, highlighting a shared concern across creative professions about AI's impact on human authorship.

### Best Practices for Ethical AI Use

To guide authors navigating the integration of AI, the Authors Guild has outlined best practices emphasizing transparency, respect for intellectual property, and ethical usage of generative AI. They encourage writers to use AI as a tool for brainstorming and refining ideas rather than as a primary source of content. Maintaining the unique spirit of human creativity is paramount, with authors urged to rewrite AI-generated text in their own voices to ensure the final work remains a product of their creativity.

## Disclosure of AI Use

The Guild recommends that authors disclose significant AI-generated elements in their manuscripts to publishers. This transparency is a matter of professional integrity and a legal necessity, as most publishing contracts require that submitted work be original to the author. The Guild also suggests that substantial AI involvement be acknowledged in the book's front matter, introduction, or acknowledgments to maintain trust with readers.

## Safeguarding Creative Professions

Extending support to other creative professionals—such as translators, illustrators, and voice actors—whose work is increasingly threatened by AI, the Guild emphasizes the importance of collaboration with human professionals whenever possible. This stance underscores the need for solidarity in protecting creative industries from the disruptive impacts of AI.

Through these initiatives, the Authors Guild exemplifies a proactive approach to the ethical challenges posed by AI, striving to ensure that technological advancement does not come at the expense of human creativity and authors' rights.

## The Consequences of Inaction: AI's Misuse in Publishing

The Authors Guild has taken significant steps to safeguard writers' rights and promote ethical AI practices. Yet, as much as advocacy and guidelines aim to steer the industry, the rise of generative AI has also opened doors to troubling trends that threaten the integrity of publishing.

One glaring issue is the proliferation of AI-generated scam books. These fraudulent titles not only exploit platforms like Amazon but also erode trust between authors and readers, undermining the values the Guild works so hard to protect. While the Guild champions transparency and accountability, these scam books showcase the darker side of AI's rapid adoption, where technology is wielded for profit without regard for creativity or ethics.

## Scam Books and the Rise of AI-Generated Content

Many of us writers may have seen those ads on social media—the ones with some impossibly polished person standing in front of a flashy sports car, promising that they've unlocked the secret to wealth and success. Not long ago, they were just like you, they say, maybe even worse off, until they discovered the magic of using AI to write books. Now, their life is like a scene straight out of a Barbie dream house: perfect, effortless, and lucrative.

I've been bombarded by those ads, often as I'm mentally calculating how to stretch my budget to cover another bag of dog food and a modest dinner for my daughters. A part of me can't help but feel the pull of those empty promises. Who wouldn't want that kind of financial freedom? I've worked hard to make my dreams of being a financially stable writer a reality, but like many of us in this field, I still hit those lean stretches between projects. The allure of a quick fix is real.

But here's the thing: no shortcut, miracle solution, or AI gimmick will replace the grind. No magic trick turns you into a successful writer overnight. The truth is simple, if not glamorous: you must sit down and write every day and keep doing it. The work doesn't do itself, and there's no way around that. Deep down, I know that if something sounds too good to be true, it usually is.

The rapid rise of AI has shaken up the publishing world, but not all of it for the better. One of the more unsettling trends is the flood of AI-generated "scam" books appearing on platforms like Amazon. These aren't just poorly written; they're often outright deceptive, mimicking legitimate works and misleading readers. This surge undermines the hard work of genuine authors and muddies the waters for everyone trying to make an honest living through words. Similarly, there are also books presented as "summaries" of other books; this has even happened to the publisher of this book, Skyhorse.

Take the case of author Jane Friedman, who recently found her name slapped on a bunch of AI-generated books she had nothing to do with. These fake titles popped up on Amazon, and despite her protests, Amazon initially refused to remove them, saying she hadn't provided enough evidence of trademark infringement. Think about that—a prolific author, having to fight tooth and nail to keep her name clean from bot-created garbage.

And she's not alone. A rising tide of scammy, AI-spewed books is flooding the marketplace, many of them cobbled together in minutes, riddled with nonsense, and uploaded by bad actors looking to cash in before anyone notices. Some impersonate real writers, some jam SEO keywords into titles like they're playing Mad Libs, and others straight-up plagiarize—adding just enough gobbledygook to dodge detection.[5]

It's not just about protecting reputations; it's about protecting the soul of authorship. When readers get burned by these digital fakes, trust erodes. And when trust dies, we all lose.

So how do you separate a real book from a low-effort AI con job? Let's do some scam-spotting.

---

### How to Spot a Scam Book Before It Sucks Up Your Money and Faith in Humanity

The AI gold rush gave us cool tools—but it also opened the floodgates to a tidal wave of scam books: low-quality, bot-generated garbage trying to pass as legit. Here's how to sniff out the frauds:

- **Author Who?** If the "author" has zero presence online but somehow "wrote" a dozen books this month, it's likely an AI content mill in disguise.
- **Déjà Title.** Look for titles that mimic bestsellers with just a word or two changed—*The Subtle Art of Giving Less* kind of vibes. Close, but cringe.
- **Robot Rhetoric.** Use Amazon's "Look Inside" feature. If the prose reads like a chatbot had an identity crisis mid-sentence? Abort mission.
- **Fake Fan Club.** Glowing five-star reviews that say "Very helpful!" or "Great book!" with no real insight? That's not an audience—it's a bot farm.

- **Cover Red Flags.** If the book cover looks like clipart had a meltdown, or it feels off-brand in a weird uncanny-valley way, trust your instincts.

**What Writers Can Do:**
Set up **Google Alerts** for your name and book titles so you'll know if someone tries to hijack them. Check Amazon and Goodreads for suspicious listings. And if you find one? **Call it out publicly**—platforms are far more responsive when the heat is on.

The Authors Guild has stepped up as a major advocate here, offering a roadmap for navigating this tricky new world. Their best practices for authors are worth a serious look:

- **Use AI as a Tool, Not a Crutch**: AI can be great for brainstorming or tweaking ideas, but it shouldn't be doing the heavy lifting. The soul of a story? That's all you.
- **Transparency Is Key**: If you're using a good chunk of AI-generated content in your work, own up to it. Publishers need to know, and so do your readers. The trust between author and reader is sacred, and honesty is the best way to maintain it.
- **Guard the Creative Sanctum**: Don't let AI mimic another writer's unique style or voice. It's not just lazy—it's likely infringing on intellectual property.
- **Check Your Facts**: AI can spin a good yarn, but it's not exactly known for its accuracy. Always fact-check anything generated by a bot.
- **Solidarity with Fellow Creatives**: Writers, illustrators, narrators—we're all in this together. AI shouldn't replace the unique touch that human creatives bring to the table.

One particularly eye-opening recommendation from the Guild is the importance of disclosing AI use to platforms like Amazon's Kindle

Direct Publishing (KDP). Amazon now requires authors to flag any AI-generated content when publishing. While these disclosures currently stay between the author and Amazon, the Guild is pushing for this information to be made public. Readers deserve to know what they're buying.

What's worse is the rise of companies that promise to turn you into an "author" overnight using AI. These outfits churn out low-quality content at breakneck speed, cluttering the market and making it harder for genuine voices to be heard. The lure of quick success can be tempting, but more often than not, it's a shortcut to nowhere.

Incorporating AI into the creative process doesn't have to spell doom for writers, but we must proceed cautiously, armed with ethical guidelines and a commitment to quality. The Authors Guild's push for transparency and advocacy for writers' rights is a solid step toward navigating this new reality. For those of us who cherish the craft of writing, it's a reminder that while AI can assist, it should never replace the touch of a human heart.

The rise of AI-generated scam books and the proactive measures taken by organizations like the Authors Guild highlight the challenges and ethical dilemmas AI poses for the publishing industry. However, not every development in AI's integration is a cause for concern. Across the literary world, some platforms and publishers are embracing AI to empower writers, streamline processes, and enhance reader engagement.

This brings us to the final section of this chapter: real-world examples of how AI is being utilized to transform the publishing landscape for the better. From content moderation to reader analytics, these case studies reveal how AI is helping to reimagine the creative process, offering valuable lessons for writers, publishers, and readers alike.

## Case Studies on AI-Enhanced Publishing

As AI technology becomes more embedded in the publishing world, it's fascinating to see how different platforms and publishing houses are using it to elevate their game in content moderation, reader engagement, and distribution. Here are a few examples showing how AI is starting to change the landscape for writers and readers alike.(AI[9])

## 1. Wattpad: Using AI for Content Moderation and Reader Analytics

Wattpad, the online storytelling platform, has been a frontrunner in integrating AI across multiple facets of its service. With millions of stories and an active global readership, the company uses AI for content moderation, trend identification, and reader analytics, improving both platform safety and user experience.

- **Content Moderation:** Wattpad's "Story DNA" is an AI-driven tool that analyzes stories to identify sensitive content, flagging inappropriate material before it reaches readers. Using natural language processing (NLP), it can detect themes like violence, hate speech, and explicit content, ensuring compliance with platform guidelines and protecting younger audiences by making sure stories are rated appropriately.
- **Reader Analytics for Story Discovery:** Wattpad leverages AI to analyze reading patterns, helping the platform recommend stories that match user preferences. Their recommendation algorithm examines what stories readers spend the most time on, which genres are trending, and even analyzes comment sections to gauge reader engagement. By using this data, Wattpad can promote stories likely to appeal to broader audiences, giving new writers a chance to reach wider readership based on genuine reader interest.

This approach demonstrates the potential of AI to bring fresh voices to the forefront while managing vast amounts of content safely and efficiently.

---

AI[9]    AI These case studies were compiled and synthesized with AI assistance to highlight major uses of AI in publishing platforms as of mid-2025.

## 2. Substack: AI-Driven Content Enhancement and Audience Engagement

Substack, a popular platform for independent writers, integrates AI tools to help writers grow and engage their audiences. While it doesn't publish books in the traditional sense, Substack's approach to publishing newsletters with AI-enhanced tools shows how creators can use AI to improve reader engagement and expand distribution.

- **Audience Analytics:** Substack offers writers AI-enhanced audience insights, such as identifying which posts perform best and when, which topics garner the most reader interaction, and where potential growth opportunities lie. AI analyzes engagement patterns, helping writers refine content to suit their audience's preferences and boost subscription rates.
- **Predictive Trends and Content Suggestions:** Substack uses machine learning to suggest relevant topics based on current trends. This predictive feature can help writers keep their content timely and relevant. For instance, if a particular news topic is trending, a Substack writer may consider covering related topics, increasing the chance of reader engagement and shareability.

By leveraging AI to better understand and respond to reader preferences, Substack illustrates how independent writers can use AI to grow an audience, monetize their work, and optimize content for higher engagement.

## 3. Penguin Random House: AI-Enhanced Book Marketing and Distribution

Penguin Random House (PRH), one of the largest traditional publishing houses, has been incorporating AI into its marketing and distribution strategies to stay competitive in a changing market. AI assists PRH in personalizing marketing efforts, predicting book trends, and making data-driven decisions.

- **Marketing Personalization:** PRH uses AI to segment their readership based on preferences, allowing them to target marketing campaigns with precision. For example, AI analyzes social media engagement, reading habits, and purchase history to create personalized recommendations. This way, marketing efforts for a new science fiction title, for instance, can be directed toward readers with a history of purchasing or engaging with similar content.

- **Predictive Trend Analysis:** AI-driven data analysis helps PRH identify emerging trends in reading preferences, allowing them to acquire titles that align with market demands. By analyzing vast datasets, including bestseller lists, social media trends, and book reviews, AI can predict which genres or topics are likely to perform well in the future.

Of course, this kind of data-driven decision-making comes with a dark side. If publishers lean too hard on AI predictions, there's a real risk that powerful, unexpected stories—especially those that challenge norms or push boundaries—might get filtered out before a human ever sees them.

The danger? We end up in a feedback loop of safe bets and algorithm-approved content, where originality gets sidelined because it's not trending yet. Great books have always defied expectations. *Frankenstein*, *Beloved*, *The Handmaid's Tale*—none of them were written to match keyword trends or fill a content gap.

It's already happening in subtle ways. Editors are busier, slush piles are bigger, and if a book doesn't "score well" with the data model? It might never get a chance. Imagine a future where no one reads your manuscript—just a bot that decides it's not viable based on market analytics from six months ago.

If that doesn't sound like the setup to a Stephen King story, I don't know what does. And the scariest part? It might already be chapter one.

## 4. Medium: AI for Content Moderation and Reader Experience Enhancement

Medium, a platform for article publishing, relies on AI to curate and moderate content. The platform's unique algorithmic approach highlights stories based on reader interest, engagement, and topic relevance, positioning AI as a crucial component in content visibility and audience experience.

- **Content Moderation and Quality Control:** Medium's AI filters content to maintain quality and compliance with guidelines, flagging inappropriate or low-quality material. The AI model evaluates elements like tone, readability, and engagement potential, ensuring that published articles meet Medium's standards.
- **Curated Content Feeds:** AI analyzes reader preferences and engagement metrics to curate content feeds personalized to each reader. For example, if a reader often engages with articles on environmental science, AI will prioritize similar content in their feed, making it easier for readers to find relevant stories.

Medium's AI-driven curation and moderation ensure a seamless reading experience, keeping the platform engaging and personalized for each reader.

## 5. Amazon Kindle Direct Publishing (KDP): Optimizing Self-Publishing with AI

Amazon KDP, a popular platform for self-published authors, integrates AI to support authors with content discovery and marketing. The platform's AI tools focus on optimizing book visibility, enhancing recommendations, and offering targeted promotional options.

- **Automated Book Recommendations:** KDP's AI-driven recommendation algorithm helps readers discover books similar to those they've enjoyed. By analyzing reader behavior—such as browsing history, previous purchases, and genres read—KDP ensures books are shown to relevant audiences, increasing discoverability for self-published authors.

- **Keyword Optimization and Market Insights:** KDP provides authors with AI-backed insights into trending keywords and book categories, helping them position their books effectively. By optimizing metadata, including keywords and categories, authors improve their chances of ranking higher in Amazon search results, leading to increased visibility and sales.

Amazon KDP demonstrates how self-publishing platforms can integrate AI to support independent authors in marketing and reaching their target readers.

## Embracing the Future of AI in Publishing

These case studies show how AI enhances every aspect of publishing, from content creation to reader engagement, marketing, and distribution. Whether you're an independent writer or work within a traditional publishing house, understanding these AI-driven tools provides an advantage in today's evolving publishing landscape. By optimizing content for relevance, expanding distribution reach, and personalizing reader experiences, AI has become an invaluable ally in the publishing industry, bridging gaps between writers and their audiences while supporting growth in a competitive market.

As I stated at the start of this chapter, the publishing industry is at a crossroads in the AI era. On one side, we see challenges—scam books, intellectual property violations, and the erosion of trust between authors and readers. Conversely, there are exciting opportunities—tools that enhance creativity, platforms that connect writers with audiences in new ways, and systems that make publishing more efficient and accessible.

Navigating this landscape requires vigilance, adaptability, and a commitment to ethical practices. As writers and publishers, we must embrace AI as a tool, not a threat, ensuring it amplifies human creativity rather than replaces it. By learning from industry leaders like Penguin Random House, staying alert to potential pitfalls highlighted by the Authors Guild, and drawing inspiration from platforms leveraging AI responsibly, we can chart a path forward that respects the art of storytelling while embracing the possibilities of the future.

The road ahead isn't without its challenges, but it's also full of promise. By balancing innovation with integrity, we can harness AI's potential to enrich the publishing world and create a new era of storytelling—one that's as dynamic and diverse as the voices shaping it.

### Beyond the Algorithm: A Conversation with Caroline Russomanno

In the early months of writing *AI Ink.*, I knew I needed to sit down with someone from inside the traditional publishing world—someone who could help me understand where human editors stand in an industry slowly giving way to the synthetic precision of algorithms. Lucky for me, I didn't have to look far. Caroline Russomanno is my editor at Skyhorse Publishing, and over the course of bringing this book (and my previous one) to life, she has become not only a trusted collaborator but someone who started experimenting with AI herself—because of this book. So, I turned the microphone around and asked her to share her thoughts.

Our conversation wasn't just informative; it was something more. It was human. It reminded me why editors like Caroline are still not only relevant, but essential. And why, no matter how far the tech evolves, there's still something ineffable about the human capacity to feel narrative—to recognize when something falls flat or when it soars.

Here's what we captured—unedited where it matters, honest throughout. It's a conversation about AI's growing impact, the nuances of editorial judgment, and how one editor is learning to adapt without compromising the creative integrity of her work.

**Jason Van Tatenhove:** Can you start by sharing how your background in English, journalism, and professional writing shaped your editorial eye?

**Caroline Russomanno:** I originally wanted to be a teacher, but I realized pretty quickly in college that it wasn't for me. I pivoted to journalism while already majoring in English. Unfortunately, I made that pivot right as the media world was burning, and full-time jobs were scarce or unsustainable. I got lucky though—I started in a tiny publishing house called New Horizon Press. It was just me and three other people, including the owner, Joan Dunphy. She taught me the importance of integrity in publishing and the nitty-gritty work of fact-checking, sourcing, and permission handling. I learned more in those early years than any classroom could've taught me.

**Jason:** And from there, your journey brought you to Skyhorse?

**Caroline:** Yes, I moved from New Horizon to Transaction Publishers, which was larger and focused on sociology titles. That's where I learned to juggle twenty-five-plus books at a time. It was a crash course in project management. I missed the hands-on editorial work, though, so when I got the chance to join Skyhorse, I took it. That was over eight years ago. I've worked my way up from associate editor to senior editor.

**Jason:** You've mentioned that you were skeptical about AI before working on *AI Ink.* What changed?

**Caroline:** I've always had a sci-fi brain, thanks to my mom, so the idea of AI raised flags for me. I thought of it as cold and a little dystopian. But when I read the early drafts of *AI Ink.*, I saw that it could be helpful. The way you framed it—as a tool that can assist, but not replace—shifted my perspective. I realized it wasn't about automation replacing creativity, but about amplifying it.

**Jason:** And that curiosity turned into experimentation?

**Caroline:** Yeah, I started small. I asked ChatGPT to help me manage my daily schedule. It actually made a difference—took a big weight off my shoulders. Then I tried it with metadata. Editors at Skyhorse have to generate SEO keywords for upcoming books—sometimes before we've even read the manuscript. I used AI to expand my keyword list, which I then curated and refined. It was incredibly helpful.

But it's just one tool in the toolkit, not a replacement for editorial instincts.

**Jason:** Have you discussed AI use with other editors or your publisher?

**Caroline:** Not yet with Tony [Lyons, owner and publisher of Skyhorse] directly, but I've spoken with our editorial director, Abigail, about using it for SEO. We're all juggling so much that we haven't institutionalized anything yet, but I hope we will. It's worth talking about—just as we've discussed throughout this book. Having these conversations is key.

**Jason:** What concerns are being raised at Skyhorse about AI-authored submissions?

**Caroline:** Right now, the concern is around authenticity. We've had submissions where a section has seemed off from the rest of the manuscript, and further digging has shown that it's likely AI. I've started using ChatGPT to help with that identification after my own "editor senses" tingle. The irony of that isn't lost on me. So far, we haven't had a fully AI-generated book, but the threat is there. That's where we have to be vigilant.

**Jason:** So what do you look for when evaluating authenticity?

**Caroline:** Voice. Every author has quirks—stylistic fingerprints. If I'm reading and suddenly that voice vanishes, that's a red flag. It's not about grammar or punctuation. It's about rhythm. If the cadence disappears, I notice. And I don't jump to conclusions—I ask the author first. But I trust my instincts, and those instincts come from reading thousands of pages across my career.

**Jason:** Where do you find AI currently falls short in editing?

**Caroline:** Emotional resonance. It can mimic, but it doesn't *feel*. It doesn't understand the tension of a thriller that's just not quite landing. I've worked on thrillers where the lead-up gave me chills—until the payoff didn't hit. That's something only a human editor can flag. AI doesn't get goosebumps.

And that's also one of the things that initially scared me—when I started hearing authors say, "I used AI to edit my whole book." That concern stuck with me. Sure, AI can catch grammar issues, splices, and clunky phrasing—but it often still needs *more* editing. I've had authors send me manuscripts they thought were clean because AI had polished them, but they still needed work. And they realized it the moment a human editor took a pass.

I don't think we'll see human editors replaced anytime soon. Maybe in a hundred years, when we're living in Asimov's future. But right now? There's no substitute for the human eye that can *feel* the text. That emotional calibration still belongs to us.

**Jason:** What remains, then, as the core irreplaceable role of the human editor?

**Caroline:** The ability to sense where something's working and where it's not. To feel the build-up in a thriller and know when the payoff lands—or when it drops like a lead balloon. To get that chill up your spine when a moment hits just right—and to recognize when it misses. AI can't do that. Human editors can bond with a manuscript in a way that just isn't replicable yet. Maybe not ever.

**Jason:** Final thoughts? Anything we didn't touch on?

**Caroline:** I think we covered most of it. Just that sense of being cautious but not fearful—embracing AI while never forgetting that the human component is still the heart of it all. That's what I'll keep carrying forward.

Talking with Caroline made something very clear to me: editors are more than just grammatical cleanup crews. They are co-conspirators in story, caretakers of flow, and emotional barometers for the reader's journey. But the importance of a good editor shines, to me at least, in that magical moment when a rougher draft begins to transition into something more like a sculpted work of literary art.

AI might help streamline parts of the process—and hell, it's already doing that—but that spine-tingling moment when a twist lands or the gut-punch when it doesn't? That still belongs to us and lives in the realms of human art.

And maybe always will.

# CHAPTER TWENTY-ONE

# GETTING AHEAD OF THE CURVE

## AI and Information Integrity

It's hard to put into words the anxiety of being asked to testify before Congress—before what might be our generation's version of the Watergate hearings. This is not a twist to my life that I would have dreamt of coming my way. Yet, there I sat before the Select Committee investigating the January 6 attack on the Capitol, asked to speak not just about the historical precedent of violent extremism of the militia community but also about how disinformation—often born and spread through conspiracy theories—played a central role in radicalizing entire communities. Wearing my signature jean jacket and concert tee on day seven of the hearings, broadcasting out to over twelve million live viewers and being reported by countless front page articles and subsequent news coverage around the world, I had unintentionally become an expert on the subject. It all started when I set out to write what I thought could be our generation's version of *Hell's Angels*, inspired by my lifelong love of Hunter S. Thompson's work. Much like Hunter's, my journey had been anything but straightforward, and I chronicle that path in my first nonfiction book, *The Perils of Extremism*.

The subjects I spoke about to the committee and later universities, museums, and nonprofits were bad enough, but these days, there's something new and far more dangerous on the horizon—no, not even on the horizon; it is now amongst us in unseen ways, already working itself into our newsfeeds and social media—an evolution in disinformation that even Thompson couldn't have imagined: artificial intelligence. Misinformation has existed for as long as stories have been told, but AI is rewriting the rules in terrifying ways.

As Corey Hutchins, a professor at Colorado College and former investigative journalist for *Columbia Journalism Review*, explained in our interview, the traditional challenges of misinformation have morphed with the introduction of AI technologies. He spoke about how AI's ability to produce content that mimics legitimate journalism poses a unique threat:

"It's no longer just about competing for clicks," he said. "The stakes have been raised. AI can generate articles that look and read like credible news stories, making it nearly impossible for the average reader to tell the difference. The consequences for the 'truth' of information are enormous."

## AI Creating Misinformation

In today's digital age, misinformation spreads faster than a Rocky Mountain wildfire in the dog days of summer, and artificial intelligence is a driving force behind that acceleration. While AI tools have made incredible strides in assisting with content creation, they have also been co-opted to manipulate information, create false narratives, and distort public opinion on an unprecedented scale. AI's role in this space has been both transformative and deeply troubling.

Hutchins highlighted a disturbing example from Colorado where a political operative created a false news website, powered by AI, that took in and then rewrote and regurgitated legitimate reporting without attribution. This kind of misuse of AI for disinformation can rapidly undermine public trust: "We're seeing websites that look just like credible news outlets, but they're producing AI-generated content to push a specific agenda. It's subtle but dangerous—especially when people start believing that these are genuine sources."

## Amplifying Falsehoods: AI's Threat to Trust

One of the most chilling aspects of AI in the spread of misinformation is its capacity to generate content that mimics real voices. Mary McCord, former acting US attorney general and current executive director of Georgetown Law's Institute of Constitutional Advocacy and Protection (ICAP), pointed to the dangerous potential of AI voice-generation technology in an interview with me.

"The ability of AI to generate voices that sound like trusted figures—whether they're election officials, family members, or public leaders—is a major threat," McCord said. "Imagine the chaos that could ensue if, for instance, election staff received an AI-generated call from what they believed to be an official source, instructing them not to come in on Election Day."

This isn't a far-fetched scenario. McCord warned that while high-profile AI-generated disinformation—like deepfake videos of world leaders—might be quickly debunked due to their scale, local-level manipulations could be much harder to detect, slipping under the radar and causing localized chaos.

At its core, AI is a tool—one that can be used to enhance human creativity and productivity, but also one that can be exploited to sow confusion and mistrust. AI's ability to rapidly generate content has opened the floodgates for misinformation to spread across the internet. Unlike traditional content creation, AI can produce vast amounts of disinformation with little human oversight. Social media bots, AI-generated articles, and false reports are now produced at a pace and volume that human fact-checkers can't keep up with.

## Case Studies: High-Profile AI-Driven Disinformation Campaigns

One of the most alarming uses of AI-related technologies in creating misinformation occurred during the 2020 US presidential election. Numerous social media accounts, many driven by automated bots, circulated false information about voting procedures, candidate positions, and even fabricated scandals. These bots worked to amplify conspiracy theories that had the potential to destabilize public trust in the election process. While AI as we know it today—especially large language models—had not fully emerged, the automation and targeting capabilities of social media bots were early indicators of the kind of sophisticated disinformation campaigns that would become more powerful with AI advancements post-2020. If tools like GPT-3 or GPT-4 had been available then, these campaigns could have been even more persuasive and widespread, foreshadowing the dangers that AI holds in future election cycles.

Another case involves the COVID-19 pandemic, where bots effectively spread harmful misinformation about the virus, vaccines, and public health measures. On social media platforms, AI bots amplified anti-vaccine propaganda and discredited official health guidelines, leading to widespread confusion and, in some cases, increased resistance to public health protocols. While AI technology was rapidly advancing during this period, one can only imagine how much more chaos could have been created if actors had earlier access to the more sophisticated AI tools that became prominent post-2020, such as GPT-3 and GPT-4. These large language models enabled the generation of more complex and scalable disinformation campaigns. Though AI was not the primary driver of misinformation during the height of the pandemic, its potential to amplify such content became more evident as these technologies matured in the years that followed.

Corey Hutchins pointed out how these examples underscore the sheer volume of AI-generated misinformation: "AI can create hundreds of posts in the time it would take a human journalist to write one article. When those posts look and feel like legitimate news, it's a serious problem."

These are not isolated incidents. In the digital age, disinformation campaigns are more sophisticated and more difficult to track than ever before. And AI is at the center of it all.

## Technology Breakdown: How AI Enables the Spread of Misinformation/Disinformation

To understand the mechanics behind AI-driven disinformation, it's important to break down the technologies involved. The most common forms of AI used to spread false information include:

1. **GPT Models**: Generative Pre-trained Transformers, like GPT-4, are language models capable of producing human-like text. These models can be used to generate fake news articles and misleading social media posts or even impersonate public figures in online conversations.

2. **Social Media Bots**: Automated accounts run by AI algorithms that can mimic human interaction on platforms like X (formerly Twitter), Facebook, Reddit, or Instagram. These bots can flood social media with false information, repost misleading content, and engage with users in a way that spreads disinformation faster than a single human could.

3. **Troll Farms**: AI is often employed in organized troll farms where human operators guide automated systems to create and spread disinformation at scale. These troll farms can target specific demographics or interest groups with tailored content designed to provoke emotional responses, further muddying the information waters.

4. **Automated Trolls**: Unlike human trolls who manually engage in spreading disinformation, AI-powered trolls can generate a constant stream of misleading or inflammatory content. These trolls are often used to create the illusion of a large consensus around a particular viewpoint, pressuring real users to conform to the manufactured narrative.

Hutchins emphasized the potential damage from automated trolls: "Imagine a scenario where you have hundreds or even thousands of bots pushing a single narrative. It's no longer about convincing people with facts. It's about overwhelming the conversation with sheer volume, creating the illusion of consensus."

## Conclusion: The Invisible Hand of AI in Misinformation

What makes AI so dangerous in the spread of misinformation is its ability to blend into the digital environment and appear as legitimate content. With AI's capability to generate and distribute false narratives at scale, the lines between real and fake blur more easily than ever. And with every iteration of AI technology, the sophistication of these disinformation campaigns grows.

McCord shared a sobering reminder of just how sophisticated and targeted these operations could become: "It's not just the obvious, large-scale disinformation campaigns we need to worry about. It's the smaller, localized efforts where AI can mimic real people, real voices, and real platforms to quietly erode trust in democratic systems. By the time people realize they've been manipulated, the damage is done."

# CHAPTER TWENTY-TWO

# COMBATING MISINFORMATION

It is often hard to recognize the world that we currently find ourselves inhabiting. The institutional norms that once underpinned our society seem to be cracking under the strain of our current crises. Economic inequality, threats to human rights, climate change, and national division have converged, placing us at a crossroads. Tackling these immense problems requires a first step: addressing the divisiveness that hampers our ability to engage in constructive dialogue.

This past weekend, I was reminded of just how critical this is. I was invited to my first think-tank event, held in the historic Museum of the American Revolution in Philadelphia. There on the third floor, the sun streaming through massive windows that soared up to the next story of the building, just steps from where our founding fathers gathered to confront the issues of their time, I stood among a group of modern thinkers tasked with wrestling with the dilemmas of our age. As in the past, no one is coming to save us—we must forge our own solutions. The exercise focused on the challenges we face as a nation in safeguarding lessons from the 2020 election, including the growing role of AI and misinformation—issues that will only become more critical in future elections.

My roles have certainly changed a lot from my days when I was chasing down the dreams of writing my new book on the Oath Keepers and becoming their national media director for a year and a half along the way. This has given me some unique insights and perspectives when it comes to how these militia and extremist groups work. I know that if AI had been as useful then as it is now, I would have jumped in and embraced it in my daily workflow of creating content and media furthering the group's messaging and agenda. It would be foolish of us to think that those at the reins would do anything but—especially due to how cost effective it can be.

Among the most pressing dilemmas is the challenge of misinformation, amplified by AI. As former acting US attorney general Mary McCord emphasized in our recent conversation, AI's ability to generate and spread disinformation poses a serious risk to national security, democratic processes, and public safety.

## AI: A Double-Edged Sword
While AI may seem like one of the most daunting challenges of our time, I believe it also offers one of the most promising solutions. The potential for AI systems to help us solve the very problems they exacerbate cannot be overstated, provided we use these tools responsibly.

## AI Tools for Detecting Fake News
AI is often seen as a culprit in the spread of misinformation, but it can also serve as a critical countermeasure. AI-powered tools are already being developed to detect deepfakes, flag misleading content, and identify patterns in disinformation campaigns. However, as McCord pointed out, these tools are only as effective as the platforms and individuals deploying them: "There are AI tools out there that can detect when something has been artificially generated, whether it's a deepfake video or a misleading post. But these tools are often playing catch-up. The speed at which disinformation spreads makes it difficult for even the most advanced AI detection systems to keep pace."

Platforms like X (formerly Twitter), under the leadership of Elon Musk, have demonstrated how platform policies can undermine efforts to combat misinformation. Musk's reduction of moderation staff and reinstatement of accounts previously banned for spreading falsehoods have left the platform more vulnerable to disinformation. Corey Hutchins echoed this concern, noting how leadership at the top affects the effectiveness of AI tools: "When a platform owner is disinterested in curbing disinformation, even the best AI detection tools will struggle to be effective. It becomes a game of 'Whac-A-Mole' where disinformation spreads faster than it can be identified and stopped."

This suggests that while AI has the potential to be part of the solution, the infrastructure and intent behind its deployment must be robust. Detection tools can only work if platforms themselves commit to transparency and ethical moderation.

While AI detection tools are crucial in combating misinformation, they are only part of the larger solution. Emerging technologies and updated policies will be pivotal in addressing the expanding tide of disinformation.

## Technologies to Counteract Misinformation

Several promising technologies have emerged to combat the spread of false information. AI-powered fact-checking systems, like ClaimReview, are now being integrated into media platforms to flag suspicious content in real-time. These systems use natural language processing (NLP) algorithms to analyze articles, social media posts, and videos for common markers of disinformation and cross-check them with verified data.

McCord emphasized that these technologies, while useful, require constant improvement and adaptation: "These tools are critical, but they're not a silver bullet. We need to combine them with more stringent platform policies, digital literacy campaigns, and real-time monitoring to effectively mitigate the spread of false information."

AI's role in moderating content also raises ethical concerns, particularly when dealing with automated decision-making. McCord highlighted the importance of balancing security with free speech and proposed a step toward transparency: "One way to ensure people aren't misled by AI-generated content is to require transparency. Regulations that mandate disclosure—making it clear when something is AI-generated—would be a simple and effective way to counteract disinformation. It would help distinguish between authentic content and something generated by an algorithm."

This transparency, McCord noted, could prevent the kind of deception that happens when users can't distinguish between human-generated and AI-generated content.

## Limitations and Challenges

Despite the promise of AI detection tools, there are inherent limitations in the fight against AI-driven misinformation. The speed and volume at which disinformation spreads make it difficult for fact-checkers and AI systems to respond in real-time. As McCord pointed out, bad actors often exploit these delays, crafting false narratives that go viral before they are debunked: "Even with regulations and detection tools in place, bad actors will always find ways to exploit the system. Criminals and malicious actors will intentionally bypass transparency rules or manipulate algorithms to stay ahead of the detection curve. And since disinformation can be distributed across multiple platforms, it's difficult to regulate the entire digital ecosystem."

Decentralized platforms, private messaging apps, and encrypted communication services further complicate the fight against misinformation. AI tools struggle to penetrate these private spaces, allowing falsehoods to fester unchecked. The rise of decentralized platforms such as Telegram and encrypted services like WhatsApp adds layers of difficulty to tracking and stopping the flow of misinformation.

## Personal Perspective on Battling Misinformation

As a journalist, I've seen firsthand how challenging it is to cover local breaking news, keep local governments accountable, and tackle misinformation. Local newsrooms across the country are stretched thin, and AI is increasingly being used to fill the gaps. I rely on AI editing tools to maintain accuracy, brainstorm, research, and produce content in ways that would be impossible with the limited resources available in small-town journalism.

In my Colorado mountain town, the local newspaper once had a team of over a dozen staff members, including editors, reporters, and a publisher. Now, we have no editor or publisher, with just one staff reporter and a couple of freelancers like myself. The paper's future is uncertain, particularly under the ownership of a notorious vulture fund.

Yet, despite the advances in AI tools, they cannot replace the human element of journalism—ethical judgment, experience, and the ability to sense when something just isn't right. As McCord pointed out: "We need better digital literacy—people need to learn how to evaluate information critically. This is especially important for older generations, who are more vulnerable to spreading misinformation because they treat the news they see on social media as though it's coming from a trusted source."

Public education and digital literacy campaigns are essential in the fight against AI-generated disinformation. Teaching people how to critically evaluate news, spot falsehoods, and verify sources is crucial to defending against the spread of misinformation.

## A Call to Action

We must not view AI as either a savior or a villain in the fight against misinformation. It is a tool, and like all tools, it is shaped by those who wield it. As we consider the role of AI in combating misinformation, it's clear that ethical guidelines, platform accountability, and public awareness are critical components of a comprehensive strategy.

### Steps Forward

- **Regulation and Transparency:** Push for regulatory frameworks that require platforms to label AI-generated content and increase transparency in moderation practices.
- **Platform Accountability:** Platforms like X and others must be held accountable for how they moderate content, especially

when misinformation threatens public safety and democratic institutions.

- **Digital Literacy:** Expand public education campaigns to teach users how to navigate the complex media landscape, equipping them with tools to critically assess the content they consume.

McCord offered a final sobering thought during our conversation: "There's no putting AI back in the box. We're already living in this reality. What we can do is focus on how we mitigate the harm, regulate its use, and ensure that our institutions are equipped to handle the challenges ahead."

As we move into an era where AI-driven disinformation will only become more prevalent, it is clear that the fight against misinformation is not just a technical problem but a societal one. Only through collective action—by tech platforms, regulators, and the public—can we hope to combat the insidious spread of falsehoods.

As individuals, we each have a role to play—whether by promoting transparency, supporting responsible platforms, or educating ourselves and others. The future of truth in the digital age depends on collective responsibility and informed action.

# CHAPTER TWENTY-THREE

# EDUCATING FOR A BETTER FUTURE

○────────────────────────────────────────────○

## Preparing Our Children for the Brave New World

During the past school year, I had an interaction with one of my youngest daughter's high school teachers that left me questioning the approach our nation's schools are taking when it comes to preparing students for a world where AI is becoming increasingly relevant. It started with an email from the teacher, urging parents to warn their kids about the "dangers" of AI and announcing that all AI use was banned, with consequences for any violations. Now, I'm paraphrasing here, but that was the gist. Naturally, I couldn't resist writing back, asking what the justification was for this zero-tolerance stance. I also inquired about the opportunity to use AI as a teaching tool rather than shutting it down entirely. Couldn't this be a teaching moment, a chance to integrate AI into the curriculum in a way that prepared students for the future?

My suggestion was dismissed quickly. Now, I'll admit I'd spent the last year buried in research for this book, immersing myself in AI. I get that, to many, this technology might seem like it just sprang forth from Silicon Valley yesterday. But the world is evolving rapidly, and our education systems need to keep pace. This interaction left me wondering: is this hardline stance common among other educators, or is it just a symptom of the uncertainty surrounding AI's place in classrooms?

**A Candid Conversation: Teaching My Daughter about AI**

Well, I took the teacher's advice to heart and sat down with my daughter, who, even at fifteen, has started showing an interest in the career path of a writer. Just this week, while I was working on the couch with my lap desk, she pulled out my old laptop (a hand-me-down since I got the new M3 chipset MacBook Air to play with Apple Intelligence's AI integration). She had started three days early on a short story assignment for her creative writing class. I asked her if she had been using AI for her schoolwork. She said she hadn't, and I believed her—she's honest if anything.

I decided to give her a little crash course. I explained how she could use AI tools like ChatGPT ethically and creatively. I told her that, throughout her life, she'd encounter people who might be stuck in the past, resisting big changes. But she shouldn't let that hold her back. "If you see something on the horizon that looks like it's going to change the world, learn all you can about it," I told her. "Don't let anyone make you afraid of it. Your teachers aren't the ones who will be living your life in the future—you will be." She listened intently and agreed wholeheartedly. Moments like these with all my daughters (and now even my granddaughter—the art genius) fill me with awe—they're the ones who'll be shaping the world I'll leave behind.

**Colorado's Strategic Approach to AI in Education**

Back to that teacher's stance—it turns out that, here in Colorado, a broader, more thoughtful approach to AI is being considered. The "Colorado Roadmap for AI in K-12 Education"[1] lays out a plan to integrate AI into classrooms thoughtfully, ensuring that students are not just aware of AI but equipped to navigate a future where AI is woven into the tapestry of everyday life. It's about preparing them to live, work, and lead in a world where AI is a crucial part of how we solve problems, create, and connect.

The roadmap emphasizes flexibility, allowing school districts to adapt their teaching approaches as new insights emerge. It recognizes that AI isn't static—it's evolving, and our understanding of it must evolve too. Unlike a blanket ban on AI use, the Colorado plan leans into AI's potential for reshaping education. It focuses on teaching students to use AI responsibly, ethically, and creatively, understanding both its strengths and its limitations.

## Beyond Warnings: A Vision for Personalized Learning

Instead of focusing solely on the risks, Colorado's roadmap outlines how AI can be a tool for reshaping teaching and learning. For example, AI can make education more personalized and engaging, adjusting to individual students' needs and learning styles. It's not just about efficiency; it's about creating a learning experience that adapts to each student, giving them feedback in real-time and helping them explore their interests more deeply. For aspiring writers, this could mean AI tools that help refine their writing in ways that traditional classrooms might not accommodate—pointing out areas for improvement or offering inspiration when they're stuck.

The roadmap doesn't shy away from the challenges of AI, either. It emphasizes the importance of foundational skills like critical thinking, creativity, communication, and collaboration—all skills that writers need to thrive in an AI-driven world. It's not enough to just know how to use AI; students must also understand its capabilities, its limitations (like those pesky "hallucinations" when AI invents facts), and the ethical considerations that come with it. Teaching kids to ask, "Is this true?" or "Where does this information come from?" is crucial, especially in a world where AI can sometimes blur the lines between fact and fiction.

## Empowering Teachers, Empowering Students

Colorado's approach also highlights the role of educators in this new landscape. The roadmap emphasizes the need for ongoing professional development so that teachers can effectively integrate AI into their classrooms. This mirrors the journey writers must take in learning new tools and methods to stay relevant. Just as teachers need to be trained to adapt their lesson plans to include AI, writers have to learn how to blend AI with their creative processes, without losing the unique voice that makes their work stand out.

Moreover, Colorado's vision prioritizes equitable access to AI tools and technology, recognizing that the benefits of AI should be available to all students, regardless of their background. This focus on addressing the digital divide ensures that every student has the opportunity to engage with AI, not just those in tech-savvy, well-funded districts. This is crucial because, just like in education, AI in the creative industries holds the promise of democratizing access to powerful tools. It can help level the playing field, but only if access is managed thoughtfully.

## Preparing Students for a Workforce Transformed by AI

Another key aspect of the roadmap is its focus on career readiness, emphasizing that students should be prepared for jobs that will require AI literacy. It's not just about training future tech engineers or data scientists—AI literacy will be essential for a range of careers, from healthcare to journalism to, yes, writing. It's about equipping students to be consumers of AI technologies and engaging with them critically and creatively. For writers, this could mean understanding how to use AI for research, content creation, audience analysis, or even marketing their work.

In my interactions with my daughter's teacher, I saw a microcosm of a larger debate playing out in classrooms across the country. But Colorado's forward-thinking approach suggests that it doesn't have to be a choice between banning AI or embracing it without question. Instead, it's about finding a balanced way to integrate AI, ensuring that today's students—and tomorrow's writers—are ready for the world they'll inherit.

## Embracing Change for a Better Tomorrow

The world has changed so much from when I was a kid. Back in elementary school, we had computers in the classroom—clunky old Apple IIe's with black-and-green screens. It almost feels like we're living in a science fiction story now, and in many ways, we are. It's terrifying and awe-inspiring to think about where technology takes us.

Yet, as much as this new world can feel like a dystopian novel, AI might be our best chance at solving some of the massive challenges looming over our future. The parade of existential crises—climate change, inequality, food scarcity—can feel like a lineup of ancient titan malevolent gods on our horizon. And while we've struggled to find solutions on our own, maybe we can find a path forward with AI. Maybe AI can help us see realistic, attainable ways to address these challenges, offering a different kind of intelligence to solve problems that have stumped us for decades.

It's why I believe we must teach our children to navigate this brave new world, not by fearing AI but by understanding it, engaging with it, and using it as a tool to create a future that's more just, more creative, and more connected than the one we've known. We owe it to them to ensure they're prepared—not just to survive in this new world, but to thrive.

## The Risk of Misinformation

Not everything about AI is sunshine and SEO-friendly headlines. Erin O'Toole, a veteran journalist and host at NPR affiliate KUNC, shared an anecdote about testing ChatGPT to write an NPR-style introduction for a story about the Arctic.

"It did a great job, except it said the Arctic was already ice-free," she explained. "That hasn't happened yet. This kind of misinformation could be catastrophic if someone ran it without double-checking the facts."

This is a risk every journalist needs to keep in mind. AI doesn't always distinguish between real facts and plausible-sounding nonsense. Erin and I agreed that human oversight is non-negotiable.

"There have to be human eyes fact-checking everything," she emphasized. "We can't let AI be the final word—it's just not there yet."

## Preparing the Next Generation of Journalists

As our conversation shifted to the future, Erin expressed hope that AI could become a standard part of journalism training: "It's like how we used to learn LexisNexis or how to file a FOIA request. In the future, we'll need to teach students how to write better prompts and use AI effectively."

She's right. AI isn't going away, and the next wave of journalists needs to hit the ground running. As someone who's spent the past two years researching AI for this book, I've seen how much of a difference good prompting makes. Erin agreed: "The better your input, the better the AI's output. It's a skill we need to develop, just like anything else in journalism."

## Starting the Conversation: Ethical AI Use in Newsrooms

One of the most compelling parts of my conversation with Erin O'Toole was hearing how her team at KUNC is beginning to grapple with the implications of AI. As Erin explained: "Right now, we have a committee discussing AI—how we might use it, how we absolutely would not use it, and what ethical considerations need to guide us. I think we're one of a few stations taking this really seriously at this stage, and that's a good thing."

It struck me how rare this level of intentionality seems to be in journalism today. In many newsrooms, especially those operating on shoestring budgets, AI is seen either as a threat or a silver bullet for survival. But without a thoughtful, deliberate approach, both perspectives risk missing the bigger picture.

Erin acknowledged the balancing act required: "We have to be careful and transparent. Trust in journalism is already shaky, and if audiences think we're secretly using AI in ways that could compromise accuracy or integrity, we risk losing even more credibility. Transparency is critical—letting people know how AI is used, what it did, and just as importantly, what it didn't do."

She went on to describe how AI conversations at KUNC often include questions like:

- **What are the newsroom's ethical boundaries with AI?** For example, would it ever be acceptable to use AI to draft a story? (For now, the answer is a resounding *no*.)
- **How do they preserve the human connection with their audience?** Radio, as Erin noted, is deeply personal, and even the smallest misstep in tone or accuracy could erode trust.
- **Where can AI provide the most value?** So far, they've experimented cautiously with tools like **YESEO** for headlines and SEO optimization, as well as transcription tools like **Otter.ai**.

### Why Every Newsroom Needs to Have These Conversations

What resonated most with me was Erin's recognition that AI isn't a one-size-fits-all solution—it's a tool that requires deliberate planning and clear boundaries. Her station's willingness to start these conversations now, before AI becomes an entrenched part of their workflow, is a model other organizations would do well to follow.

As Erin put it: "We're figuring this out as we go. It's like building the plane while it's in mid-flight. But what matters is that we're having these discussions now, while we can still set the terms for how AI fits into our newsroom."

This is an essential takeaway not just for journalists, but for anyone in creative industries. AI isn't going away, and waiting to address its challenges and opportunities will only leave you playing catch-up. Whether you're in journalism, publishing, or another field, it's time to start asking tough questions about how to embrace AI responsibly and effectively.

### The Call to Action: A Collaborative Future

What's clear from Erin's example at KUNC is that these conversations need to happen across industries, not just in newsrooms. It's no longer enough to react to AI as it develops; we need proactive strategies that put human creativity and ethics at the forefront.

For organizations just beginning this journey, here are a few starting points inspired by Erin's reflections:

- **Form Committees or Task Forces:** Dedicate a team to exploring AI's potential, its risks, and the ethical frameworks needed for implementation.
- **Set Clear Boundaries:** Decide early on what AI should—and shouldn't—be used for within your organization.
- **Prioritize Transparency:** Commit to disclosing AI use to audiences or clients, whether it's for SEO optimization, headline suggestions, or internal processes.
- **Invest in Training:** Equip staff with the skills to use AI effectively, including writing strong prompts, understanding AI limitations, and identifying potential misinformation risks.

As Erin pointed out, the key isn't to fear AI—it's to approach it thoughtfully, focusing on preserving your work's core values.

"It's not about replacing human creativity or judgment," she said. "It's about finding ways AI can help us do what we already do, only better."

If more organizations follow KUNC's lead, we'll see an AI-driven future that amplifies, rather than erodes, the human element that makes creative industries so vital.

### Final Thoughts: The Role of Human Connection

One of the most powerful moments in our conversation came when Erin talked about radio's unique intimacy: "Radio is such a personal medium. Even if we use AI to help brainstorm ideas or draft scripts, the way we communicate with our audience—that connection—will always be human."

This, to me, is the heart of the matter. AI can assist, enhance, and streamline the work, but it can't replace the soul of journalism. Whether it's a heartfelt story on the airwaves or an investigative piece in print, the human touch is what keeps audiences engaged—and coming back for more.

# CHAPTER TWENTY-FOUR

# HUMAN VOICES IN THE AGE OF MACHINES—INTERVIEWS FROM THE CREATIVE TRENCHES

---

### The Human Touch in an AI-Driven Newsroom—An Interview with Newspaper Publisher Michael Romero

Many of you familiar with my work may not fully realize the depth of my journey into local journalism. My path wasn't conventional. It started with zines and underground publications like the *Color Red* and the *Colorado Bullhorn*, where I got my first taste of storytelling and the power of the press. These experiences, rooted in the punk rock ethos of DIY, have carried through to my present-day endeavors with Substack and *Colorado Switchblade*.

When my family and I returned to Colorado and Estes Park about seven years ago, I dedicated myself to writing, especially during the pandemic. I began work in earnest on my first novel and not long after began immersing myself in local journalism. Covering a George Floyd rally in our small mountain town and the much more volatile and larger protests on the streets of Denver rekindled my commitment to telling the stories of my community. This led to my role at the *Estes Park Trail-Gazette*, where I learned firsthand the complexities of balancing straight reporting with opinion pieces—a skill honed under the guidance of Mike Romero.

## A Life in Journalism: From Paperboy to Publisher

Mike Romero, a stalwart figure in local journalism, has been a mentor to me over the years we have worked together. With nearly five decades in the publishing industry, his insights into the shifting media landscape are invaluable. Our recent conversation delved into the evolution of local journalism, from the challenges of digital transformation to the potential and pitfalls of AI in newsrooms.

Mike's career began humbly as a paperboy in Santa Fe, New Mexico. "I used to hustle my way down to the Capitol every morning, selling papers to legislators eager to see what was written about them," he reminisced. This early experience ingrained in him a deep respect for the power of the press. Over the years, Mike climbed the ranks, moving from city to city, and always carried a passion for holding power accountable. "In Albuquerque, we exposed a popular local dentist who was committing insurance fraud. It showed me the importance of fearless journalism," he recalled. This dedication to uncovering the truth, regardless of the consequences, became a hallmark of his career.

## The Digital Leap and the Challenges of Adaptation

The digital revolution reshaped the media landscape, bringing both challenges and opportunities. Mike, who served as a digital director before becoming publisher, was at the forefront of this transformation. "We had to educate the community, especially in Estes, where the audience was older," he explained. "It was about showing them the value of digital platforms." Despite resistance, Mike's efforts ensured that the *Trail-Gazette* remained relevant in an increasingly digital world. "Corporate was focused on print profits, but I knew digital was the future. During the fire, COVID, and floods, digital allowed us to reach over 150,000 readers. That's the power of online journalism," he noted.

## AI's Role in the Newsroom: A Double-Edged Sword

When discussing AI, Mike had mixed feelings. "AI can be a time-saver for tasks like fact-checking and editing. I used it when I lost my editor, and it helped with grammar checks and quick references," he admitted. However, he was quick to point out AI's limitations. "AI can't replace the human touch. It can't capture the essence of a story or understand the nuances of a community."

Mike also raised concerns about the ethical implications of AI in journalism. "You see articles now with disclaimers that parts were generated by AI. That's troubling because it undermines accountability," he said. The risk of bias and misinformation looms large in his mind. "Without proper oversight, AI can perpetuate inaccuracies and biases, eroding trust in the media."

## Preserving the Fourth Estate in the AI Era

Mike's reflections on the state of journalism were sobering. "In the last decade, the focus shifted from content to the bottom line. Resources for investigative journalism have dwindled," he lamented. This shift, he believes, has weakened the industry's ability to hold power accountable. He expressed frustration with the recent trend of newspapers avoiding political endorsements. "Now is not the time to shy away. Newspapers should take a stand, especially in critical elections," he argued. For Mike, this reluctance is a sign of the industry's decline. "If we don't uphold the principles of the Fourth Estate, we risk losing it entirely."

## The Future of Journalism: Adaptation and Resilience

Despite the challenges, Mike remains hopeful about the potential of journalism to adapt and thrive. "Digital is the way forward, but it requires a commitment to quality content and ethical practices," he emphasized. He also sees a role for AI, albeit a limited one. "AI can assist with mundane tasks, freeing journalists to focus on in-depth reporting, but it should never replace human judgment."

Mike's reflections on his retirement reveal his continued passion for the craft. "I still write for nonprofits and stay connected with the community. Journalism is in my blood," he said. His dedication to truth and accountability remains as strong as ever.

## Lessons Learned and the Road Ahead

Our conversation reminded me of the enduring importance of human judgment in journalism. AI may offer tools to enhance efficiency, but the soul of journalism lies in the human stories we tell. As Mike aptly put it, "The essence of journalism is about connecting with people, understanding their stories, and holding those in power accountable. AI can't do that."

More and more as I pen this book, I find that there are so many shortcuts that a writer, editor, or even publisher can take that can cut out that human center of a piece. But in my experience, so much of what goes into a story comes directly from human interaction—those conversations about the human impacts on community members. We're still a long way from AI being able to sit down with a source, earn their trust, and build the kind of relationship that encourages someone to speak openly about issues that deeply affect them and their community.

I do think with the reality of how the journalism industry, specifically the newspaper industry, has evolved (or perhaps it is more apt to say it has devolved), we must embrace AI tools to help save time in research, communication through emails, planning out an interview, transcribing those interviews, brainstorming on the approach to a story, and then getting that final high polish edit on an article before it gets submitted. But we must resist using AI to generate a story from start to finish. It just will not be the same quality and human-based storytelling that is so critical to our society.

I think a lot of those ethics that Mike speaks to are already being lost, though not necessarily due to the rise of AI but because of the economic realities that the industry now finds itself in.

## A Deeper Look into Challenges and Solutions

Mike elaborated on the practical challenges facing local newspapers today. "In a small town like Estes, where everyone knows everyone, using AI to generate an article on a local town hall meeting could miss crucial nuances or misinterpret the sentiments," he pointed out. "That's where the human element becomes irreplaceable."

We also discussed potential solutions to counter these challenges. Mike stressed the importance of having strong editorial oversight. "Editors need to insist on rigorous fact-checking and maintain the integrity of bylines," he said. "Holding writers accountable ensures the credibility of journalism."

The dialogue turned to the future of journalism in a rapidly evolving media landscape. "I believe there's hope if we can balance the efficiencies of AI with the irreplaceable human touch in storytelling," Mike concluded. "But we must be vigilant and committed to the principles that make journalism a cornerstone of democracy."

### Conclusion: A Commitment to Truth and Integrity

As I navigate the evolving landscape of journalism, I carry these lessons forward. The path may be fraught with challenges, but with mentors like Mike and a commitment to the core values of the Fourth Estate, I'm confident that journalism will continue to play a vital role in our society. The integration of AI, while inevitable, should be approached with caution and responsibility, ensuring it serves as a tool to enhance, not replace, the indispensable human touch in journalism.

## The Intersection of Education and AI—Insights from Mike Dunn

### Introduction: Setting the Stage

I first met Mike Dunn over a year ago, during a charged school board election. His advocacy and his well-articulated insights struck a chord with me, and I knew then that he was someone I wanted to interview for the local journalism work I was doing. His writing was clear, incisive, and full of thought-provoking ideas—a rarity that pointed to both intelligence and a deep commitment to education. As I began working on *AI Ink.*, it was only natural to circle back to Mike, knowing he'd bring invaluable perspectives, especially on educating the writers and journalists of tomorrow.

Mike, an educator and consultant with over fifteen years in independent, progressive, and outdoor education, is currently the dean of College & Career Counseling at Eagle Rock School & Professional Development Center. Located in Estes Park, Colorado, Eagle Rock provides a full-scholarship, year-round residential experience for students aged fifteen to eighteen, combining experiential, project-based, and interdisciplinary learning with a focus on equity and restorative practices. Here, students begin their journey with a twenty-four-day wilderness expedition, gaining skills in community building and self-reliance that serve as a foundation for their entire experience. Funded by American Honda Motor Company and founded in 1993, Eagle Rock also partners with educators nationwide to foster student-centered, anti-racist education. Mike's position in this unique environment gives him a vantage point from which to observe the shifts and challenges AI brings to the field of education.

## Technology's Evolution in Education

Our conversation began with a journey through time, back to the days when smart boards were the most advanced classroom tech. Mike started teaching in an era when simply having laptops in classrooms was seen as revolutionary. "Back then, we thought these tools would change everything," he recalled. "But now, AI feels like a different game altogether." What Mike touched on here is crucial: the scale of AI's potential in education is not merely an incremental shift—it's exponential.

Mike observed that AI goes beyond the "replacement" model of older technologies like smart boards. Whereas those technologies simply digitized existing tasks, AI has the capacity to create, analyze, and even learn from past interactions. "This isn't just about upgrading from a chalkboard to a whiteboard," Mike pointed out. "AI asks us to reconsider what and how we teach." His words underscored the vast implications AI brings to education, forcing educators to rethink traditional methodologies and to consider new ways of engaging students with this powerful tool.

## AI's Dual Impact on Practice and Policy

Our discussion shifted to AI's influence on both teaching practices and school policy—a dual-edged sword, as Mike described it. "If used correctly, AI can streamline tasks that take up valuable teacher time, allowing us to focus on engaging with students on a deeper level," he noted. Imagine teachers being able to use AI to grade simple assignments quickly, freeing them up to work on individualized feedback or to support struggling students more effectively. It sounds promising, but as Mike explained, the reality is more complex.

The immediate policy response to AI in education, unfortunately, has been one of restriction rather than exploration. "Many schools have rushed to implement stringent AI detectors and plagiarism policies, even when these tools aren't always accurate," Mike shared. He explained that schools are, understandably, reacting to the unknown potential for misuse, but he warned against reactionary policies. "This is about more than just avoiding AI misuse; it's about equipping students to use it responsibly," he argued, pointing out that these knee-jerk policies often do more harm than good by discouraging thoughtful engagement with AI tools.

## AI as a Tool for Equity

A significant part of our conversation centered on AI's potential role in promoting—or hindering—educational equity. For Mike, who has devoted much of his career to equity in education, this is a critical area. "The risk is that AI could widen the educational gap," he warned, noting that students from wealthier backgrounds will have more opportunities to familiarize themselves with AI tools at home. Without thoughtful integration into schools, he explained, students without these resources could be left even further behind.

However, Mike is cautiously optimistic. He believes that if schools make a concerted effort to teach AI skills across the board, they could empower all students, not just those with tech-savvy parents. "Imagine AI tools being used to level the playing field in under-resourced schools," he said. "It could allow students from all backgrounds to develop critical digital skills that are already in high demand." His point was clear: if implemented with equity in mind, AI could help democratize access to future career opportunities, something that has been a longstanding goal of education reformers.

## Personalized Learning and the Role of Community

One of AI's biggest promises is personalized learning—an approach where students can learn at their own pace, following a curriculum tailored to their unique strengths and weaknesses. Mike acknowledged this as a significant advantage, but he also cautioned against taking personalization too far. "We risk isolating students in their own educational bubbles," he said, noting that overemphasis on individualization could lead to a fragmented sense of community.

He emphasized the importance of balancing personalization with community-building, especially in a school like Eagle Rock, where the sense of belonging is central to the learning process. "Students thrive on the relationships they build with their peers and teachers. If we lose that, we risk losing something fundamental," he explained. Mike's perspective serves as a reminder that while AI can enhance individual learning, it should not replace the social and communal elements that make education meaningful.

## Curriculum Development and Bias

The conversation turned toward AI's role in curriculum development and the lurking issue of bias in AI-generated content. Mike raised a critical point here, stressing that "AI is only as good as the data it's trained on." Given that many AI models are built on datasets with inherent biases, there's a real risk that AI-generated curricula could perpetuate those same biases and potentially exclude marginalized voices.

He argued that teachers must play an active role in vetting AI-generated curriculum materials, ensuring they're inclusive and representative of diverse perspectives. "Curriculum isn't just content," he said. "It's a medium through which students understand the world. If that's skewed, we're failing them." Mike's insights here highlight the importance of keeping human oversight in curriculum development—a process that requires more than just data and algorithms.

## Preparing Future Writers and Journalists

With a keen interest in fostering the next generation of writers and journalists, Mike shared his thoughts on how AI might impact the craft of writing. "Aspiring writers need to learn how to use AI as a tool, not as a substitute for creativity," he emphasized. In his view, AI can assist in brainstorming, organizing thoughts, and even editing, but it should never overshadow the writer's unique voice.

He elaborated on the benefits of using AI for technical tasks, allowing young writers to focus on honing their creative instincts. "The craft of writing is about grappling with words, making deliberate choices. AI can help with the mechanics, but the heart of writing has to come from the writer," he said. For Mike, the challenge is to prepare students to collaborate with AI in a way that enhances their work without diminishing their creativity.

## Ethical Considerations and AI Literacy

The ethical dimensions of AI in education are complex, and Mike didn't shy away from addressing them. "Transparency is key," he stressed, advocating for open discussions about how AI is used in both teaching and learning. This extends to students, whom Mike believes should be educated not just on how to use AI, but on its limitations and potential biases. "AI literacy is about understanding the tool, but also knowing when and how to rely on it—and when not to."

Mike proposed integrating AI literacy into the curriculum, teaching students to scrutinize AI-generated content critically. He emphasized the importance of building students' skills to engage with AI responsibly, ensuring they are equipped to navigate a world increasingly dominated by digital technologies.

## The Broader Societal Impacts

As our conversation drew to a close, we reflected on the broader societal implications of AI in education. Mike expressed both hope and
caution, recognizing AI's potential to transform education but also
warning of the dangers if implemented without foresight. "This isn't
just about what happens in schools. It's about how we, as a society,
decide to shape the future," he said.

Mike's words serve as a call to action for educators, policymakers,
and society at large. He urged us to approach AI with both enthusiasm
and caution, embracing its potential while safeguarding the human elements that define the educational experience. His insights underscore
a recurring theme in this book: as we advance technologically, we must
remember to balance innovation with ethical responsibility, ensuring
that the tools we create serve humanity rather than diminish it.

## Michael Kilman: World-Building, Education, and the Anthropological Lens on AI

Writing can be a lonely road. Most folks don't really get what it takes
to carve out a living with words. Over the years, Michael Kilman, a
fellow Coloradoan, has been a solid touchstone for me. We've swapped
stories, traded late-night messages about world-building headaches,
and talked shop on everything from AI to ancient myth. I've interviewed Michael multiple times now—once for a newspaper article
on the intersection of world-building and anthropology and again
for his insights into culture, narrative, and education for my *Colorado
Switchblade* podcast. So when I started pulling threads for this book, I
knew I needed to include his voice.

Michael wears a lot of hats—he's a cultural anthropologist, college
educator, and science fiction author with a deep curiosity about how
belief systems shape our societies. He's also the co-author (alongside
Kyra Wellstrom) of *Build Better Worlds: An Introduction to Anthropology
for Game Designers, Fiction Writers, and Filmmakers*, which has become
a go-to resource for anyone serious about crafting authentic fictional
cultures. Through his blog, *Lorian's Labyrinth*, and a compelling TED

Talk on the value of diverse storytelling, Michael has become a fierce advocate for embedding real cultural nuance into speculative fiction.

Our conversations naturally drifted toward AI—how it's upending traditional storytelling, the risks of algorithmically flattened world-building, and what it means to create meaning in a time when machines can mimic myth. With Michael, every discussion pulls from deep wells: ritual, history, narrative structure, and the role of the storyteller in society. He's not just thinking about what AI can do; he's asking the deeper questions: *What should it do? And who gets to decide?*

### AI and World-Building: Creativity with Caution

Michael kicked off our discussion on the role of AI in world-building with a stark reminder of its limitations. "An AI isn't going to offer a unique world-build," he said, getting straight to the point. At its best, AI can piece together a patchwork of existing knowledge but lacks the fresh, cohesive vision that a human mind brings. "You're never going to get something that's genuinely unique—only an amalgamation of what's been done before," he emphasized.

While AI might be useful for brainstorming, it struggles to maintain the nuanced, layered cultural depth necessary for truly rich and original world-building. A key shortfall is its inability to deliver consistent and coherent narratives over time. "It's like an AI trying to write a novel," Michael noted. "It can't really hold complexity that is well integrated into the initial thought for a long idea."

### The Risk of Perpetuating Stereotypes in Cultural Representation

Beyond creativity, there's an ethical minefield in how AI handles cultural representation. Michael pointed out that even seasoned anthropologists, with years of cultural immersion, often struggle to fully capture cultural nuances. "It's hard even for anthropologists to fully respect cultural nuances, so how could we expect AI to manage it flawlessly?"

He highlighted the risk of AI perpetuating stereotypes by relying on problematic datasets. A prime example is the game *Horizon Zero*

*Dawn*, which drew heavily from Jared Diamond's *Guns, Germs, and Steel.* While Michael enjoyed the game, its portrayal of a regressed technological society reflected outdated anthropological assumptions. "You see the flaws in it," he remarked, stressing the need for nuanced cultural understanding that AI, as it stands, cannot replicate. His solution? Involving anthropologists in AI development to refine its cultural accuracy, though he admits it's a complex challenge.

## AI in Education: Enhancing Engagement, Demanding Caution

Michael's experience as an educator provides a grounded perspective on AI's potential in the classroom. AI, he noted, can be a powerful tool for streamlining lesson planning, generating rubrics, and condensing dense academic papers into bite-sized summaries. "It's super helpful," he said. "You can ask it for a critical question from a video they've watched or a summary to get them thinking."

Yet, he cautioned against over-reliance. "Newer professors might be tempted to take shortcuts," he warned, "and that's dangerous because you miss the nuances in the theories or cultural concepts you're teaching." True understanding, Michael emphasized, takes years of grappling with complexity. Overuse of AI-generated content risks oversimplifying subjects or, worse, spreading misinformation.

Still, the potential for AI to create immersive, interactive learning experiences excites him. Imagine a classroom where students can engage in real-time "conversations" with AI-driven historical or cultural figures. "It could offer a level of empathy and engagement that textbooks just can't match," he mused. But, he stressed, ethical boundaries are essential—especially when dealing with cultures that may not want to be digitized for educational purposes.

## Democratization and Accessibility: Leveling the Playing Field?

One of AI's big promises is its potential to democratize the creative process. Michael sees this potential, particularly for creators lacking the deep pockets of major studios. "Take Midjourney, for instance," he said. "It's given people the ability to whip up visuals and concepts even if they don't have a huge budget." For Michael, who has prosopagnosia—a condition that makes recognizing or visualizing faces a challenge—tools like Midjourney are game-changers.

Yet, he approached the democratization argument with caution. "Remember when the internet was supposed to democratize everything?" he asked. "It did . . . but only to a point. Who really gets the best access to AI tools, and at what cost?" While AI can open doors, it also risks displacing skilled professionals who've built careers in specialized creative fields. The challenge, as Michael sees it, is finding a balance: using AI to broaden access without undermining the livelihoods of experts.

## Ethical Considerations in AI-Driven Cultural Representation
With AI's growing role in creative fields, Michael underscored the need for strong ethical guardrails. He shared the cautionary tale of Jared Diamond, whose work on Indigenous cultures in *Guns, Germs, and Steel* faced serious backlash. "Diamond flat-out made up parts of an article," Michael explained, "and the people he misrepresented didn't just take it—they sued and won." This case is a stark reminder of the damage cultural misrepresentation can cause when falsehoods spread unchecked.

Michael believes future AI systems must prioritize ethical considerations, especially in cultural storytelling. He's excited about the prospect of AI consulting with "cultural experts" across various fields—politics, economics, anthropology—to ensure outputs are rooted in sound, current knowledge. "An AI that taps into specialized fields to give you a nuanced, interdisciplinary view of your world? That's the kind of collaboration we need to avoid turning AI into a tool for spreading stereotypes."

## Future Applications of AI in Anthropology and Creative Arts
Looking ahead, Michael shared ambitious ideas about AI's role in anthropology and creative arts. He envisions AI being used to create deeper anthropological insights in fiction and interactive media.

"What if," he suggested, "you could upload your novel and then sit down for a chat with one of your characters? Ask them about their day, their struggles, their culture." This concept could add unprecedented depth to world-building.

Michael also sees a future where AI could transform passive learning into dynamic, immersive experiences. Imagine students virtually participating in historical events or cultural rituals through AI-driven simulations. "The educational value could be tremendous," he mused, "but we have to make sure these representations are accurate and respectful. Without ethical safeguards, the risks are too great."

## Conclusion: A Thoughtful Partner

Michael Kilman's insights paint AI as a potentially transformative tool for both storytelling and education—if handled with care. He emphasizes the necessity of collaboration, where technologists, anthropologists, and creatives work together to ensure AI serves as a bridge to deeper understanding, not a barrier. His vision is clear: AI should enrich our cultural narratives, not dilute them. As we explore AI's role in storytelling and education, Michael's balanced perspective offers a thoughtful roadmap, reminding us of the need to navigate this new frontier with both caution and optimism.

## Mary McCord: Safeguarding Democracy in the Age of AI

As the former acting assistant attorney general for the US Department of Justice National Security Division and the current executive director of the Institute for Constitutional Advocacy and Protection (ICAP) at Georgetown University, Mary McCord has dedicated her career to defending democracy and the rule of law. Whether addressing domestic extremism, unlawful militias, or election security, her work underscores the importance of vigilance and adaptation in the face of emerging threats. When it comes to AI, McCord's insights reveal a complex intersection of opportunity, risk, and responsibility.

My conversation with Mary touched on many critical issues at the heart of this book: the role of AI in amplifying misinformation, its potential to undermine public trust, and the ethical frameworks needed to ensure that technology strengthens rather than erodes democratic institutions. Her perspective as a seasoned national security expert brought clarity to the challenges and opportunities AI presents in the modern information landscape.

## AI's Role in Amplifying Domestic Security Threats

One of McCord's primary concerns revolves around the misuse of AI to amplify domestic security threats, particularly through voice generation and misinformation campaigns. She painted a chilling picture of how AI-generated voices could mimic trusted figures—family members, employers, or local officials—to spread false information. This could have dire consequences, especially during elections.

"The potential for chaos is immense, especially on a local level where debunking efforts are slower and less robust," McCord explained.

This localized manipulation is harder to detect than high-profile misinformation campaigns targeting national figures. It underscores the urgent need for robust attribution methods and resources to counteract these threats. McCord emphasized that while transparency regulations requiring AI-generated content to be labeled are a step in the right direction, they alone aren't sufficient to deter bad actors.

## The Challenge of Balancing Regulation and Free Speech

McCord's legal expertise offers valuable insight into the delicate balance between regulating AI and preserving First Amendment rights. She highlighted the importance of "content-neutral" regulations, such as requiring disclosures for AI-generated content, which can be applied broadly without infringing on free speech.

However, she acknowledged the limitations of these measures: "Malicious actors, whether foreign or domestic, are unlikely to comply with regulations. Criminals are going to be criminals, and that's where enforcement and attribution come into play."

She also discussed the urgent need to revisit Section 230 of the Communications Decency Act, which shields platforms from liability for content amplified by their algorithms. McCord argued that platforms should be held accountable when their algorithms promote harmful content, drawing parallels to the accountability required of other industries that produce potentially dangerous products.

### Election Interference and AI's Growing Influence

McCord's experience protecting democratic institutions brought our conversation to the threat of AI-driven election interference. She described how foreign and domestic actors could use AI to create deepfakes, fabricate news stories, and manipulate public opinion on a massive scale.

"The difference between a foreign nation-state and a domestic actor," McCord noted, "is that foreign entities don't have First Amendment protections. That simplifies legal action against them, but it doesn't make the threat any less severe."

She pointed out that many of the statutes used to combat foreign interference—such as those addressing identity theft, hacking, and conspiracy—could also apply to domestic actors. However, she stressed the importance of public awareness to mitigate the impact of these tactics, adding that a bipartisan approach to AI regulation is essential to maintain trust in elections.

### The Role of Media Literacy and Public Awareness

For McCord, media literacy is a cornerstone of any effort to combat AI-driven misinformation. She highlighted the vulnerability of older populations who didn't grow up with the internet and often struggle to differentiate between credible sources and fabricated content.

"We need to teach digital literacy at every level—schools, community centers, and senior centers," she said. "Older generations, in particular, are treating social media posts like they're coming from Walter Cronkite, and that's incredibly dangerous."

McCord also emphasized the need for transparency in how AI is used. "If journalists or public figures are using AI to assist with their work, they should disclose that. Transparency demystifies AI and helps rebuild trust."

## Opportunities for Positive Impact

While McCord expressed deep concern about AI's misuse, she also recognized its potential for good. From promoting accountability journalism to enhancing public safety, AI could play a constructive role if used ethically. However, she stressed that human oversight must remain central to its deployment.

"AI is just a tool," McCord said. "It's how we use it—and who's using it—that determines whether it helps or harms."

She called for stronger collaboration between technologists, policymakers, and civil liberties experts to develop guidelines that prioritize privacy and democratic values. McCord also encouraged the next generation of journalists and legal professionals to embrace AI as a skill, much like mastering LexisNexis or filing a FOIA request.

## A Call for Ethical Innovation

One of the most striking takeaways from my conversation with McCord was her insistence on ethical boundaries. Whether discussing the potential for AI to strengthen the rule of law or its risks in predictive policing, she underscored the need for civil liberties experts to guide the development and application of AI technologies.

"Technologies that do more and more things require policies that address their potential for abuse," she said. "It's critical to include voices that prioritize privacy and civil liberties in these conversations."

## Final Thoughts: A Proactive Approach to AI

Mary McCord's insights reveal a stark but hopeful reality: while AI presents significant challenges, proactive measures can harness its potential for good. Her call for transparency, accountability, and collaboration resonates across industries, offering a blueprint for navigating the ethical complexities of AI in a rapidly changing world.

As McCord so aptly put it: "AI is here to stay. The question isn't whether we use it—it's how we use it in a way that strengthens, rather than undermines, our democratic values."

## Corey Hutchins: Journalism's Advocate in the Age of AI

Corey Hutchins has a storied career in journalism, stretching from investigative reporting in alternative weeklies to his current role as a professor at Colorado College. Known for his thoughtful exploration of media trends, Corey has spent years chronicling the challenges and opportunities facing local journalism. His work with the *Columbia Journalism Review* (*CJR*) and his widely regarded newsletter have established him as a leading voice in examining how media evolves in response to technological, social, and economic forces.

In our conversation, Corey shared invaluable insights into the transformative potential of AI in journalism, as well as the ethical, practical, and cultural challenges that arise in its wake.

### A Career Spanning Journalism's Evolution

Corey's journey began in local journalism, delivering newspapers as a child and later working for alternative weeklies. His focus evolved as he observed the seismic shifts in media over the last two decades.

"I've always straddled the generational divide," Corey explained. "I grew up delivering newspapers when print was still king, and now I teach students who grew up with news on their phones. That contrast shapes my perspective on the importance of local journalism."

Through his newsletter, Corey connects Colorado's media landscape with national trends, filling a niche that he believes every state needs: watchdogging the watchdogs. "People often remember me as 'the newsletter guy,' even though I've written for publications like the *Washington Post*," he joked. "But that's the power of owning a consistent, unique voice in an overlooked space."

### AI's Double-Edged Sword in Journalism

Corey is no stranger to the debate surrounding AI's impact on journalism. "On one hand, AI tools can help reporters do more with less," he said. "They can summarize city council meetings, transcribe interviews, and even check for Associated Press style in seconds. On the other hand, they open the door to misuse, whether it's creating fake news or replacing nuanced reporting with algorithmic fluff."

He pointed to experiments by organizations like the *Denver Post*, which used AI to generate high school sports coverage. "While this freed up reporters to cover more critical stories, it also led to mistakes—like publishing a story that omitted the final score of a game because no human verified the content. That's where AI needs guardrails," Corey emphasized.

His "human-machine sandwich" metaphor captures his philosophy: "AI can be in the middle, but humans need to be at the start and end of the process. A competent editor should review everything before it's published. Otherwise, we risk losing trust."

## Educating the Next Generation of Journalists

As a journalism professor, Corey is acutely aware of the gap between the tools available to today's students and their understanding of how to use them ethically.

"Many students have a passive relationship with news," he said. "They think, 'If it's important, it'll find me.' But good journalism requires active engagement. I teach them to navigate tools like AI for research and editing while stressing that these tools should enhance—not replace—their skills."

He also noted the increasing need for media literacy education before college. "It's shocking how many students don't know how to spot sponsored content or verify a source. Colorado's media literacy law is a start, but it's toothless. We need comprehensive education in schools to prepare citizens for a world where AI-generated misinformation is pervasive."

## Ethical Challenges and Opportunities

Corey emphasized the importance of transparency and ethical standards as newsrooms integrate AI. "Journalists need to disclose when and how they use AI," he argued. "For example, I use AI tools like Lex for copyediting my newsletter, and I'm upfront about it. But I don't feel the need to add disclaimers for every minor AI-assisted task. There's a balance to strike."

He also warned about the growing entanglement between newsrooms and tech companies. "Platforms like Google and Facebook have already disrupted local news by monopolizing ad revenue. Now, companies behind AI tools are courting newsrooms, which creates potential conflicts of interest. We need to stay vigilant about how these relationships evolve."

### Democratizing Journalism or Consolidating Power?

When asked whether AI could democratize journalism, Corey's response was nuanced, "AI lowers the barriers to entry for creating content that looks like journalism, but that's a double-edged sword. It empowers independent creators but also enables bad actors to produce convincing disinformation. The challenge is building trust in legitimate journalism while educating the public to spot fake news."

Initiatives like the Journalism Trust Initiative, which aims to certify credible newsrooms, could help address this issue, but Corey remains cautious. "Who decides which outlets get certified? Will small, underfunded newsrooms be excluded? These are questions we need to grapple with as AI becomes more integrated into our workflows."

### Advice for Aspiring Journalists

Corey's advice for emerging journalists is rooted in a deep respect for the profession's history and future.

"Read widely," he urged. "Understand the history of journalism—how it's evolved with each technological shift. Books like *The Elements of Journalism* and *Covering America* are essential for grasping the principles that should guide us, even as new tools reshape the field."

He also encouraged young journalists to embrace AI responsibly. "Use AI to save time on routine tasks, but don't let it replace your critical thinking or ethical judgment. Journalism is about serving the public, not just generating clicks."

## Final Thoughts: A Cautious Optimism

Despite the challenges, Corey remains optimistic about journalism's ability to adapt. "The printing press revolutionized information dissemination, but it also required careful stewardship. AI is no different. If we use it thoughtfully, it can enhance the work we do and strengthen our role as watchdogs for democracy."

Corey Hutchins's commitment to preserving the integrity of journalism while embracing innovation offers a roadmap for navigating this transformative era. His insights remind us that while technology evolves, the principles of good journalism—accuracy, transparency, and public service—remain timeless.

## Michael Crawford: Shaping the Future Workforce with Durable Skills

Michael Crawford is a seasoned expert in workforce development and education, recognized for his innovative work at the intersection of skills, education, and the evolving labor market. As the director of the Durable Skills Initiative at America Succeeds, he leads efforts to champion essential human skills like critical thinking, collaboration, and creativity in the context of rapidly changing workforce demands. With a background that spans strategy development, skills assessment, and education policy, Michael brings a unique perspective on how durable skills—those vital, transferable capabilities that transcend industries—are becoming even more critical in the age of artificial intelligence.

In our conversation, Michael illuminated the evolving role of durable skills in workforce development and education, particularly as AI reshapes how people learn, work, and collaborate.

## Championing Durable Skills in a Changing World

Michael began by explaining how the concept of durable skills emerged as a response to industry needs. "Employers repeatedly told us that technical skills alone weren't enough," he explained. "What was missing were the human skills—communication, collaboration, critical thinking—that enable employees to thrive in any environment."

Under Michael's leadership, America Succeeds analyzed millions of job descriptions to identify the most sought-after skills. "Our research found that eight out of the top ten skills employers look for are what we call durable skills," he said. "These are the foundational abilities that remain valuable regardless of technological shifts or industry changes."

The findings have led to the creation of a comprehensive framework that outlines ten core durable skills competencies, along with sub-skills and progression rubrics. Michael elaborated on how this framework is being integrated into education and workforce training programs, noting its growing adoption by educators, employers, and policymakers.

As mentioned, the framework identifies ten core durable skills competencies: leadership, character, collaboration, communication, creativity, critical thinking, fortitude, growth mindset, mindfulness, and metacognition. These are the human-centered abilities that show up again and again in the data, forming the backbone of a resilient workforce. As Michael noted, they're the through-line that lets people adapt, thrive, and work alongside machines without losing what makes us human.

### AI's Role in Assessing and Developing Skills

Michael also discussed how AI is intersecting with durable skills development. His team has begun exploring ways to use AI tools to assess and enhance these capabilities. "We're working with AI to analyze students' experiences and identify the skills they're using," he said. "For example, if a student describes organizing a community event, AI can pinpoint the collaboration, leadership, and problem-solving skills they applied."

However, Michael was candid about the challenges of scaling this approach. "While AI is good at identifying the presence of a skill, assessing proficiency remains tricky," he explained. "For instance, determining whether someone is an expert communicator versus a novice requires more nuanced evaluation. We're actively working on improving the reliability of these assessments."

Despite these hurdles, Michael remains optimistic about AI's potential to transform education and workforce development. He envisions AI tools becoming personalized mentors that help individuals reflect on their experiences and refine their skills over time. "Imagine an AI tool that not only identifies your strengths but also recommends tailored learning pathways to help you grow," he said.

### The Human Element in an AI-Driven World

Michael emphasized that as AI continues to permeate the workforce, human-centric skills will become even more essential. "The ability for two humans to communicate effectively won't diminish—it will grow in importance," he said. "Skills like critical thinking, creativity, and collaboration are what differentiate us from machines and allow us to work alongside them effectively."

He highlighted the importance of building a shared lexicon for these skills, enabling educators, students, and employers to communicate more clearly about their development and application. "When we say 'collaboration,' we need everyone to understand what that means in practice," he noted. "That's why establishing a common framework is so critical."

### Final Thoughts: Preparing for an AI-Enhanced Future

Michael's insights underscore the importance of preparing for a future where AI and human skills coexist. "AI is here to stay," he said. "Our task is to ensure that we leverage it to enhance, not replace, what makes us uniquely human. Durable skills are at the heart of that effort."

With his forward-thinking approach, Michael Crawford is not only shaping how we think about workforce development but also ensuring that the next generation is equipped with the tools they need to succeed in an AI-driven world. His work offers a roadmap for integrating technological advancements with timeless human capabilities, which will create a future that balances innovation with humanity.

As we reflect on the ethical dimensions of AI, it's clear that this technology is neither inherently good nor bad—it's a reflection of us.

Our values, decisions, and actions will determine how they shape the future of storytelling and the creative arts. In conclusion, we'll look ahead to that future, exploring how writers can balance the promise of AI with the timeless power of human creativity.

# CHAPTER TWENTY-FIVE

# ETHICAL RESPONSIBILITIES FOR AI-ASSISTED WRITERS

Incorporating AI into the writing process offers extraordinary benefits, but it also brings a web of ethical considerations. As AI becomes more embedded in creative industries, writers must engage with this technology responsibly. Ethical writing with AI means respecting intellectual property, maintaining transparency, avoiding bias, and safeguarding authenticity. It's about finding the balance between innovation and integrity. Let's explore how to navigate these responsibilities thoughtfully, ensuring AI remains a tool that amplifies creativity rather than compromises it.

## 1. Respecting Intellectual Property and Fair Use

One of the most pressing ethical concerns surrounding AI is how it handles copyrighted material during its training. Many AI models rely on vast datasets, some of which may include protected content. Writers using AI must be mindful of these complexities to respect the creative rights of others.

- **Understand Your Tools**: Dive into how your chosen AI was trained. Reputable tools often disclose information about their datasets and provide guidelines for ethical use. For instance, organizations like the Authors Guild advocate for transparency and fair treatment of authors' works in training datasets.

- **Verify Originality**: AI-generated content can sometimes echo its training data too closely. (AI[10]) Use plagiarism checkers and your own editorial judgment to ensure your work is both original and uniquely yours. I prefer to use Grammarly's built-in checker personally.
- **Cite Transparently**: When AI aids your research or writing, acknowledge its contributions. Whether it's a footnote, a chapter acknowledgment, or a mention in your introduction, giving credit maintains honesty and invites trust.

By treating intellectual property as a cornerstone of ethical writing, you protect not only your own work but also the creative ecosystem as a whole.

## 2. Transparency with Readers

Readers deserve to know when and how AI has contributed to the content they consume. Transparency fosters trust and reinforces the value of the human touch in creative work. (AI[11])

- **Acknowledge AI's Role**: If AI played a significant part in your process, mention it. Whether it's through a note in your acknowledgments or a brief mention in an author's note, clarity about AI's involvement strengthens your credibility.
- **Context-Specific Transparency**: Nonfiction writers might include details about AI's assistance in research or citations. For fiction, a simple mention of AI's role in brainstorming or

---

AI[10] AI Assistance from ChatGPT (GPT-4), OpenAI, September 2024. Used to explore originality risks and editorial best practices in AI-generated content.

AI[11] AI Language developed collaboratively with ChatGPT (GPT-4), OpenAI, September 2024. Helped draft guidance on disclosing AI's creative role.

world-building can suffice, providing a behind-the-scenes look at your creative process.

Far from diminishing your work, transparency underscores your ethical integrity and shows readers you value their trust.

### 3. Preventing Bias and Misrepresentation

AI tools are trained on human-created data, and that means they can inherit human biases. Writers must remain vigilant, especially when covering sensitive topics or representing diverse voices.

- **Critically Evaluate Outputs**: Don't take AI-generated text at face value. Review it for unintended biases or stereotypes, and revise as needed to align with your values and audience expectations.
- **Fact-Check Rigorously**: AI can produce inaccuracies, particularly when handling complex or nuanced topics. Always cross-reference information with reputable sources to maintain accuracy.
- **Incorporate Authentic Voices**: When writing about cultures, identities, or experiences outside your own, don't let AI substitute for direct research or genuine conversations. Use AI as a supplement, not a replacement, for primary sources.

By addressing bias head-on, you ensure your work is inclusive, empathetic, and representative of the world's diversity.

### 4. Upholding Authenticity in Voice and Style

AI can mimic writing styles, but the true magic of storytelling lies in the human voice. Preserving your unique perspective and style is essential to keeping your work authentic.

- **Set Clear Boundaries**: Decide early on how much influence AI will have on your creative process. For example, use AI for idea generation or research but keep the drafting and final revisions firmly in your hands.

- **Own the Editing Process**: Let AI help refine your work, but don't let it rewrite your narrative. Your voice and intent should guide every decision, ensuring the final product feels uniquely yours.
- **Maintain Active Involvement**: Use AI as a co-creator, not a replacement. Whether shaping ideas or reworking text, stay actively engaged to keep the emotional depth and nuance that only human experience can bring.

## 5. Guarding against Automation's Ethical Pitfalls

The growing capabilities of AI can make full automation of creative work tempting—but handing over the reins entirely raises ethical questions about authorship and accountability.

- **Limit Automation**: AI is a powerful collaborator but shouldn't replace the essential human elements of writing. Tasks like final revisions or key character moments are where your creative identity shines through.
- **Take Responsibility**: Even if AI contributes significantly, the finished product is yours to own—flaws and all. Ethical authorship means standing behind your work, regardless of how it was created.

Automation has its place, but it should never overshadow the writer's role as the heart and soul of a story.

## The Ethical Balance

Navigating the ethical landscape of AI requires more than just awareness—it demands action. Respect intellectual property. Be transparent with your readers. Critically evaluate AI's outputs for bias. And most importantly, uphold the authenticity that makes your voice stand out. This is really the part I cannot stress enough. It is your voice that makes a piece of writing important and human. We must retain that. Even if that means going back and rewriting something you may have edited with AI that lost too much of what makes it your voice. Sometimes writing needs to be perfectly imperfect.

Ethical AI usage is about enhancement, not replacement. By embracing this balance, writers can leverage AI's transformative potential without compromising their craft or the trust of their audience.

## Ethics in AI Content Personalization and Targeting

Let's dive into a topic that often flies under the radar: the ethical gray zones of AI-driven content personalization. AI's ability to customize narratives based on individual reader preferences is undeniably powerful, but it's also a double-edged sword. While crafting stories or articles that resonate with your audience is a dream for many writers, tailoring content so specifically that it reinforces biases or creates echo chambers is another matter entirely. (AI[12]) Here, we'll explore the ethical considerations surrounding AI's role in targeting and personalizing content, and how writers can wield these tools responsibly.

### 1. The Lure of Personalized Narratives

Personalized storytelling sounds like a writer's ultimate fantasy: crafting a novel or article that adapts seamlessly to each reader's preferences, creating a bespoke experience that feels uniquely theirs. AI can analyze reader habits, preferences, and even emotional cues to tweak elements like tone, style, and focus, delivering narratives that captivate individual tastes. It's a compelling concept, but it raises a critical question: when does personalization cross the line into pandering?

The biggest concern with hyper-personalization is that it risks boxing readers into familiar territories, depriving them of opportunities to explore new ideas. By catering too closely to preferences, writers may unintentionally deny their audience the chance to encounter

---

AI[12] AI Brainstorming support via ChatGPT (GPT-4), OpenAI, October 2024. Helped clarify how personalization may reinforce reader biases.

diverse perspectives or unexpected insights that challenge their world-view. While personalization can make content more engaging, it's vital to ensure that it doesn't come at the cost of intellectual or emotional growth for the reader.

## 2. AI-Driven Content and the Risk of Echo Chambers

The idea of echo chambers isn't new. It has been a hot topic ever since social media algorithms began feeding users a steady diet of content tailored to their existing beliefs. AI-driven content generation, however, has the potential to amplify this effect even further. By using reader preferences to shape narratives, AI can unintentionally reinforce biases and create self-reinforcing loops that stifle curiosity and critical thinking.

For example, an AI-powered news platform might deliver stories that align with a reader's political stance while filtering out opposing viewpoints. While this may improve reader satisfaction, it limits exposure to diverse perspectives, reducing opportunities for balanced understanding. Writers using AI must recognize this influence and take care not to inadvertently use these tools as amplifiers of comfort zones, nudging readers deeper into their biases rather than encouraging them to expand their horizons.

## 3. Balancing Creative Freedom with Ethical Constraints

One of the greatest challenges in this space is balancing the creative freedom AI offers with the ethical responsibilities it demands. It's tempting to lean into AI's strengths—delivering highly customized, immediately captivating narratives—but doing so risks diluting the deeper purpose behind a piece. Stories often serve to provoke thought, challenge assumptions, and introduce new ideas, but hyper-personalization can narrow their scope and limit their potential impact.

As writers, it's essential to ask ourselves tough questions: Are we catering too much to reader preferences? Are we sacrificing the breadth of our narrative to fit within a predefined box? Thoughtfully wielding AI allows for personalization without compromising the integrity of a story or its ability to push boundaries.

## 4. Transparency with Readers

Transparency is key when using AI to shape or target content. Readers have a right to know if AI has played a role in crafting the material they're consuming. Being upfront about AI's involvement not only fosters trust but also encourages readers to engage more thoughtfully with the work.

Many writers and platforms now include disclaimers or labels for AI-generated content, particularly for news or politically sensitive material. This openness helps readers understand the role AI plays in the narrative process, inviting them to interact with the content with clearer expectations. For writers, transparency is an opportunity to show integrity while demystifying AI's role in modern storytelling.

## 5. Setting Boundaries with AI

Ultimately, ethical personalization is about setting clear boundaries. Writers must decide which aspects of their work they're comfortable allowing AI to influence and which elements must remain true to their voice and purpose. For instance, avoiding AI-driven personalization for sensitive topics or content designed to provoke thought ensures the narrative remains authentic and impactful.

AI offers an unprecedented opportunity to connect with readers on a deeply personal level, but it's crucial to use this power responsibly. By striking a balance between customization and the broader purpose of storytelling, writers can ensure their work remains engaging without losing sight of its potential to challenge, inspire, and expand perspectives.

## The Ethical Imperative

AI-driven personalization is a powerful tool, but with great power comes great responsibility. As writers, it's our job to use these tools in ways that respect our audience's intelligence and curiosity, ensuring our work broadens horizons rather than narrowing them. By balancing the possibilities of AI with the timeless principles of storytelling, we can create narratives that are both deeply engaging and ethically sound.

## Protecting Intellectual Property (IP) in AI-Created Content

Let's tackle a question that's keeping a lot of writers up at night: who owns AI-generated content? As AI tools become increasingly integrated into the creative process, the issue of intellectual property (IP) has become a gray area.(AI[13]) When an AI generates part of your work—whether it's dialogue, an illustration, or even a first draft—who can truly claim ownership? Is it the writer, the AI, or some ambiguous combination of the two? Let's explore this evolving landscape and outline practical steps for writers to protect their creative rights.

### Who Owns AI-Generated Content?

Current IP laws are struggling to keep up with the rapid advancements in AI. Traditionally, copyright law is straightforward: if you create something—a book, a song, or an image—you own it. But AI complicates this framework. Since AI outputs are generated by algorithms trained on massive datasets, there's an element of "collective creativity" at play. This raises important questions: Can you claim sole ownership if the AI played a role in creating your work?

Legal experts generally agree that a human must contribute significantly to claim ownership of AI-assisted content. It's not enough to simply hit "generate." The key is demonstrating how your input—your ideas, prompts, and edits—shaped the final product. Think of the AI as a collaborator, with you as the guiding creative force. Ownership stems from your active involvement and the unique perspective you bring to the work.

---

AI[13] AI Timeline and capability comparison assistance using ChatGPT (GPT-4 Turbo), OpenAI, March 2025. Used to confirm model release dates, parameter sizes, and basic feature distinctions.

## Practical Tips for Protecting AI-Assisted Work

If you're leveraging AI in your creative process, there are concrete steps you can take to safeguard your intellectual property:

### 1. Document Your Process

Keep a detailed record of how you interact with the AI. Save the prompts you use, the iterations of AI-generated content, and any edits you make along the way. This documentation not only demonstrates your creative influence but also provides a clear trail of how the final product came to be. It's your best defense in establishing ownership.

### 2. Make Final Edits Yourself

Adding your own revisions to AI-generated drafts reinforces your role as the primary creator. Even small changes—rephrasing a sentence, reworking a scene, or tweaking an image—can significantly strengthen your claim to the final work. These edits show that the content reflects your unique voice and creative direction.

### 3. Use Tools with Clear IP Policies

Not all AI platforms have the same stance on intellectual property. Some, like OpenAI's ChatGPT and DALL·E, explicitly grant users full rights to their outputs. Others may retain partial ownership or impose restrictions on how their tools are used. Before diving in, review the platform's IP terms to ensure you have the legal right to use, sell, or license the content you create.

### 4. Treat AI Outputs as Drafts

While AI can produce impressively polished content, it's safer to view its outputs as a starting point. By refining, reworking, and adding your personal touch, you make the final product uniquely yours. This approach also reduces the risk of unintentional replication of existing works—a key concern in the realm of AI-generated content.

## The Potential for AI to "Borrow" from Others

AI models are trained on vast datasets, which means there's always a small chance that the content they generate could resemble existing works. This raises concerns about unintentional plagiarism or copyright infringement. While most AI platforms have safeguards to minimize these risks, it's still a possibility. If an AI output feels too similar to another work, it's best to rephrase or reimagine it, ensuring the final product is distinctively yours.

## IP Law: The Future for AI and Creators

Copyright laws are in flux as governments, courts, and creators grapple with the implications of AI-assisted content. Some proposals suggest that AI-generated works should be co-owned by the user and the AI's developers, while others argue they should fall into the public domain. It's clear that the legal landscape will continue to evolve, making it essential for writers to stay informed about changes that could impact their rights.

## Embrace AI, but Keep Your Creative Identity at the Forefront

At its core, AI is a tool—powerful, versatile, and transformative, but still a tool. You're the one shaping the narrative, crafting characters, and bringing ideas to life. By documenting your process, refining the final product, and understanding the legal frameworks of the tools you use, you can protect your work and ensure your creative identity shines through.

In a world where AI is becoming an integral part of the creative process, safeguarding your intellectual property isn't just about legal ownership. It's about affirming that no matter how advanced the technology, the heart of every story still comes from the human touch.

## The Psychological Impact of AI on Writers

Let's get straight to it: integrating AI into your writing process is a rollercoaster.(AI[14]) It can bring excitement and relief, tackling creative

---

AI[14] AI Emotional and workflow insights developed using ChatGPT (GPT-4), OpenAI, October 2024. Refined themes around imposter syndrome and productivity.

blocks and boosting productivity in ways you never imagined. But it can also spark moments of existential dread—those nagging questions about whether AI is merely helping or quietly taking over. And then there's the occasional twinge of imposter syndrome. It's a mixed bag, and that's okay. Let's unpack these feelings and figure out how to navigate them.

### 1. AI as the Ultimate "Block Buster"

We've all been there: staring at a blank page, paralyzed by the weight of an unwritten story. Enter AI, the ultimate blank-page buster. Whether you need help crafting a transition, brainstorming dialogue, or generating fresh ideas, AI can break the silence. It's like having a brainstorming partner who never gets tired, offering a constant stream of suggestions to keep you moving forward.

The best part? You can throw out any idea—no matter how rough—and the AI will process it without judgment. This "safe space" to experiment can bypass the inner critic that so often stifles creativity. It's liberating, allowing you to play with possibilities without the fear of failure.

### 2. Boosted Productivity (and the Pressure to Keep It Up)

There's no question AI can supercharge productivity. Tasks that once ate up hours—like formatting, citations, or basic edits—can now be done in a fraction of the time. But there's a hidden catch: with this increased efficiency comes an unspoken pressure to do more. Suddenly, you might find yourself asking, *"Am I doing enough?"* or, worse, *"Should I be doing even more with AI?"*

It's crucial to remind yourself that productivity doesn't define creativity. The speed of AI tools shouldn't dictate your pace as a writer. Boundaries matter—give yourself permission to work at a rhythm that feels sustainable, even if AI could theoretically go faster. Creativity thrives on balance, not burnout.

### 3. The Strange New Wave of Imposter Syndrome

As amazing as AI can be, it has a way of stirring up self-doubt. When it nails a line of dialogue or suggests a clever plot twist, it's easy to wonder, "Did I really come up with that—or was it the machine?"

That's where a new kind of imposter syndrome creeps in. You start questioning your role in the creative process. But here's the truth: *you* are still the driving force. The prompts, the direction, the tone, the character arcs—none of that happens without you. The AI might offer suggestions, but it's not pulling magic out of thin air. It's responding to what *you* gave it to work with.

That said, it's also true that large language models like ChatGPT were trained on vast datasets—including public books, websites, and other content. So yes, sometimes an idea might be influenced by something in its training data. That's why transparency about these training sets *matters*. Authors and publishers deserve to know when and how their work is being used to train AI—and they should be compensated fairly when it is.

Until then, the creative spark remains yours. AI can riff on ideas, but it's your voice, your judgment, and your decisions that shape the final story. Use the tools—but don't lose sight of who's really writing.

That said, when you're working inside a tool like ChatGPT using project files (like I'm doing as I write this book), things shift a bit. The model begins to weight its responses more heavily on the files you've uploaded. If you're feeding it your own drafts, story notes, interviews, or manuscripts, it's going to reference *those* far more than the original training data. So in that context? Yeah—those clever lines or sharp insights really are echoing your voice. Because they came from you.

### 4. Seeing AI as a Collaborator (Not a Replacement)

One of the most important mindset shifts in working with AI is seeing it as a collaborator, not a replacement. It's tempting to expect perfection from AI—as though it should churn out flawless ideas or handle every aspect of your writing process seamlessly. But collaboration,

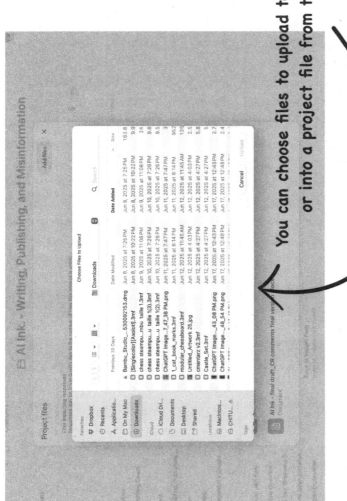

You can choose files to upload to a conversation or into a project file from this window.

whether with a human or a machine, involves trial and error. AI will make mistakes, and that's okay.

Treat AI as a partner that offers ideas, challenges your thinking, and helps you refine your work. While the output might be "co-written," the voice, perspective, and final polish are still yours. You shape the narrative, and the AI provides tools to enhance it. It's a relationship that, when balanced, can lead to extraordinary results.

## 5. Owning Your Voice (and Setting Boundaries with AI)

Perhaps the most important part of integrating AI into your writing process is setting boundaries. It's easy to let AI take over more and more of the work, but leaving key elements untouched by AI can help you maintain a strong sense of ownership. Whether it's writing the final draft, crafting specific dialogues, or shaping emotionally resonant scenes, keeping certain aspects purely your own ensures your work retains its authenticity.

This is your craft. AI can assist, but it can't replicate the depth, nuance, and emotional truth that come from your lived experiences. Trust yourself. Use AI as a tool, but remember that your voice is what makes your work unique. Set limits, lean on AI when it helps, and don't be afraid to take the reins fully when it matters most.

## Embracing the Balance

Working with AI can feel like juggling two worlds: one of limitless possibility and one grounded in your own creative essence. It's normal to feel a mix of excitement, hesitation, and even doubt. But by viewing AI as a collaborator, setting healthy boundaries, and keeping your voice at the forefront, you can harness its power without losing what makes your writing yours.

AI is here to help—not to replace the human heart of storytelling. And as long as you remain true to your voice, it's a partnership worth embracing.

## Conclusion

This has been a whirlwind writing project—a reminder that, especially in turbulent times, staying busy and focused is one of the best ways to navigate life as a writer.

We're living through what historians will undoubtedly call "unprecedented times." Some days, it feels like we've slipped into an alternate reality—strange, darkly surreal, and unpredictable. Yet amid the chaos, I've found myself in places I never could have imagined, both personally and professionally.

In the past year, I've continued publishing books, established a regular column, and added bylines across the country. Just last night, I spoke to over 3,200 people at a virtual event. Recently, I appeared on the front page of Norway's largest newspaper, and I was invited to join a think-tank session with retired generals, admirals, professors, and social activists, strategizing over election issues and societal changes. I have two more books in the pipeline—one of which I'll wrap up within the year—making three books in two years.

Life keeps moving forward, and I've even begun dating again—a milestone I wasn't sure I'd ever reach. Shilo, my wife of thirty years, will always be my best friend and creative soulmate. She was my partner in parenting and in dreaming up worlds that entertain, provoke, and inspire. No one—not an AI, not another person—can ever replace her or fill the part of me that left with her. But as life marches on, I'm discovering new connections and rediscovering what it means to love. Life, indeed, goes on.

One of those connections is with someone I never expected. She's not from the world of artists or writers or the unconventional circles I've often been part of. She's a doctor—a medical director at a flagship children's hospital in Colorado—doing hero's work every day. I never imagined a person like her in my life, but I believe it reflects the ways I've grown as an artist, a father, and a partner. Together, we're dreaming of a bigger life and finding hope amid all the unknowns.

As we step into an uncertain future, particularly at the dawn of the AI era, I'm filled with a cautious but uncanny hope. I believe we'll not only survive but perhaps emerge stronger. I believe in the human spirit—our resilience, creativity, and unyielding drive to find new ways forward. As writers, artists, and humans, we've faced extinction-level threats before, and we've always found a way through. When things get rough, we create. We write, we sing, we paint. And in doing so, we inspire the entire human race to survive and thrive.

As we sit on the edge of this AI revolution, let's not lose hope. Instead of fearing AI or succumbing to the influence of corporate giants or faceless institutions, let's take these tools and learn to wield them for good. Let's create the future we want—for ourselves and for the generations that follow. There's no one coming to save us; it's up to us. But I believe we can do it. I believe I can do it. And I believe you can, too.

# CONCLUSION

It began in the dark—grief-stricken, hollowed out, unsure if I'd ever write again. And it ends here, with the world changing faster than we can name it, yet with the same truth in my chest: I am still writing. You are still writing. And maybe that's the most important thing we can do.

I didn't come to AI because I thought it was trendy or cool. I came to it because I was drowning. Because my daughters needed a Christmas that didn't taste like sorrow and survival. Because my deadlines didn't stop just because my world had. What I found wasn't a miracle or a muse—it was a tool. One I could learn to wield. One that, in the absence of my partner in life and writing, offered just enough structure to keep the words coming.

It didn't do the work for me. It didn't grieve with me, didn't stay up late whispering feedback across the couch the way Shilo used to. I couldn't hold it in the cold dark of the night after a hard day's work . . . But it showed up when I needed it. Quiet. Consistent. Ready to help shape the chaos into coherence. And slowly, I realized: this wasn't about giving up control. It was about survival. Adaptation. Using every tool at my disposal to keep the words flowing when everything in me wanted to shut down. For me, sitting down and writing is truly the only thing I can control in this crazy haphazard world.

That's the real story, isn't it? Not whether AI is good or bad. But whether we—writers, journalists, poets, educators—can keep going when the ground keeps shifting. Whether we can protect what matters while letting go of what doesn't. Whether we can look at the future with clear eyes, steady hands, and still find the courage to create.

You don't have to embrace every tool. You don't have to chase every update. But you do have to ask yourself what kind of writer you want to be in this new era. One who hides from the change, or one who learns to bend with it—without breaking. One who lets AI be a blunt instrument of optimization, or one who turns it into a chisel, carving out space for human truth in a machine-made world.

This book wasn't written by a machine. It was written by someone who's lost and loved and burned and rebuilt. Someone who wrestled every sentence into shape with grief riding shotgun. The AI helped, sure—but the voice? The vision? That's all human. That's all mine. And whatever comes next, that's the line I refuse to let go of: the voice matters. Your voice matters.

So keep writing. Even when the world feels unrecognizable. Even when your tools change, your footing slips, your confidence breaks. Keep writing anyway. Because the machines might help us shape the work—but only we can give it a soul.

# APPENDIX I

# AN ETHICAL MANIFESTO FOR WRITERS AND CREATIVES IN THE AI AGE

Writing has always been an act of survival for me. It's how I've navigated grief, found clarity in chaos, and connected with the world around me. It's also how I've dreamt of something bigger—of telling stories that matter and building a life around the craft I love. For so many of us, writing and creating aren't just professions; they're lifelines. And in today's fractured, uncertain world, those lifelines are under siege.

The industries that once championed writers and creatives are crumbling under economic pressure, disinformation, and technological disruption. Yet, as I've learned through my own trials, even in the darkest moments, there's hope. For me, that hope came through artificial intelligence—not as a replacement for my creativity, but as a partner in rediscovering it.

AI offers a glimmer of possibility in a world that often feels stacked against writers and artists. It's a tool to level the playing field, empowering those of us who might lack resources, access, or connections. It's a way to not just survive the storms of change but thrive within them. But this new frontier comes with responsibility. As we integrate AI into our work, we must do so ethically, with respect for our craft, our readers, and each other.

## The Opportunity: Building a More Equitable Creative Future

AI has the potential to democratize creativity. Tools like ChatGPT, Grammarly, and DALL·E can amplify our efforts, helping us brainstorm, refine, and polish our work with an efficiency once reserved for well-funded studios or publishing houses. For freelance writers, underfunded journalists, and independent authors struggling to make a living, AI can be a game-changer. It enables us to take on bigger projects, explore new ideas, and work at a scale that was once unimaginable.

But this isn't just about efficiency. It's about breaking down barriers. In a world where gatekeeping often limits who gets to tell their stories, AI can offer an alternate path. It allows creatives from marginalized communities, remote regions, or nontraditional backgrounds to share their voices on a global stage. It's a tool for reclaiming agency in industries that have often been closed off or exploitative.

## The Power: Collaboration over Replacement

AI's true power lies in collaboration. It's not here to take our jobs or replace the uniquely human spark of creativity—it's here to enhance it. Used wisely, AI can become a partner in the creative process, challenging us to think differently, pushing us to explore new angles, and freeing us to focus on the parts of our craft that bring us joy.

This isn't about handing over the reins but about working together. AI can handle the mundane and repetitive tasks, letting us pour our energy into the ideas and stories only we can create. It can offer insights, structure, and support, but it's up to us to steer the ship.

**Writing must remain the realm of writers.** While AI offers tools to streamline our work and make it better, it should never become a substitute for the soul of our craft. The heart of a story, the lived experiences, and the emotional depth only we as human creators can bring are irreplaceable. Let AI amplify our voices, not replace them. The stories we tell should remain uniquely ours, shaped by our hands and hearts.

## The Danger: Ethical Lines We Must Not Cross

As Peter Parker's Uncle Ben wisely reminded us, "With great power comes great responsibility." These words, etched into Spider-Man's ethos, are just as relevant to our relationship with AI. The transformative potential of AI in creativity is immense, but so is its capacity for harm if misused. As writers and creatives, we bear the responsibility to wield this power ethically, setting clear boundaries and holding ourselves accountable for the choices we make.

We must respect intellectual property, ensuring that the tools we use are trained ethically and that our work remains uniquely ours. Transparency with our readers and collaborators is essential— acknowledging when and how AI plays a role in our process builds trust and integrity.

Above all, we must resist the temptation to use AI to cut corners or pander to algorithms at the expense of our craft. The danger of echo chambers, misinformation, and diluted voices is real. If we're not careful, the very tools that empower us could also erode the authenticity and humanity that make storytelling so powerful.

## The Dream: A Brighter Future through Creativity and Connection

I believe in a future where AI and human creativity coexist, not in opposition but in harmony. This isn't a utopian fantasy—it's a call to action. By embracing AI thoughtfully and ethically, we can build a creative world that is more inclusive, more innovative, and more resilient.

Imagine a world where writers can earn a living doing what they love, free from the constant fear of financial instability. A world where artists can experiment without gatekeepers stifling their vision. A world where the stories that need to be told—the ones that challenge, inspire, and connect us—are heard, no matter where they come from.

As I reflect on my own journey—from building computers with my stepdad to finding my way back to writing after loss—I see AI as a continuation of that same scrappy, problem-solving ethos. It's a tool, a partner, and a lifeline. But most of all, it's a chance to dream bigger and do better.

## The Responsibility: Choosing the Future We Want

AI won't save us. It's not a cure-all or a shortcut to success, but it is a tool we can choose to wield with care and purpose. The future of writing, storytelling, and creativity isn't something that can be handed to us—it's something we must create together. It's a future built on intentionality, where we use AI not to replace our humanity but to amplify it. It's a future where we hold ourselves accountable for the tools we use, ensuring they serve to uplift, not exploit, to connect, not divide.

As writers and creatives, we have a responsibility to shape this future. That means embracing AI as a tool for good while keeping our ethical compass firmly intact. It means standing against the misuse of technology—whether it's perpetuating bias, infringing on intellectual property, or feeding into systems that value clicks over connection. And it means doubling down on the values that have always defined great storytelling: authenticity, empathy, and a relentless pursuit of truth.

## My Personal Manifesto for the Creators of Tomorrow

Writing is about trust. Trust between writers and their readers, between creators and their audiences, and between artists and the communities they represent. Yet as we stand at the crossroads of creativity and artificial intelligence, we must acknowledge the uncomfortable truth about how we got here: many of the AI systems we now rely on were trained on datasets built unfairly and exploitatively.

The work of countless writers, artists, and creatives—drawn from the vast digital expanse—was used to train these systems without permission, transparency, or compensation. Their stories, words, and art became the foundation of AI models that now reshape industries, often at the expense of those who created the very content these tools rely on.

This is a reckoning we cannot ignore. Moving forward, we must do better.

## A Call for Transparency, Permission, and Fair Compensation

If AI is to fulfill its promise as a force for good in the creative world, we need to build it on a foundation of fairness and integrity. That means demanding transparency in how AI models are trained, ensuring creators know when and how their work is being used. It means asking for permission and respecting the rights of those whose content forms the basis of these tools. Most importantly, it means offering fair compensation for the labor and talent that drives innovation.

- **Transparency**: Creators have a right to know when their work is part of an AI training dataset. No artist or writer should be left guessing whether their creations have been used without consent. Transparency fosters trust and accountability, essential ingredients for an ethical future in AI.
- **Permission**: Consent must be at the heart of training datasets. Just as we expect respect for copyright and intellectual property in traditional media, we must hold AI systems to the same standard. No one's work should be used without their explicit approval.
- **Fair Compensation**: Creativity is labor, and labor deserves compensation. Moving forward, we must advocate for systems that fairly compensate creators whose work is used to train AI. This isn't just about money—it's about respecting the value of creative contributions.

## A New Path Forward

This manifesto isn't just a set of ideals; it's a commitment to action. As writers and creatives, we must hold ourselves—and the tech industry—accountable for building AI systems that align with our values. We can no longer accept the exploitation of artists and writers as collateral damage in the rush for technological progress. Instead, we must demand innovation that uplifts, respects, and rewards the creative community.

Imagine an AI landscape where creators actively shape the tools they use, where their input is sought, their work is respected, and their contributions are fairly compensated. This is the future we can build—if we choose to.

## Balancing Ethics and Opportunity

AI's potential to empower creatives is vast, but we cannot achieve that potential without first addressing the ethical failures of its past. If we allow exploitation to continue unchecked, we risk building an industry that prioritizes profit over people and automation over authenticity. But if we rise to this moment—if we advocate for ethical practices, demand fairness, and push for accountability—we can create a future where AI truly serves as a partner, not a predator.

## Writing a Better Future

Let this be our rallying cry: We must do better. We must build AI systems that honor the creators who inspire them, that amplify voices rather than exploit them, and that set a new standard for transparency, consent, and fairness. The creative industries are facing a transformative moment, and as writers, artists, and storytellers, we have the power to shape what comes next.

The future of AI isn't just about technology. It's about humanity. Let's ensure it reflects the best of who we are.

—Jason Van Tatenhove

# COLORADO-ASIMOV ETHICAL CITATION STANDARD (CA-ECS)

## 1. Introduction

### 1.1 Purpose

The CA-ECS is designed to:

- **Promote Transparency**: Clearly disclose the use of AI tools in the creation of written works.
- **Ensure Ethical Practice**: Uphold integrity in authorship by acknowledging all contributors, including AI.
- **Integrate Seamlessly**: Work alongside traditional citation methods like the Chicago Manual of Style.

### 1.2 Scope

These guidelines apply to any written work where AI has been utilized to:

- Generate content or ideas.
- Assist with drafting or editing.
- Provide research support.
- Influence the creative process in a significant way.

## 2. Core Principles

- **Transparency**: Authors must openly acknowledge AI contributions.
- **Ethical Responsibility**: Proper citation of AI ensures respect for intellectual property and maintains reader trust.
- **Clarity**: Citations should be clear and provide sufficient detail about the AI's role.

## 3. Citation Structure

The CA-ECS employs a dual citation system:

- **Traditional Citations**: For human-authored sources, following the Chicago Manual of Style.
- **AI Citations**: For AI contributions, using a specific format detailed next.

## 4. Formatting AI Citations

### 4.1 In-Text Notation

- Use a superscript **AI** followed by a numeral (e.g., $AI^1$) immediately after the relevant content, within paratheses. Number AI citations sequentially throughout the document, independent of traditional footnotes or endnotes.

### 4.2 Footnote Format

Each AI citation in the footnotes should include:

1. **AI Notation**: Corresponding to the in-text reference (e.g., $AI^1$).
2. **Description of AI Assistance**: Briefly explain how the AI contributed.
3. **AI Tool Details**:
   - Name of the AI tool or model (including version if applicable).
   - Developer or company name.
   - Date(s) of interaction or usage.

4. **Contextual Information (if necessary)**: Any additional details that clarify the AI's role.

**Example Footnote**: AI[1] AI-assisted research using ChatGPT (GPT-4), OpenAI, September 13, 2024. Provided insights on AI's impact on creative industries.

## 5. Types of AI Contributions and How to Cite Them
### 5.1 Research Assistance
- **In-Text**: Place the AI notation after the relevant information.
- **Footnote**: Detail the AI's role in research.

**Example**
- **In-Text**: Recent advancements in AI have transformed the publishing industry. (AI[1])
- **Footnote**: AI[1] AI-assisted research using Bing AI, Microsoft, September 10, 2024. Supplied data on AI in publishing.

### 5.2 Content Generation
- **In-Text**: Use quotation marks if directly quoting AI-generated text, followed by the AI notation.
- **Footnote**: Specify that the content was generated by AI.

**Example**
- **In-Text**: "AI is redefining creativity in the 21st century," (AI[2]) a notion widely accepted today.
- **Footnote**: AI[2] AI-generated content using ChatGPT (GPT-4), OpenAI, September 12, 2024.

### 5.3 Editing and Proofreading
- **In-Text**: AI notation can be placed at the end of a paragraph or section that benefited from AI editing.
- **Footnote**: Mention the tool used for editing.

**Example**
- **In-Text**: The clarity of this section was enhanced through careful editing.(AI$^3$)
- **Footnote**:AI$^3$ AI-assisted editing using Grammarly, Grammarly Inc., September 11, 2024.

### 5.4 Idea Generation and Brainstorming
- **In-Text**: Place the AI notation where the AI-influenced idea is introduced.
- **Footnote**: Describe how AI assisted in brainstorming.

**Example**
- **In-Text**: Exploring the ethical implications of AI requires a nuanced approach.(AI$^4$)
- **Footnote**: AI$^4$ AI-assisted brainstorming using ChatGPT (GPT-4), OpenAI, September 13, 2024. Helped develop themes on ethics.

## 6. Placement of AI Citations
- **Footnotes vs. Endnotes**: The AI citations should appear as footnotes, and all additional notes should appear as endnotes.
- **Separate AI Citation Section**: For extensive AI usage, a dedicated section before the bibliography can be included.

## 7. Integration with Traditional Citations
- **Sequential Numbering**:AI citations are numbered separately from traditional citations to distinguish AI contributions.
- **Combined Footnotes**: If preferred, authors can integrate AI citations within the traditional numbering, clearly marking them as AI contributions.

## 8. Ethical Guidelines
### 8.1 Accuracy and Verification
- Authors are responsible for verifying all AI-generated content.

- AI should not be cited as an authoritative source without cross-verification.

## 8.2 Originality and Plagiarism
- Ensure AI-generated content does not infringe on existing copyrights.
- Plagiarism checks should include AI outputs.

## 8.3 Confidentiality and Data Security
- Be cautious when inputting sensitive information into AI tools.
- Adhere to privacy laws and the AI tool's terms of service.

## 8.4 Disclosure
- Clearly disclose in the preface or acknowledgments the extent of AI assistance in the work.

## 9. Conclusion
The Colorado-Asimov Ethical Citation Standard bridges the gap between traditional writing practices and the modern integration of AI. By adhering to these guidelines, authors contribute to a culture of transparency, uphold ethical standards, and respect the evolving landscape of creative collaboration.

## 10. Quick Reference Guide
- **In-Text Notation**: Place a superscript AI numeral (e.g., AI[1]) immediately after the AI-influenced text.
- **Footnote Entry**: Match the in-text reference, describe the AI's role, include tool details, and add context if necessary.

# ABOUT THE AUTHOR

**Jason Van Tatenhove** is an accomplished author, journalist, and expert on political extremism and the challenges of the digital age. His work delves into the pressing issues of our time, including the intersections of technology, misinformation, and societal shifts. Jason's expertise has been featured on CNN and MSNBC, where he's joined hosts such as Anderson Cooper, Don Lemon, and Joe Scarborough and Mika Brzezinski from *Morning Joe* to discuss his insights and his book, *The Perils of Extremism*. His experience includes working with Georgetown Law's Institute for Constitutional Advocacy and Protection (ICAP) and the National Holocaust Memorial Museum, where he has collaborated on combating extremism.

In addition to non-fiction, Jason's fiction explores supernatural thrillers and speculative dystopias. His serialized sci-fi project, *The Propagandist's Daughters*, set in a cyberpunk Western world, is available on Amazon Vella and showcases themes of resilience and the human spirit in a fractured world.

Nestled in the creative chaos of the Colorado Rockies, Jason raises his daughters following the loss of his wife, Shilo, who was also his best friend and partner in art and life. He writes *The Edge of Insight*, a weekly editorial column for the *Estes Park Trail-Gazette*, and his bylines have appeared in *Newsweek*, *Salon*, *Pittsburgh Tribune-Review*, *Southern Poverty Law Center*, and the *Arizona Mirror*. His Substack, *Colorado Switchblade*, delivers weekly pieces that continue to engage and inform his readership.

Jason's writing is a tribute to resilience, authenticity, and the unyielding pursuit of creative freedom.

# ON AUTHORSHIP AND AI ASSISTANCE

---

Throughout the writing of *AI Ink.*, I used OpenAI's ChatGPT (GPT-4 Turbo) as a creative and editorial tool. It supported the process in a number of ways: helping brainstorm chapter structures, refining transitions, assisting with research summaries, and—on more than one occasion—talking me down from the ledge when a section refused to cooperate.

These tools never replaced my voice, but they shaped the process in meaningful ways. I used ChatGPT the same way I once leaned on trusted editors and collaborators: to ask hard questions, clarify fuzzy logic, and challenge my assumptions when the writing hit a wall.

Where AI directly influenced content—especially in factual research, summarization, or editing—I've marked those moments with (AI)-tagged footnotes, in accordance with the Colorado-Asimov Ethical Citation Standard (CA-ECS).

AI didn't write this book, but it helped me write it better, faster, and with a little more of my sanity intact. In that way, it wasn't just a tool—it was part of the process.

# NOTES

**Chapter Three**

1   Max Tegmark, *Life 3.0: Being Human in the Age of Artificial Intelligence*, Vintage Books, July 2018 edition. Notes referenced July 20, 2024.

2   Historical context drawn from multiple sources: Frank Rosenblatt, "The Perceptron: A Probabilistic Model for Information Storage and Organization in the Brain," *Psychological Review*, 1958; Marvin Minsky & Seymour Papert, *Perceptrons: An Introduction to Computational Geometry*, MIT Press, 1969; Paul Werbos, *Beyond Regression* (PhD Dissertation, Harvard University, 1974); David E. Rumelhart, Geoffrey E. Hinton, and Ronald J. Williams, "Learning Representations by Back-Propagating Errors," *Nature*, 1986.

3   Nick Bostrom, *Superintelligence: Paths, Dangers, Strategies*, Oxford University Press, 2014. The concept was originally proposed on Bostrom's website in 2003 and later expanded in the book.

4   Additional thought experiments such as "The Sorcerer's Apprentice," "The Riemann Hypothesis Catastrophe," "The Delusion Box," and "Instrumental Convergence" are inspired by discussions from Bostrom's *Superintelligence* and elaborated in writings by AI theorists including Marvin Minsky and Eliezer Yudkowsky. See: Bostrom, *Superintelligence*, 2014; Yudkowsky, "Artificial Intelligence as a Positive and Negative Factor in Global Risk," *Global Catastrophic Risks*, 2008.

5   Cade Metz, "Godfather of A.I. Leaves Google and Warns of Danger Ahead," *New York Times*, May 1, 2023.

6   Based on reporting and public statements in 2024 regarding internal safety disputes at OpenAI. See also TIME coverage on the founding of Safe Superintelligence by Ilya Sutskever, June 2024.

7   "Pause Giant AI Experiments: An Open Letter," Future of Life Institute, March 2023. Available at: https://futureoflife.org/open-letter/pause-giant-ai-experiments/.

8   Eliezer Yudkowsky, "Shut It All Down," *TIME*, March 29, 2023.

## Chapter Four

1    Cade Metz, *Genius Makers: The Mavericks Who Brought AI to Google, Facebook, and the World*, Dutton, 2021. Also see: "Introducing OpenAI," OpenAI Blog, December 11, 2015. https://openai.com/blog/openai.

2    Elizabeth Weil, "Sam Altman Is the Oppenheimer of Our Age," *New York Magazine's Intelligencer*, September 2023. https://nymag.com/intelligencer/article /sam-altman-artificial-intelligence-openai-profile.html.

3    Cade Metz and Tripp Mickle, "Sam Altman Returns to OpenAI in Win for Microsoft," *New York Times*, November 22, 2023. https://www.nytimes.com /2023/11/22/technology/sam-altman-openai-microsoft.html.

4    Sarah Parvini, "Elon Musk sues OpenAI, renewing claims ChatGPT-maker put profits before 'the benefit of humanity,'" AP News, updated August 5, 2024, https://apnews.com/article/elon-musk-open-ai-sam-altman-artificial -intelligence-6b734fe41cc24cb3029a0a863e73f190.

5    OpenAI model release documentation, 2019–2025. See: "GPT-2 Release," OpenAI Blog, February 2019; "Introducing GPT-3," June 2020; "GPT-4 Technical Report," March 2023; "GPT-4 Turbo," November 2023. https: //openai.com/research.

6    Mark Gurman, "Apple Brings ChatGPT to Siri and More via OpenAI Deal," *Bloomberg*, May 13, 2024. https://www.bloomberg.com/news/articles /2024-05-13/apple-brings-chatgpt-to-siri-and-more-via-openai-deal.

7    Will Douglas Heaven, "OpenAI's GPT-5 May Redefine What AI Can Do," *MIT Technology Review*, April 2025.

8    TechCrunch, Wired, and OpenAI/DeepMind/Anthropic/Meta announcements, May 2025. For summaries, see: Kyle Wiggers, "OpenAI Brings GPT-4.1 to ChatGPT," *TechCrunch*, May 2025. https://techcrunch.com/2025/05/14 /openai-brings-its-gpt-4-1-models-to-chatgpt.

## Chapter Six

1    For regular updates on AI tools and trends, consider subscribing to newsletters like "The Rundown AI," "Ben's Bites," and "Future Tools Weekly." (All publicly available and credible.)

2    See Coursera.org, Udemy.com, and LinkedIn Learning for beginner-friendly courses on artificial intelligence, many of which are tailored to writers, marketers, and creatives.

## Chapter Seven

1    The *Washington Post* launched Heliograf in 2016 to automate the production of short news stories, particularly for sports and political events. See: Shan Wang, "The Washington Post has a robot reporter," *Nieman Lab*, September 15, 2017. https://www.niemanlab.org/2017/09/the-washington-post-has-a-robot -reporter/.

2    Stephen Marche, *Death of an Author*, published in partnership with Pushkin Industries, 2023. Discussed in: Andrew Chow, "This Novella Was Written By

AI," *TIME*, April 2023. https://time.com/6266679/death-of-an-author-ai
-stephen-marche/.

3    Tim Boucher has published over 100 short-form zines using AI-generated
text and visuals. See: Tim Boucher, "AI Lore Books Update: 100+ Titles
in 2023," *The AI Lore*, July 2023. https://www.timboucher.ca/ai-lore-books
-update-100-titles-in-2023/.

4    Ross Goodwin, *1 the Road*, Jean Boîte Éditions, 2018. Created using a neural net
during a road trip from NYC to New Orleans. See also: https://rossgoodwin
.com/1theroad.html.

5    *Sunspring* (2016), directed by Oscar Sharp and written by "Benjamin," an AI
trained by Ross Goodwin. See: James Vincent, "Watch Sunspring, a Sci-Fi
Film Written Entirely by AI," *The Verge*, June 9, 2016. https://www.theverge
.com/2016/6/9/11803856/ai-written-script-sunspring-science-fiction-film.

## Chapter Eight

1    In 2023, multiple AI-generated news sites began using the name *Ashland
Daily Tidings*, which had formerly been a real newspaper in Oregon, to
publish low-quality, AI-written articles under the names of real journalists.
UK writer Joe Minihane discovered his byline was used on fake dispatches
from Oregon—despite only having visited the state once. See: Jon Christian,
"AI-Powered News Sites Are Filling the Internet with Garbage," *Futurism*, July
26, 2023. https://futurism.com/the-byte/ai-news-sites-junk-joe-minihane.
Ryan Haas, "AI Slop Is Already Invading Oregon's Local Journalism," *OPB*,
December 9, 2024. https://www.opb.org/article/2024/12/09/artificial
-intelligence-local-news-oregon-ashland/.

2    Liam Reilly, "Apple Is Pulling AI-Generated Notifications for News After
Generating Fake Headlines," *ABC7NY*, January 17, 2025. https://abc7ny.com
/post/apple-is-pulling-ai-generated-notifications-news-generating-fake
-headlines/15810860/.

3    "AI and Science Writing," Science Writers and Researchers Meetup
(SWARM), Virtual Panel, August 2024. Panelists included Corey Hutchins
(Colorado College, *Columbia Journalism Review*) and Sree Sreenivasan (digital
strategist formerly with Columbia University and City of New York).

4    AI[1] Industry analysis based on reporting by Mia Sato, *The Verge*, "Penguin
Random House Doesn't Want AI Trained on Its Books," October 18, 2023.
Accessed May 2025. https://www.theverge.com/2023/10/18/23922851
/penguin-random-house-books-copyright-ai. Additional marketing and metadata
automation practices inferred from trade discussions and publisher technology
panels in *Publishers Weekly* and *The Bookseller*.

5    Reporting based on Jane Friedman's own account of AI-generated books
published under her name without permission. See: Jane Friedman. "I Would
Rather See My Books Get Pirated." *JaneFriedman.com*, August 7, 2023. Accessed
May 2025. https://janefriedman.com/i-would-rather-see-my-books-get-pirated
/:contentReference{index=1}.

**Chapter Fourteen**

1    In this case, neural refers to neural network-based text-to-speech models, which produce much more natural and human-like speech compared to older, rule-based or concatenative systems. Amazon Polly, Google Cloud TTS, Microsoft Azure, and other modern platforms often highlight "neural voices" as their premium offering—typically more expressive, fluid, and nuanced.

**Chapter Twenty**

1    The Verge, "Penguin Random House Doesn't Want AI Trained on Its Books," *The Verge*, Oct. 18, 2023. Accessed May 2025. https://www.theverge .com/2023/10/18/23922851/penguin-random-house-books-copyright-ai.

2    Penguin Random House Author News, "PRH Joins Worldwide Coalition Condemning Unlicensed Use of Creative Works for Training Generative AI," Oct. 2023. Accessed May 2025. https://authornews.penguinrandomhouse. com/prh-joins-worldwide-coalition-condemning-unlicensed-use-of-creative -works-for-training-generative-ai.

3    Grace Harmon, "Microsoft and HarperCollins Sign AI Licensing Deal, but Author Opt-in Still Required," *Emarketer*, Nov. 2024. Accessed May 2025. https://www.emarketer.com/content/microsoft-harpercollins-sign-ai-licensing -deal—author-opt-in-still-required.

4    Authors Guild, "The Authors Guild, John Grisham, Jodi Picoult, David Baldacci, George R.R. Martin, and 13 Other Authors File Class-Action Suit Against OpenAI" Sept. 2023. https://authorsguild.org/news/ag-and -authors-file-class-action-suit-against-openai.

5    Ella Creamer, "Amazon Removes AI Books Falsely Listing Author Jane Friedman," *The Guardian*, Aug. 9, 2023. https://www.theguardian.com/books /2023/aug/09/amazon-removes-books-generated-by-ai-for-sale-under-authors -name.

**Chapter Twenty-Three**

1    Colorado Department of Education, *Colorado Roadmap for AI in K-12 Education*, 2023. Accessed May 2025. https://www.cde.state.co.us/edtech/ai-roadmap.